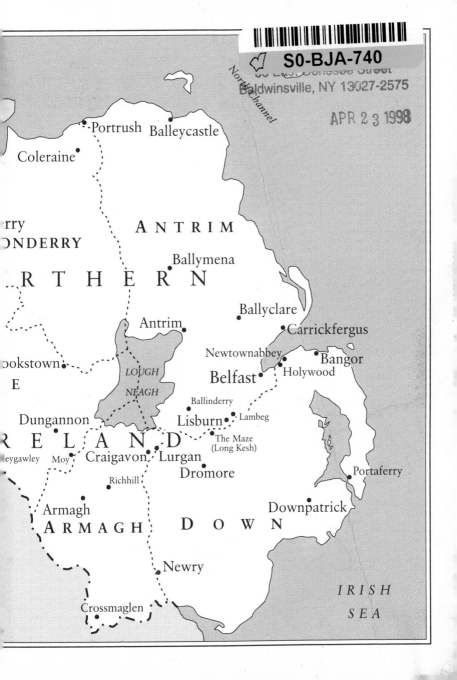

North Channel

Portrush Balleycastle

Coleraine

A N T R I M

Ballymena

R T H E R N

Ballyclare

Antrim

Carrickfergus

Newtownabbey

Bangor

okstown

LOUGH

Belfast Holywood

E

NEAGH

Ballinderry

Dungannon

Lisburn Lambeg

The Maze
(Long Kesh)

R E L A N D

eygawley Moy Craigavon Lurgan

Dromore

Richhill

Portaferry

Armagh

Downpatrick

A R M A G H

D O W N

Newry

I R I S H

Crossmaglen

S E A

rry
ONDERRY

CHILDREN
OF
"THE TROUBLES"

Also by Laurel Holliday

CHILDREN IN THE HOLOCAUST AND WORLD WAR II
Their Secret Diaries

Published by POCKET BOOKS

CHILDREN

OF

"THE TROUBLES"

OUR LIVES IN THE CROSSFIRE OF NORTHERN IRELAND

Laurel Holliday

POCKET BOOKS

New York   London   Toronto   Sydney   Tokyo   Singapore

POCKET BOOKS, a division of Simon & Schuster Inc.
1230 Avenue of the Americas, New York, NY 10020

Copyright © 1997 by Laurel Holliday

APR 2 3 1998

Library of Congress Cataloging-in-Publication Data

Children of "the troubles" : our lives in the crossfire of Northern
Ireland / [edited by] Laurel Holliday.
    p. cm.
  Includes bibliographical references.
  ISBN 0-671-53736-9 (hc)
  1. Children's writings, English—Irish authors.   2. Children and
violence—Northern Ireland—Literary collections.   3. Political
violence—Northern Ireland—Literary collections.   4. Children and
violence—Northern Ireland.   5. Northern Ireland—Literary
collections.   6. English literature—Northern Ireland.   7. English
literature—Irish authors.   8. English literature—20th century.
I. Holliday, Laurel, 1946–
PR8891.N672C48   1997
820.8'09282'09416—dc21   96-49217
                                                                     CIP

First Pocket Books hardcover printing March 1997

10 9 8 7 6 5 4 3 2 1

POCKET and colophon are registered trademarks of
Simon & Schuster Inc.

Text design by Stanley S. Drate/Folio Graphics Co. Inc.

Printed in the U.S.A.

DECEMBER 20, 1976

I would love to risk sleeping some Christmas night with curtains flung back from the windows, nothing but shiny black glass between me and the stars and sky, the drizzle and the horses, but [IRA] bombs ruthlessly silence my wishes, for a while at least.

From the diary of Sharon Ingram
Eighteen years old, Ballygawley

28th APRIL, 1994

I am frightened living on this street across from the Protestants. I am frightened they will come and kill us because this is the eleventh time they have shot people in our street. I don't know why they want to kill us.

From the diary of Bridie Murphy
Eleven years old, Belfast

CONTENTS

Part I

BELFAST: Bullets and Bombs

Part II

THROUGHOUT THE DIVIDED COUNTRY

CONTENTS

Part III

PIGS IN THE MIDDLE: Bridges to Peace

ACKNOWLEDGMENTS

I would like to sincerely thank all of the writers who submitted their writing for publication in this book. Difficult decisions had to be made and not everyone's work could be included, but I appreciated the efforts of each and every one of you and learned much from the stories and poems you sent me.

Heartfelt thanks to all of the writers who met with me in Northern Ireland! I learned so much from you and I enjoyed it thoroughly. Thanks also to the families who invited me into your homes and to the teachers and principals who hosted my visits at the various schools. I will never forget your kindness and hospitality.

And thanks to all the photographers whose work appears in this book, including Cassandra Lindquist, who did the author portrait.

I would like to thank the following people for providing me with background information about the Troubles: Jane Bell, Belfast; Reverend Bernard J. Canning, Scotland; Paddy Bogside Doherty, Derry; Louise Foresman, Seattle; Dominic Gates, Seattle; Nancy Gracey, Belfast; Charles McAleaf, Seattle; Derek McCauley, Derry; Paul Neeson, Kirkland, Washington; Will Pegg, Belfast; Dr. Michael Roe, Seattle; and Jim Watson, Belfast.

The following people have my heartfelt appreciation for helping me to connect with writers in Northern Ireland: Anne Carr, Belfast; Pat Campbell, Belfast; Dr. Michael J. Carr, Derry; Margaret Dolan, Belfast; Francis Donnelly, Crossmaglen, Northern Ireland; Ann Gaughan, Blue Bell, Pennsylvania; Mary Jo Jackson, Northfield, Minnesota; Dan O'Kennedy, Livonia, Michigan; Joanne Mulcahy, Derry and Portland, Oregon; Miss C. O'Reilly, Belfast; Ms. Pettigrew, Belfast; Miss S. Simpson, Lisburn, Northern Ireland; Anne Tannahill, Belfast.

Special thanks to Kevin Byers, Portaferry, Northern Ireland, and Dr. Michael Roe, Seattle, for their review of the introduction to this anthology and many helpful comments.

I could not even have begun to put this book together without the help of newspaper editors throughout Northern Ireland. Many thanks for printing my letter and subsequent articles about the book. Thanks also to all the folks at *Fortnight* who forwarded mail and answered questions from interested writers and to the Irish-American magazines who've let their readers know about this book as well.

As with all of my books, this book owes much to the hard work of librarians, particularly the international network of interlibrary loan librarians. Thank you all! I would also like to thank the Quick Information librarians at the Seattle Public Library, who were always happy to track down some obscure fact for me, and the Ballard Branch librarians, who never shrank from the long lists of book requests I handed them.

Very special thanks to Yvonne Murphy, Librarian for the Northern Ireland Political Collection of the Linen Hall Library in Belfast. Your guidance through the maze of books and pamphlets in a library that long ago overflowed its premises was oh so welcome. (If anyone is looking for a worthy cause in Northern Ireland to which to donate—please consider contributing to the continued existence of this very special and impressive collection.)

I would like to thank John O'Neill, of Belfast, for serving as a consultant for this book during its early stages. Just knowing you were only a phone call or fax away really helped.

Many thanks to professor and poet Frank Ormsby, Belfast, and novelist Kathleen Ferguson, Castle Rock, County Derry, for serving as adjudicators for a literary award connected with this anthology.

I am very grateful for the intelligence, the care, and the diligence of my editor, Paul McCarthy, at Pocket Books/Simon & Schuster. He believed in this project from the beginning and has provided expert guidance all along the way. Thanks for letting me try my wings in a country I love, Paul.

Special thanks go to my agent, Sarah Jane Freymann. Just knowing you're working in Manhattan and loving it lets me hide out in Seattle and write—or fly off to Northern Ireland! Thanks for all of your insights about this book and those to come, Sarah Jane.

One of my oldest friends, silent partner, and sometimes personal assistant, Cheri Brown, kept me together through my visit to Northern Ireland. Although you're somewhat invisible here, you know how much I appreciate you.

And finally, heartfelt thanks to Kate, who fed and cared for all my furry, four-legged creatures in Seattle while I was in Northern Ireland, kept a hilarious diary of their beastly antics so I'd know what I'd missed, and kept the light in the window burning till my return.

CHILDREN
OF
"THE TROUBLES"

INTRODUCTION

In 1969 animosities between Catholics and Protestants in Northern Ireland escalated into what is called "the Troubles," now nearly three decades of violence during which thirty-four thousand shootings and fourteen thousand bombings resulted in the wounding of over forty thousand people and the loss of more than thirty-one hundred lives.

Eyewitness to this widespread violence, the generation that is known in Northern Ireland as "children of the Troubles" has never known a permanent peace. In this collection of their own true stories, memoirs, essays, diaries, letters, and poems, sixty of them tell what it has been like to grow up in a painfully divided country and what it means to them that, after decades of murder and destruction, there is now a possibility of a lasting peace.

In September and October 1994, Catholic and Protestant paramilitary organizations in Northern Ireland announced cease-fires in an effort to work out a peace agreement. Sadly, the Catholic paramilitary cease-fire ended in February 1996 with an Irish Republican Army (Nationalist Catholic paramilitary organization) bomb blast in London in which two people were killed. The Protestant paramilitary cease-fire, although still officially said to be holding, has been brought into serious question by what appears to be the sectarian murder of a Catholic taxi driver during the summer of 1996. Although sectarian violence was still an everyday reality in Northern Ireland during the cease-fires, seventeen months without a sectarian murder or bombing was no small accomplishment and many people in Northern Ireland thought it signaled the end of the Troubles.

In addition to the sheer joy of being able to walk down a street knowing that any blasts one heard were more likely to be firecrackers than bombs, the seventeen-month respite opened some people's hearts and decreased the fear of reprisal enough to allow Catholics and Protestants to begin to speak their truths in each other's hearing. This book of their own writings about growing up in the Troubles is a testament to what can be accomplished in the absence of bullets and bombs.

Many of us who have not grown up in Northern Ireland have difficulty understanding what would bring members of two Christian communities to fight to the death with one another. How could religious differences possibly be that important? In fact, the Catholic/Protestant conflict is more of an ethnic conflict between two culturally distinct groups over land and civil rights than a war about religious doctrine.

One clear indicator that the violence stems from an ethnic conflict rather than a religious one is that it predates the Protestant Reformation by several centuries. In fact, ethnic violence has been the rule rather than the exception for over eight hundred years in Northern Ireland. Still, some of the major roots of the current Troubles can be found in the seventeenth century when the British government sent thousands of Scottish Protestants (many of them Presbyterians) to confiscate land owned almost entirely by Catholics. By 1703 the Scottish settlers, backed up by British military force, had taken 95 percent of the land in the six counties that make up Northern Ireland today.

Not only did the Scottish Protestant settlers take the land from the Irish Catholics, who had barely managed to scrape a living from it as it was, but when many of the Protestants were successful in the new country because of the wealth they had brought and the support of the British government, they were not inclined to share the bounty with the Irish Catholics, whom they regarded as a somewhat primitive and barbaric people.

Massacres and rebellions defined the next two centuries in Ireland. All in all, the Protestants killed more Catholics than Catholics killed Protestants, and the northeast corner of the country became a Protestant stronghold while most of the Catholics who had lived there migrated to the south and west of Ireland. This mass displacement of the majority of the people who had inhabited Northern Ireland was in many respects more consequential than the loss of lives that occurred on both sides. Events connected with this displacement are firmly etched in the ethnic memory of both communities, and annual commemorations of these events reinforce and maintain the centuries-old sectarianism that characterizes Northern Ireland today.

Great Britain was seen by the Catholics as the real enemy behind the persecution they had received at the hands of the Scottish Protestants. Even many descendants of the Scottish planters were none too fond of England's control of them and their land. Protestants were, in fact, some of the major leaders of the home rule movement that culminated in the Easter Rising, an armed rebellion of Irish patriots against British troops on Easter Monday of 1916 in Dublin.

Great Britain's execution of these Irish patriots sharply increased Catholic demands for home rule and eventually led to a war for independence. At the conclusion of that war in 1921, Britain relinquished its hold on the southern twenty-six counties of Ireland that had a strong Catholic majority while firmly retaining control of the Protestant-dominated, northeast six counties that are known as Northern Ireland today.

If the populations of what had become two separate countries in 1922—what is now known as the Republic of Ireland and Northern Ireland—had been exclusively of one religion or the other, perhaps the peoples of Ireland could have peacefully coexisted on the same island. But a sizable Catholic minority remained in Northern Ireland when Ireland was divided, and the division of the country did nothing to decrease the sectarian strife there.

Gerrymandering and oppressive voting regulations in Northern Ireland gave the Protestants nearly complete control of local and national government, including the police force of the country, the

Royal Ulster Constabulary. Public housing was unfairly allocated, and Protestants were encouraged to hire only Protestants so that many more Catholics than Protestants were forced into poverty in the years following the division of Ireland.

With the relative prosperity that followed World War II came changes in social policies in Northern Ireland. Free education—albeit nearly completely segregated education—was extended to Catholics as well as Protestants, and Catholics began to hope for a better future for their children. Still, there remained widespread inequities in employment, housing, and the administration of civil rights. Many Catholics in Northern Ireland believed that the only way to redress these ills would be to join the Republic of Ireland—with its 95 percent Catholic majority—and become one nation again, free of British rule. Obviously, this prospect had little appeal for Protestants, who would become the minority in a united Ireland.*

During the nineteen fifties and sixties Catholic resentment mounted, and violence erupted at times over what is generally acknowledged, even by many Protestants, to have been two centuries of unfair treatment by the Protestant majority. Catholics and Protestants continued to live together in the six counties called Northern Ireland but they were far from a unified country.

On August 24, 1968, the history of Northern Ireland changed forever when, inspired in part by Dr. Martin Luther King, Jr., and also by Vietnam War protests and the 1968 Paris student revolt, four thousand nonsectarian civil rights activists, who were perceived by Protestant Unionists as Catholic Nationalists, took to the streets in what they intended to be a peaceful protest against discrimination and injustice. They marched again on October 5 in the city of Londonderry (Derry) and were attacked by the Protestant-dominated Royal Ulster Constabulary.

A march, similarly intended to be nonsectarian, was held in Janu-

---

*Demographic experts estimate that if current population trends continue, Protestants could become a minority in Northern Ireland by the year 2015 and perhaps even sooner in certain areas of the country.

ary of 1969. Caught on film and broadcast round the world, police and civilian attacks on peaceful civil rights marchers set the stage for the decades of murder and mutilation carried out by paramilitary organizations on both sides of the sectarian divide as well as by the police and the British military.

In 1969 bombings on both sides began in earnest, and Bernadette Devlin (a very outspoken twenty-one-year-old Catholic political activist) won a seat in Parliament, a wake-up call to the level of unrest in the Catholic community. On the fourteenth of August of that year British troops arrived on the streets of Northern Ireland, and by September they had erected the Berlin Wall of Belfast, the first of many so-called Peace Lines, that confirmed the absolute division between the two communities and the fact that they could not live together in peace.

Of course, calling all this the beginning of the Troubles is hindsight. No one could have guessed in 1968 or 1969 the level or the duration of the violence that was to come.

Most of the writers whose work appears in this book have known since they were toddlers that because they were born into either a Protestant or a Catholic family in Northern Ireland, they were destined to take sides and suffer the consequences. Yet many barely knew the "enemy." Northern Ireland is so divided that many young people do not even meet a member of the other religious community until they are in their teens.

From the moment children are born in Northern Ireland they begin to live in a majority Protestant or a majority Catholic neighborhood. They go to either a Catholic or a Protestant school, and their friends are likely to be exclusively one or the other. They are taught to shop only in their "own" shops in some towns and, eventually, to socialize only in their "own" pubs. And, of course, when they die they will go to a segregated graveyard.

Amazingly, I think, to those who haven't been raised there, in Belfast even the taxis divide along religious lines, with one fleet heading to Catholic and another to Protestant neighborhoods. In

some parts of the country even the sidewalks are painted to designate political/religious loyalties.

In addition to these very obvious distinctions that children need
to learn in order to survive in Northern Ireland, they also absorb
differences in language and perspective that set them apart from
one another for the rest of their lives. If you are Catholic, for example, you call Northern Ireland's second largest city "Derry"; if you
are Protestant, it is "Londonderry" to you. If you are Catholic, you
call the nearly three decades of the Troubles a "war"; if you are
Protestant, you are careful to point out that there has been a terrorist uprising, not a war, in Northern Ireland.

In fact, even the name you call your country will be in question.
If you are raised in a Catholic family wanting the reunification of
Ireland, you will refer to "the North of Ireland" as your homeland or
call it "The Six Counties," rather than making it sound as if it were
a separate country called Northern Ireland. And if you were raised in
a Protestant environment, you will be more likely to call your country
Northern Ireland or Ulster.

Not only are most children in Northern Ireland set on divergent
sectarian courses from birth, but from the age of seven some Protestant and Catholic children are coerced into running secret errands
for terrorists and assembling and hiding their weapons.

Although the majority of people in Northern Ireland abhor the
violence and take no part in it themselves, virtually every family in
Northern Ireland has had members beaten, tortured, or murdered,
and the country's children have been witness to it all. For this is not
a private war, conducted behind closed doors, nor a war where the
men go away to fight the enemy. This is an everyday, in-your-face
war, where the enemy lives on the next block and speaks (almost)
the same language.

In this collection of work by and about children of the Troubles in
Northern Ireland, we hear what it is like to grow up in a divided
country, a heart-stoppingly beautiful little country of 1.6 million

people, smaller than the smallest of the United States, that has only rarely known peace.

Prior to the paramilitary cease-fires, it was almost inconceivable that anyone would put his or her experiences of the Troubles into print. Reprisals could be swift and deadly, however small or unintended the provocation. The motto in Northern Ireland, taught by parents on both sides of the sectarian divide, has long been "Whatever you say, say nothing." Sadly, this has meant that a whole generation has been silenced about their fears, their anger, their losses—and that, with few exceptions, there is little in the literature of Northern Ireland to reflect the complex realities of living in a country torn apart by ethnic strife.

Now the women and men, girls and boys, in this book not only are courageous enough to tell their own stories of what has happened to them and their families during the Troubles, they also convey how much it means to them that there is, for the first time in their lifetimes, a hope of permanent peace in their country. Despite tremendous violence that occurred throughout the country in July of 1996, as this book goes to press, peace talks are continuing and at least some people hold out some hope for a peaceful resolution to the centuries-old conflict.

Over half of the writers were under twenty-one when they wrote the prose and poetry in this anthology. Half male, half female, they come from throughout the six counties of Northern Ireland and they speak from a wide range of political viewpoints. The creativity displayed here comes in a variety of forms, and some of the writers have chosen to use the tools of fiction in telling their stories, but all have assured me that their work is autobiographical and that the events they described really happened to them.

It is a testament to these writers' courage and a measure of the hopes for peace in Northern Ireland, I believe, that not a single person in this anthology asked to be anonymous although a few of the writers did, on occasion, change names and places to protect other people.

When I tell people about this book, many want to know how I came to write it . . . and, in particular, how I found all of the prose and poetry it contains. Therein lies a saga—a love story that began when I first crossed the border into Northern Ireland in September of 1983. I had chosen the Republic of Ireland for a solitary vacation because I needed the country landscapes, narrow winding roads, and sheep—lots of sheep—to heal from an overload of plain old American stress. I knew I would be safe there, free of the usual worries many women who travel alone carry with them.

After ten days of pastoral bliss, however, I found myself driving my rental minicar across the border to Northern Ireland, something I had promised friends I would not do and about which the U.S. State Department had issued stern warnings. Sometimes a little pastoral bliss goes a long way with me, and I was curious about what lay just over an invisible line that, in fact, seemed only to divide one hillside of sheep from another—all identical.

I had been in Northern Ireland only a few days when thirty-eight Irish Republican Army prisoners made their escape from the maximum-security prison near Belfast called The Maze, stabbing a guard to death as they went. This was the largest prison escape in British history, and what was already countrywide tight security was tightened even further.

But outside of Belfast, where my bags and purse were checked every time I went in or out of a store, I could see little difference . . . until one evening when I pulled off the road to consult a map, trying to find an infernally elusive bed-and-breakfast, and I looked up to find my minicar surrounded by rifle-pointing uniformed men. With utmost politeness, one of them asked for my identification and explained that he and his mates would need to examine my car and all its contents, which the six of them proceeded to do with great thoroughness. And with the same degree of courtesy, they folded and replaced every single item, packing my bags far more neatly than I usually did.

Nothing so extraordinary about such a search—it could happen in any number of countries, I supposed—but what struck me about it was the contrast between the bucolic, verdant landscape turned gold in the sunset, and sheep, fluff now gone pink, and these most serious men, polished and efficient, as if they had done this hundreds of times before and it were the most natural thing on earth.

Later I was to feel the contrast between what Northern Ireland seemed to be and what lay just below the surface even more sharply when I came to know and to enjoy the company of some of her people. How could people who were willing to share food and drink and talk and laughter so readily with an American stranger be so at each other's throats that they supposedly had to be guarded and searched like this to keep them from killing each other?

'Twas a mystery and one that wouldn't leave me alone. If people in one of the friendliest countries I'd ever encountered could not be trusted to pull over by the side of the road, then who or what in the world could be trusted? Once again, a question that has been a strong theme in other books I have written returned to haunt me. As naive and simple as it sounds, I have always desperately needed to understand why humans are violent toward one another. What, in other words, is the cause of man's inhumanity to man, and, specifically, why were the people of Northern Ireland bombing and shooting each other? Of course only a few of them did; nevertheless, I had come to understand that the sectarian divide between Catholics and Protestants in Northern Ireland was deep and wide and went back for centuries.

Fourteen years later I was to have the opportunity to ask that question and many others when I returned to collect these stories about growing up in Northern Ireland as a companion to another book of young people's autobiographical writings I had collected and edited, *Children in the Holocaust and World War II: Their Secret Diaries.*

As is the case with all the books in what has now become the Children of Conflict series, my role is to provide a place for people to find their own voice and to express their individuality. I couldn't write about growing up in Northern Ireland because I didn't, but I could listen to others who did and I could provide a showcase for their stories, a forum for their disparate opinions . . . a place where Catholics and Protestants can hear each other if they choose—not just the views of politicians but the firsthand stories of their counterparts on "the other side" who have grown up in the same sectarian violence as they have but see it very differently.

To provide such a forum I needed to find writers and, in particular, writers who were willing to take the risk inherent in sharing the details of their lives and their opinions in a country where crossing the street from one neighborhood into another can get you killed. First I read dozens of books, hoping to educate myself about the incredible complexities of Irish politics. Then I wrote letters to the editors of about seventy-five newspapers in Northern Ireland telling them what I needed. I wrote to primary and secondary schools, colleges and universities, organizations and government offices and churches . . . and to all the writers for whom I could find an address.

Manuscripts from Northern Ireland began filling my mailbox as one newspaper after another printed my letter to the editor and word of mouth spread that an American wanted to publish writing about growing up in the Troubles. Over six hundred people eventually answered my letters with marvelous examples of their own creativity. What they sent was clear evidence that, in addition to having an important story to tell, they were writers with a brilliant way of telling it.

Never satisfied, I wanted even more. I wanted to meet with these gifted writers and have them tell me their stories in person as well. I wanted to get together with them at their favorite pub or at their school or in their living room; I wanted to have tea or Sunday dinner with their families and meet their children and their grandparents and have them tell me everything! And I wanted their photographs for publication as well.

Amazingly, after years of being accused in print of being extremely tight-lipped, even "neurotic" by one American author who tried and failed to interview them, the people of the North shared their hearts and their homes and their families with me when I returned to Northern Ireland in September 1995. And they never flinched when I brought out my tape recorder or my camera. Either they'd developed nerves of steel during nearly three decades of the Troubles or—and this is what I believe—they were more than ready to let us in the outside world know about their lives and their country after years and years of requisite silence and of feeling misunderstood by a world that persisted in the mistaken belief that the conflict there was a dispute over religious doctrine. (As we've seen, the Troubles are as little about doctrinal disputes as political conflict between Democrats and Republicans is in the United States.)

So, that's the saga of how this book came to be. Now I want to talk a little about why it is so important that we listen to these writers and learn from their experience. Northern Ireland is certainly not the only violently divided country in the world, and the lessons these writers have to teach us are applicable in Bosnia, Israel/Palestine, South Africa, and Rwanda, to name a few, as well as in every city in the United States where racial and ethnic strife causes us to live in fear of one another.

As you read about the tragedy in Northern Ireland, I hope you will be thinking of your own country, your own state, your own neighborhood, and how *distinctions* we have found it necessary to make between our fellow human beings and ourselves are contributing to the destruction of our human family. For this is not really a book just about Northern Ireland, it is a book about us—all of us—who would try to live peaceably together on this planet, no matter how great our differences.

Since I have been a psychotherapist as well as a writer, I suspect that some readers might be curious about what I think the psychological impact of nearly three decades of violence has been on children of the Troubles. Those whose writing is included in this book describe a wide range of emotional responses to the division of the culture and sectarian violence, but fear and anger were the ones about which they most often wrote. Certainly, those who lost loved ones have written about those losses, but grief is not a predominant theme in this book. Perhaps it is a more private emotion about which it is more difficult to write and perhaps not everyone can afford the vulnerability of grieving when the dangers of the Troubles are still all around them.

During the cease-fires (September 1994 to February 1996) some mental-health professionals in Northern Ireland reported that patients were experiencing sudden bouts of depression and anxiety that could be described as posttraumatic stress disorders. Not until the murders and bombings were halted did these patients feel safe enough to fully experience their losses. A few writers told me that this was the case for them and, in particular, they found that they could not write about the Troubles until after the cease-fires began.

Some of the writers told me that even with the cease-fires they still suffered the same kinds of fears of terrorists that they had grown up with. Some continue to have violent nightmares. The emotional realities of a lifetime are not easily forgotten. Even though I was only a visitor in Northern Ireland—and that during the cease-fires—I know that firecrackers going off sent a jolt of adrenaline through my body because part of me was always expecting a bomb blast. As I sat and conducted interviews in the coffee shop of the Europa Hotel in Belfast, as much as I would have liked to, I could not completely put out of my mind the thought that this hotel had been bombed twenty-eight times during the first twenty-five years of the Troubles.

I imagine that it could take a generation of peace to quell the fears of the generation that has known only war. And perhaps just as long for anger and sectarian attitudes and beliefs to subside. Happily, however, I can say that, after meeting and talking at length with a fair number of people in Northern Ireland, I think they are as emotionally and mentally healthy as any folks on the planet. And this is not my observation alone. Nearly every sociological/psychological study of "Troubles children" has shown that they are no more violent, depressed, nor mentally ill than people of any other nationality although there may be a higher incidence of juvenile delinquency in Northern Ireland than in most Western European countries.

In keeping with what I have long suspected about children who grow up challenged by war, poverty, parental loss—even "dysfunctional" families, as we Americans rather mechanically call them—I found no empirical support for the idea that they will necessarily have lifelong psychological problems. Although there are people who have suffered serious consequences of many kinds of trauma in Northern Ireland, I believe that sometimes such serious challenges precipitate greater flexibility and maturity than a placid life of plenty. Sometimes truly compassionate and wise adults are born of painful, even torturous, childhoods.

I know that the adults I met in Northern Ireland evince the kind of honesty, judgment, social skills, motivation, maturity, compassion, and humor that most people can only hope their children will have when they grow up. Of course, it should be remembered that the writers in this book are well-educated and articulate and may not be entirely representative of the people of Northern Ireland as a whole. Still, it is because of the deep admiration I have for them, far more than because of any faith I might have in the machinations of the politicians, that I have high hopes for a just and lasting peace in Northern Ireland.

Some people have wondered what conclusions I would draw from all that I was hearing from people on both sides of the sectarian divide in Northern Ireland. Would I, as they suspect most Americans do, come to support the Nationalist Catholic cause and see the British as colonist interlopers intent on preserving their empire and the Protestant status quo no matter what the cost in terms of human lives? Or would I attribute most of the bloodshed to the Irish Republican Army and see it as a band of Catholic terrorists in need of life sentences, if not execution?

While I believe that in learning about any political situation one inevitably comes to a few rudimentary conclusions, I have tried in my research and in my writing to maintain the position of "the learner." That is, while I cannot pretend to maintain a position of complete neutrality, I can attempt to defer final judgment as long as possible while I take in the subtleties and complexities of the situation. I know that I will be suspected by some people on one side or the other—if not both—of playing favorites and misrepresenting positions. To those people I can only say that I have tried to be fair, to listen without preconceptions, and to divest myself of prejudice whenever I became aware of it. I have also tried to carefully balance this book by including close to an equal amount of writing by Catholics and Protestants.

I do have some regrets about the positions not represented in this book. Although I invited all comers, anyone with a story to tell about growing up in Northern Ireland, I received almost nothing from the children of British soldiers on duty in Northern Ireland and I received nothing at all from the Travellers' community, a disenfranchised and mostly illiterate people that Americans might call gypsies and who, unfortunately, are often disrespected in Northern Ireland and the Republic of Ireland as well. For both of these omissions I am sorry. I hope that someone else will take up the challenge to tell these Northern Ireland stories in another book.

I also regret that only one of the many, many people still in prison on Troubles-related charges responded to my call for stories. There may, of course, be a very good reason for this since there is no statute of limitations on the activities of illegal organizations in Northern Ireland; people can be jailed for years for simply admitting that they were once a member of a paramilitary group—even if it was twenty years ago.

I want to explain a few decisions I came to as I collected and arranged the material in this book. First, and most obviously, none of the prose or poetry in this book is in Gaelic, which some Nationalist Catholics consider to be the language of Ireland. For the obvious reason that few people outside of Ireland read Gaelic, I have chosen to limit this book to English writings.

I also want to point out that, perhaps not so obviously, I did not select writing for its level of blood and gore. Although the violence in this book is all too frequent and sometimes of a grotesque nature, I chose the writings in this book for their depth, their power, their beauty, their intellectual clarity, and their humor—regardless of the degree of violence they contained.

Perhaps also not so obvious to readers outside of Northern Ireland is the fact that words—many, many words—are politically charged and, therefore, a writer must constantly be on guard for hidden meanings. With what seem like tripwires spread from margin to margin, it is almost impossible not to set off someone's suspicions by the use of certain words. I have attempted to acknowledge the political overtones when I know them and to work out certain compromises, but that is not so simple in a country in which not even the name of the country can be agreed upon. In my introduction to the writers' work I have, for example, referred to the country's second-largest city as "Londonderry" or "Derry" depending on what the writers themselves call it. And I have chosen to use Northern Ireland as the name of the country because it is the one most frequently used throughout the world to designate what others call "The North," "The Six Counties," or "Ulster."

Some simple conventions probably need no explanation but, to be clear, I have inserted bracketed definitions of words and terms likely to be unfamiliar to readers outside of Northern Ireland. Of necessity, these explanations are brief and may not express all of the complexities of the situation. For example, while I have explained that Nationalists are nearly all Catholics and that Unionists are for the most part Protestants, it should be remembered that not all Catholics are Nationalists wanting a united Ireland with home rule and that not all Protestants are Unionists wanting continued British rule. For simplicity's sake, I have specified certain organizations as "Protestant" or "Catholic," but this does not mean that they are approved by or representative of the majority of the memberships of any church.

I have edited all work for consistency in spelling, grammar, and punctuation and occasionally decreased the length of prose pieces. I have retained the writers' own British/Irish spelling and syntax. Explanations contained in parentheses are the writers'. For authors under twenty-one years of age, I have specified the age at which their work was written at the beginning of their story or poem.

The photographs were taken as close to the age about which the writers were writing as possible. Unfortunately, some of the writers had no childhood photos and have long since left childhood behind, but their work stands just fine on its own.

This book is arranged in three parts that quite naturally emerged from the stories and essays. That is, the writing was not selected to fit any preconceived categories. Within the sections, the prose pieces were selected to complement one another and often are in the order of the ages about which the writers are writing. Poetry is more intuitively placed and sometimes serves as a counterpoint to the prose.

Part I, "Belfast: Bullets and Bombs," focuses on young people's responses to street violence in Belfast.

Part II, "Throughout the Divided Country," provides insight into the nature of sectarianism in Northern Ireland and, in particular, how it has impacted children and teenagers living throughout the country, even in the rural areas.

"Pig in the middle" is a childhood game familiar to most people in Ireland/Great Britain, and I've chosen it as the main title of Part III of this book to sum up the position of those who find themselves politically less than sectarian enough to satisfy the demands of the majority in their own community. I have tremendous respect for people who are willing to try to bridge the sectarian divide despite peer pressure, family pressure, church pressure, etc., and am happy to conclude the book with their writing in Part III, "Pigs in the Middle: Bridges to the Future." This does not mean, however, that those whose work appears in the other two sections of this anthology are not equally desirous of a peaceful solution for Northern Ireland.

Whatever the outcome of peace talks that are taking place as this book goes to press, it still must go down in history that the paramilitaries and ordinary people on both sides of the sectarian divide maintained a cease-fire for a year and a half, an unprecedented cessation of paramilitary armed conflict in Northern Ireland.

Perhaps it took some of the paramilitaries coming to a point in their lives when the welfare of their children and grandchildren was the most important thing to them. Gerry Adams, head of Sinn Fein, the political arm of the Irish Republican Army, has said as much, as have others on both sides of the sectarian divide in discussing why they agreed to cease-fires after twenty-five years of fighting.

Ultimately, I believe that a lasting peace can be achieved only by an agreement that provides for equal opportunity and justice for all in Northern Ireland. It is a matter of debate as to whether equal justice and equal access to employment, housing, and the political process really exist there today.

This book is dedicated to all who are seeking a just and lasting peace in Northern Ireland.

LAUREL HOLLIDAY
September 1996

PART I

BELFAST:
Bullets and Bombs

For the nearly three decades of the Troubles Belfast has been known round the world as the capital of sectarian violence in Northern Ireland. Only intrepid and perhaps adventure-seeking tourists included this blood-spattered city on their itineraries, and few outsiders other than media war correspondents experienced Belfast firsthand until the seventeen-month cease-fires that began in September 1994. Not only were foreign visitors afraid to venture into the city, many natives wouldn't come into the city even though they lived just a few miles away.

As some of the writers in Part I of this book tell us, it was as if Belfast were reborn when the paramilitary cease-fires were announced in 1994. Suddenly the town was filled with more international tourists than it could accommodate and one actually had to make reservations for dinner at some of the finer restaurants. The core of the city became a construction zone as glamorous boutiques and shopping arcades were almost instantly erected, a sign of tremendous economic growth and a memorial to the end of the violence.

As of this writing in September 1996, the fate of Belfast once again hangs in the balance after the IRA cease-fire tragically ended on February 9, 1996, with a powerful and murderous IRA bombing in London. It remains to be seen if another cease-fire can be instituted and all parties can be tolerant enough of each other to work out a permanent peace accord.

Meanwhile, the only thing the people of the city, who have endured so much unrest and bloodshed in their lifetimes, can count on is further uncertainty. Once again, some people of Northern Ireland are afraid to go into Belfast, and those who do must be careful of when and where they go, ever mindful that a bomb in Belfast is far from a remote possibility.

ADRIAN FOX

CRAIGAVON, COUNTY ARMAGH

Adrian Fox was born in Kent, England, in 1961. Both Irish, his parents had gone to England to find work but later returned to Northern Ireland to set up a home for their growing family and to start a business of their own. "Little did they know," Adrian says, "that in just two years they would become part of the nightmare [the Troubles] and that my father's small car repair centre in Belfast would be taken over and used as a British Army post and our home would be taken from us by force and burned."

Having spent his first six years happy and content in England, Adrian simply was not prepared for the violence he saw in Belfast. "It seemed like hell," he says. His school life was so affected by the chaos of the Troubles that he left school at age fifteen to become a butcher's boy.

"A friend of the family saved my life in a gun battle," he recalls, "and was killed just minutes after getting me home safely." Adrian himself sometimes was involved in the violence until one day everything changed for him: "As a young teenager, thinking this war a part of me and I a part of it, one day I was rioting with the British Army and I split a black soldier's head open and my friends congratulated me on such a fine shot but I ran home through the streets sick to my soul. And on the way a woman stood screaming in an alley, 'The bastards have shot my son!' Her son's busted body lay there with his intestines hanging out like snails on the concrete. Then as I cried myself to sleep I knew this war was not a part of me. I can still see those faces of the dead and injured."

Now living in County Armagh, happily married with three children he loves very much, Adrian's commitment is to his family, his writing, and peace. He has had quite a few poems published in anthologies. One of his poems, "Breath of Peace," was recently issued as a song on a CD by a Belfast band. The following story is Chapter Two of a book he is writing called *Freedom Winds*.

One for the Road

I didn't feel the beat of my heart until I was six years old. If I felt it before then it was only a faint murmur so I take it for granted that my first six years were spent cocooned in peaceful innocence.

Mum said I was a laid-back child full of wisdom. As long as my high chair tray was piled high with food I was content. Dad, who always differed, said I was a lazy child who needed too much attention. I suppose I was somewhere between the two assumptions.

My heart beat like it had never beaten before. It felt like my body was vibrating with fear. Reluctantly I stumbled up the mobile staircase, mother's strength tugging at my arm as I stopped, taking in the sight of the massive steel bird, holding the handrail like the branch of a tree when falling.

On reaching the platform, she turned to me to reassure me that everything would be alright. Seeing the fright written on my grimaced face and the buildup of tears, she took me into her arms. I clung to her like a leech—so close our heartbeats entwined.

This was my first time on an aeroplane. Flying to Belfast, of all places, with my head stuck in my second sick bag as if I had been given some premonition of what the future had in store. The year was nineteen sixty-seven.

What a rush of relief I felt when the aircraft taxied to a halt at Aldergrove Airport and we were in a taxi rolling through the lush green countryside. My heartbeat returned to normal as the beautiful rolling hills opened to me from the backseat, as we climbed hills filled with cattle, sheep, and little cottages and farm buildings. I had only glimpsed scenes like these in books or stories from my mother's childhood as my early years were spent in built-up towns and cities in England.

I was lost in a daydream of what my new home would be like, picturing fields to run and play in, rivers to fish with friends. My dream was shattered as the taxi fell from the last hill to civilization, past houses, shops, schools, churches, and hundreds of people on the streets.

The taxi turned off the main road where the sun was shining brightly. The side streets were dark and dismal as if an instant depression had erupted in the heavens. Grey clouds formed above, blending bleakly with the rows of closed-in red-brick terraced houses, like a garden filled with overgrown weeds.

I knelt on the backseat observing with disappointed eyes my new world, far from the beautiful scenery of my imagination. The nearest resemblance to trees were the old gaslights. Now converted to electricity, they lined the dreary streets. Scruffy, hard-looking kids swung around them enclosed in a strong rope.

I watched the older boys who played football on the road without any fear of the traffic. They leered at me through the glass.

"There's the school you'll be going to," said my father. It stood empty and evil behind the high rusted spiked double gates, surrounded by a brick wall. Along the top of the wall ran three layers of rusted barbed wire. My heartbeat grew wilder at the thought of attending such a school.

The taxi turned left into a narrower street and pulled up alongside the kerb. The daylight withdrew even further. It was more like dusk than late morning. This is hell, I thought, standing there on the pavement, waiting for someone to open the blood-red door of the bleak two up/two down [two rooms on the first floor/two rooms on the second] terraced house.

An old worn woman with mousy dead hair and an apron over her drab dress opened the door. We stood staring at the stern old woman, awaiting a smile or some expression of welcome. Dad approached her and they embraced, bringing a slight smile to her tired face.

Sarah was old and had lived alone since my father left her and the only home he knew as a young teenager. She had little time and energy. Working at the local mill where she had lost two fingers and all her pride, she spent the rest of her time in the chapel. She was a stern woman who never wed. Not many got to know her or wanted to as she dictated her religious beliefs too often.

I lay deep within the blankets of my temporary bed, a mattress on the cold linoleum floor. I shook with fear of the night coming into the room. My mother's voice from the room below brought a little comfort until my mind went wandering.

The story Sarah told me earlier was reoccurring in my mind, my imagination running wild. As she spoke with a hard northern brogue, she shot forward, just inches from my face, like a witch from the darkness. "The banshees cry at night," she said. "Don't let them see you. If they do, they'll throw their invisible combs and, if they hit you, you will die."

My insides were cold. Wanting to urinate, I took the chamber pot that rested on the only piece of furniture in the room.

With my left hand I tore at the tiny blemishes on my skin. I lay there looking at the only light in the room. A tiny crucifix enclosed within a glass tube shone a subtle red glow onto the picture it projected, adding to the sinister face of a man with a fixed glare, blood trickling from the thorned wounds of his forehead.

I turned away from the light and buried my head in the bedclothes, thinking this is an evil place with evil fleas and people talking of banshees and death, trying so hard to remember friends and good times from my short past. Eventually I fell into a sleep.

I rose from the floor and stumbled across the room in my brother's hand-me-down pyjamas. The turn-ups of four years fell in the night and hung around my feet like slippers.

I opened the curtains revealing the darkened street. I looked up to see a bright sunny day. The morning could not penetrate the street's shadows, the identical rows of houses on each side of the cobbled road were so close. I watched an elderly lady bending over her fire hearth with a little brush and shovel in her aching hands as if her back were locked and she was in terrible pain.

My older brother Terry told me there was no such thing as banshees. "It's only the cats crying," he said.

That night, before I retired, I went to the back room. I looked from the window. With my brother's reassurance, I tried hard not to be afraid.

The moon and stars reflected on my emotion-filled eyes, watching my new world nightmare. The moon threw shadows in the yard. The grey steel bathtub hung from a nail on the wall like a sinister doorway to hell. The toilet door creaked with the night's breeze and the memory from earlier in the day came fleeting back.

I held myself from falling into the hole in the wooden bench, surrounded by whitewashed walls, covered in massive webs and spiders crawling like the plague of sadness in my mind. And that door I closed upon myself I thought would swing open and something evil would be waiting. My fear running wild, the old rusted lift latch jammed. I kicked and thumped on the door, hurting my hand. The door swung open and no one was there.

I ran to my mother who was washing dishes in the sink and held her with all my might. "I don't like this place," I stammered and shook in her clutches. From the window the sights were eerier than they were in the daylight. Behind the yard wall was an alleyway I couldn't see into and I was glad because the dark figures of mind scurrying along the alley would only bring more frightened confusion.

A dark redbrick wall ran the length of the back alley. Like an extension to the yard wall, three rows of rusted barbed wire ran along the top of it. Three acres or so of rugged concrete lay beyond the wall. The unlit building loomed bleak in the centre of the playground. I dreaded my first days at that school with those rough-looking boys who played football in the street.

The cats hissed and whinged and fought somewhere in the darkness. Oblivious to the sounds, I was lost in the sights of hell. My sister entered the room and startled me. Noticing the buildup of sadness in my eyes, she sat on the bed reassuring me that everything would be alright. We went downstairs and had supper together. I felt good sitting with my family just like we used to before this strange upheaval.

Over the weeks, the hell within my mind dwindled as I learned to cope with a cold, rough northern way. Sarah took a shine to me, calling me the apple of her eye, hugging me and showering me with toothless kisses.

I reminded her of my father when he was a boy. "You're the spit from your father's mouth," she kept telling me.

We called her Aunt Sarah, although she wasn't. My father was left as a young baby for Sarah to rear, abandoned by a mysterious woman who ran off to some unknown freedom.

The mystery was never solved as both Sarah and my father were deep, secretive people who held the skeletons of their past secured within the vaults of their minds.

My father took a job as a panelbeater/sprayer [auto body repair person] and purchased a house for us. Before we moved from Sarah's I caught sight of a scene that would be etched in my memory forever.

I watched from the front bedroom window. My mother had tucked me into my temporary bed but I couldn't sleep. I saw a small stocky man running onto the street from a darkened alley. Dressed in a black bomber jacket and jeans, he wore a grimaced, painful expression on his white complexion, as if he were running for his life.

From the darkness came five black figures, their long coats flowing like shadows on water. The dim streetlights and the moon reflected from the shiny black peaks and the silver buttons of their uniforms.

The spectacle was like a private, disgusting entertainment for my benefit only. I stood affixed, as if I was the only punter [spectator] in the theatre.

The small stocky man was brought to the ground on the pavement below my window. The truncheon [club] flashed in the moonlight, impacting the side of his knee like thunder, sending shivers through me as if my bones were breaking. They kicked him into the gutter and took batons [nightsticks] from their coats. Hearing every contact of those batons with his body, my insides twisted. I tried to turn away or make a sound, but couldn't. I was numb with disbelief.

One of them jumped into the air and fell with the full force of his body weight, hatred and hobnailed boots opening the skull like a rotten potato. They beat him for what seemed a long time, but I couldn't be sure as I was locked within those moments. Names I did not understand rang in the night like howling gales. "Fenian!" "Bastard!" "Irish cunt!"

The men laughed a sick, horrid laugh and disappeared into

the darkness. Then one returned. I hoped he returned full of remorse and would pick the man up from the gutter. Little did I know that this incident in nineteen sixty-seven would be the norm for a quarter of a century.

The blood drained from my face as the broken body was shoved another foot along the gutter by the spit-polished boots. "There's one for the road," he said and disappeared into the night.

What sort of evil place is this, I thought, waking from the trance of hatred-ridden sights. I held my churning guts. My head grew light. I turned from the window to the picture of Jesus thorned and then to the busted body on the pavement and knew this can't be right.

As if I had all my young mind could comprehend, I slumped to my knees with exhaustion. My insides rolled and threw out their contents. The peas rolled like marbles on the cold floor.

After a sleepless night of sifting through my mind for an explanation—even now as I write this twenty-eight years later, knowing the politics of Northern Ireland, I still cannot fathom how a human can lower himself to such degrees of hatred—I dressed and went out onto the street before breakfast to see the stains and convince myself that I wasn't just dreaming. But the only signs remaining were spots on the pavement, bleached cleaner than the rest. I looked down to the blemishes of artificial purity like a lost soul.

I spun on my heel as if I knew my mother was there behind me. I gripped her and held her, pressing into her warm tummy like a newborn. "It happened. It happened," I cried.

She gripped me, knowing she was powerless. "I know it happened," she said. She dropped to my level and whispered, "Push the memory away. Everything will be alright. We'll be moving soon."

She held me and we walked across the pavement. Her tears erupted and she wiped them away and they fell behind her eyes, cascading into her heart.

BRIDIE MURPHY

BELFAST

Twelve-year-old Bridie Murphy tells me she keeps a diary because she can write down everything she feels and can't say and because she wants to remember everything. Although she says the rest of her diary is "too private," Bridie is willing to share this one particular entry with the world.

Living directly against the "peace wall" in one of the areas of West Belfast most heavily impacted by the Troubles, Bridie has seen more violence than many adults in wartime. "All my life I have been afraid," she says. "When it would get dark I would lie in bed and be frightened to move in case men would be outside who were going to smash the doors in with a sledgehammer and then shoot whoever is in the house as they have done before. Anyone who lives in my street has two ten-pound drop bars that they have to put on their doors. And they have shatterproof windows and grills on them to try to prevent these men from killing us."

Diary—28th April 1994

(Written at age eleven)

Yesterday was one of the worst days of my life. I was supposed to go to hospital but they rang up at the last moment and said an emergency came in and they needed the bed. So my mammy said I could go out to play. My friends were playing "Chase Me" at lunchtime and they were running after me. I did not look at where I was running and I ran right in front of a taxicab. The woman driving it was going slow but it still ran over my foot and leg. She drove me up to my house and took me and my Aunt Lorraine down to the hospital and my mammy followed down behind us.

My big toe and some bones in my foot were broken. They thought that my shin bone was cracked too so they put me in a plaster cast up to my knee. My mammy put me in her bed and gave me sweets and juice and it was great.

Then, later that night, my Aunt Lorraine and Mammy were worried because my oldest sister had not come home and it was getting late. Mammy had seen men on the Protestant side of the fence. They were cutting through the fence. Every time that happened before, the Protestant men came over and shot one of us Catholics. My mammy rang the police and told them what she had seen and they told her not to worry, they would make sure nothing happened, but she was still worried.

Then, about a quarter past eleven that night, my sister came home. She was talking to a young fella who was a passenger in the taxi. My aunt called to her to hurry in. They were in the hall and my mammy was telling my sister off for not coming in early. Then the shooting started. I heard a man screaming "I have been shot!" The shooting was still going on and on. Then my mammy and aunt ran out into the shooting.

I couldn't move because my leg was in plaster. The shooting went on for a few more seconds and then it was quiet except for the sound of someone moaning. Then people started to arrive on the street. I could hear them shouting that someone was dead. I could not get out of the bed—my leg was too sore—and I thought my aunt or my mammy was dead. I was sitting there on my bed crying.

Then, after a while, my aunt came in and hugged me and

told me my mammy was okay. But the boy my sister had been talking to in the taxi was dead and the taxi driver was wounded. She said my mammy was with the boy when he died.

When my mammy came in she came up to me and kissed me. She was very white and there was blood on her shirt but she was not crying.

I am frightened living on this street across from the Protestants. I am frightened they will come and kill us because this is the eleventh time they have shot people in our street. I don't know why they want to kill us.

My leg is sore today and the toes that are peeping out of the plaster are all black and blue, but at least I am getting to stay away from school.

JOHN McCONNELL

BELFAST

When I asked thirty-five-year-old John McConnell what stands out in his life, he said, "the Troubles. I've always been nervous . . . never calm . . . and with the cease-fires I'm just the same." When I interviewed him during the cease-fires, there had been no shootings for over a year, but John told me that he still jumped whenever he heard fireworks. "I've got it in my head," he said, 'Oh, that's shooting! That's shooting!' "

John was brought up in a conflict area near the Castlereagh Road in East Belfast, where he says he knew that every weekend there was going to be trouble. "Whenever you saw a gang standing on the corner, you knew they were just waiting for the Army and the police to come up so they could start trouble." Sometimes the violence was so bad that his mother kept him and his four brothers in the house.

As his story shows, John was always open to friendships on the other side of the divide and, as it turned out, his early romantic relationships were with Catholic girls. That made him a target for both sides, but somehow he was able to carry on peacefully.

Several years ago John was targeted by the IRA partly because of a mistaken identity and partly because he cooks for the Army. Of this terrifying time he says: "The police asked me if I wanted to move house or if I wanted to change my job. I said no. But I was putting things up against the doors. I thought someone was going to bust the doors down. The police asked if I wanted to arm myself. But I just wouldn't have a gun in the house."

This was just a few months before the cease-fires, which, when they were announced by both sides, helped a little to put John's mind at ease. He concludes his story, in fact, with the statement that there is peace now in Northern Ireland, which was a bit optimistic perhaps, even considering that it was written during the cease-fires.

Today John is living happily with his partner and their children, Gary, age three, and Lindsey, age two. He says, "So long as my kids are okay, I'm okay. I love my family. I live for my kids."

But one thing is missing for John. He misses Eamon, the childhood friend who is the subject of his story. He wrote this story in hopes that Eamon (whose last name is Marks) will read it and get in touch with him through the publisher of this book.

Eamon

This is my story of meeting Eamon in the times of the Northern Ireland Troubles.

I moved into an estate [housing project] on the outskirts of Belfast when I was about fifteen years old. I just hung about my house for the first few days. Then one day I was playing football by myself when two boys came up to me and asked me if I would like to play football with them. I said "yes," so we went over to a field where boys were picking teams.

One of the boys who asked me if I wanted to play football with them was called Eamon. I realised he must be a Catholic as the boys were laughing and saying that Eamon's team was Celtic. This was the first time I had met a Catholic and he was just like the rest of us. And a good footballer too!

When we stopped playing Eamon said he would walk round with me as he lived not far from me—about five doors away.

The conversation was mostly about football until I asked him if he supported the Celtics [a Catholic team with a Catholic following from Northern Ireland]. "Yes," he said and then he told me that he was a Catholic. There was a silence for a while between us and then he said he would see me later.

So later that night he called for me and we did what we did

most nights after that which was play more football and go to the school youth club.

I got to know Eamon better and he told me he'd lived on the estate for four years now and that he and his mother were the only Catholics in the estate. But he never talked about that much. He told me he was not interested in the Troubles. He only had time for his mother as his father had passed away.

Eamon was not what I thought Catholics were like—cross-eyed and dirty—although I had never met any of them up to now. Eamon was a tall, skinny lad—always well-dressed and with black straight combed hair. He was quiet and helpful.

One day he took me by surprise by saying he was going out to collect bonfire wood for the 11th July [eve of Orange Day, a Protestant holiday] and he wanted to know if I was going to help him. And I always thought that the Catholics went down to Dublin for the 11th–12th July to get away! He did his bit for the bonfire. We must have collected four doors and a lot of old tyres. Here was a Catholic lad out collecting wood for the Protestant bonfire. Nowadays we would be lucky to see a Catholic near a bonfire, let alone helping collect for one!

I saw Eamon a lot more now, but not in the daytime as he went to a Catholic school. One day I asked him would he have liked to have gone to our school and he said he would have loved to go to our school but he had to go to his own school because of his Catholic "ways."

That night I called for him. It was raining heavy and his mother, Pauline, came out and asked me did I want to come in as Eamon was upstairs. This was the first time I was in Eamon's house. I sat down and I noticed a cross and a picture of the Virgin Mary up on the wall.

Eamon's mother asked me did I like living in the estate. I said yes. After that it was quiet because I did not know what to say to her. Then she offered me some lemonade and then Eamon came in and asked his mother could I go up to his room. She said yes, so we went up. Eamon's room was like mine—pop posters and football posters—only he had Celtic posters up! He told me about the time when there were only about five Catholic families living on the estate and one night he heard a lot of shouting and screaming. He looked out the back window of his house and saw a Catholic family moving out and a crowd around his own house. He said he panicked and ran downstairs and told his mother. She locked all the doors and drew the curtains. Then there was a knock at the door.

Eamon said his mother was screaming and they heard a lot of screaming outside. He looked out the window and saw a group of women. They shouted to him to open the door and he said he opened it because he knew a lot of the women at his door. They came in and they asked where his mother was. She was in the kitchen and they got her to calm down as she was in hysterics.

I asked Eamon how did he feel and he said he felt scared and shaking. He felt like running out of the house and not stopping. But he also said he worried about his mother.

He told me that one of the women from the estate had told him that men from other areas had come into the estate to get all of the Catholic families out. The women said they would help keep Eamon and his mother safe from the men. The women stood outside their door and front window and shouted to these men to go away. He said it lasted about twenty minutes. But it was like all night to him.

Then the men went away but they shouted that they would be back. But this never happened.

His mother would not move house but she was still afraid to go out of the house for about six months and she had to get help from the doctor. Eamon told her he didn't want to move either. The women of the estate helped him and his mother a lot and this is why they stayed in the estate.

That night really told me what kind of person Eamon was—caring and helpful, and he loved his mother.

I got to know his mother well and so did my own mother.

The 11th night came and we were celebrating. Eamon was with us and we were singing "The Sash" [a Protestant anthem] and he joined in. He even sang the "Billy Boys," another well-known Protestant song!

It was not long after this that there were a lot of tit-for-tat shootings going on—Protestants shooting Catholics and Catholics shootings Protestants. The trouble was getting worse. Eamon still never said much about the Troubles that were going on. That was his nature.

After one night at the school youth club we walked home and said the usual things—"see you later," "see you tomorrow." But I never did. That night someone shot two shots through Eamon's window. I heard the bangs and went downstairs. My father told me to stay in the house, so I looked out of my brother's window and saw a crowd at Eamon's house. Then I saw an ambulance come and take someone away.

My mother came up and told me that Eamon was shot. But he was okay as he was shot in the lower leg. I felt numb. And I felt hatred for the ones who did this. Why Eamon, I just kept asking myself.

Next morning I saw a lorry moving all of the furniture out of Eamon's house. I ran downstairs and I asked one of the men where was Eamon and he just said he was in hospital and he was okay.

Later I found out it was one of his uncles moving house for him and his mother. I never heard of where he moved to, but there was a rumour going around that he moved to England and is living there now. I still think about him and wonder how he would feel now that there is peace in Northern Ireland.

JAMES BAILIE

BELFAST

One of five children, James Bailie was born at home, near Belfast's Shankill Road, in 1953. As he describes in his essay written at age fifteen—an assignment to tell what he did over the summer vacation of 1969—he grew up in a Protestant neighborhood close to the interface between the two communities in Belfast and was, therefore, an eyewitness to considerable violence. The map on page 40, with which James illustrated his school essay, is an example of how children try to make sense of the Troubles—in this case, visually.

Forty-two now, James is married with two children. He works as a quality inspector for Short Brothers Aerospace Manufacturers in Belfast and lives in a quiet area near the Holywood Road, where he and his wife Yvonne, a cleaner at Queen's University, moved in 1983 to get their children out of the worst of the Troubles.

The Riots in Belfast
(Written at age fifteen)

I am a Protestant living in the Shankill Road area of Belfast. My father is an Orangeman [member of a Protestant organization] and hates the Catholics. My mother and the rest of us have no quarrel with them although we never associate with them. The trouble is that people like my father and his Catholic counterparts cannot live in peace together as the riots have shown.

I was at the scene of the outbreak of the riots [August 3, 1969] and I feel I am qualified to give an account of what happened. I suppose it all started at Unity Walk when the Catholic inhabitants stoned our procession of juveniles [young participants in the annual Protestant Orange parades] while we were marching past. Obviously it was only a few troublemakers who started it but, nevertheless, the whole community had to suffer

Drawn by James Bailie

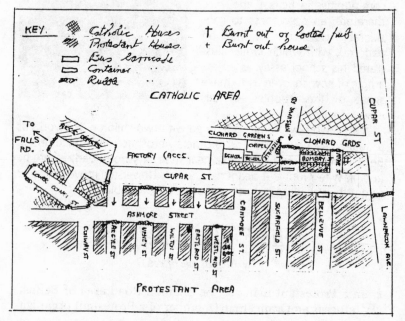

the consequences. The efforts of the police were enough to keep these troublemakers apart but tension mounted and the parade in Derry [August 12] was enough to start the fighting off again on an even deadlier scale.

My friends and I were touring our area [August 14] and saw groups of men facing a few hundred Catholics in lower Cupar Street. Suddenly the mob started running up the street, but shouts from our boys were enough to bring reinforcements from neighbouring streets.

For about twenty minutes these two forces battled but neither seemed to be gaining any headway. From nearby David Street, petrol bombs were hurled into the midst of the Protestants but these were met with equal strength by the victims.

Police trucks arrived in time to prevent serious trouble breaking out. They sped down Cupar Street right into our boys. Fortunately they jumped out of the way in time but a third truck came while our lads were running behind the previous ones in glory. This time they were not so lucky because two of them were struck down by the vehicle. Later I found out it was a neighbour of mine and a particular friend of mine who was one of the victims.

The police kept the hotheads away from each other for the night. I did not see any more fighting because I was only permitted to stand at the corner of Cupar Street.

No one was able to sleep that night since we were all put on alert. Rumours were spreading that Catholics from faraway estates [housing projects] were coming. The only place for them to get by was Kashmir Road, but to our relief it was heavily guarded by vigilantes from neighbouring streets.

Right up to about two o'clock bursts of gunfire ripped the peace of the night, but nothing more than this was visible or audible that night.

Next day [August 15], preparations for protecting ourselves were made. A nearby factory in Cupar Street was forced open and containers were rolled out and put at street corners facing the Catholic area behind Cupar Street. I helped in these preparations.

A meeting was in progress in Canmore Street where Johnny McQuade M.P. [Member of Parliament] was attending. He was talking about peace and how to protect yourselves without starting anything with the "enemy."

No sooner had the bottom of the Kashmir Road been barricaded than about twenty Catholics in a large lorry, obviously hijacked, arrived at Bombay Street and blocked off the end of the Kashmir Hill. All was set now for a pitched battle and it was not long before the first stones rained down on us.

In our street, petrol bombs were frantically being prepared while, at the scene of the battle, paving stones were being pulled up and shattered to provide ready ammunition. This time no police came and both forces were left to fight it out.

It was not long before the guns came out on their side. Incidentally, it was only four o'clock in the evening. These guns frightened our boys and kept them from advancing up the hill.

The main thing which worried us was that Mockil's [engineering works on Springfield Road] workers had not come home yet. Their usual way home was through the Catholic area but they could not possibly go that way now.

Suddenly a man ran down Cupar Street and a few remarked he'd had enough, but a few minutes later he returned with a shotgun. Until now I had not seen a gun in these riots. He positioned himself behind the Kashmir Road and from reliable sources I heard that he had shot five Catholics. One of them I was told was killed.

More Protestants took his lead and got their guns. Mainly they were shotguns or pistols but two had rifles. Altogether there were no more than six guns.

At the Catholic school which our boys unsuccessfully tried to burn I actually saw one of us shot in the face. Luckily it was a shotgun and he appeared to be alright, though streams of blood covered his face. I gave him my handkerchief and a while later he was taken to hospital in an ambulance. That was enough for me. I realized that since I was only a few feet away from him it could as easily be me that was hit by the spreading buckshot.

I ran up to our house via Eastland Street to avoid being the target of this sniper from the school, eager to tell about my close experience.

At about four o'clock the Army made a brief appearance at the scene of the trouble, but before half on four [4:30 P.M.] had elapsed they were gone.

By now our crowd had taken over the Catholic barricade, burnt as it was, and proceeded to burn every house in Bombay Street—as the Catholic houses in lower Conway Street had suffered the previous night.

It was dark by now and the fighting had been going on for about eight hours when the troops took over, firing tear gas grenades to disperse the crowd.

That was the end of the fighting. The next day the Army put up their barricades and for two days we were virtually locked in.

Now everything has quietened down, but at night organised parties of Protestants patrol our streets to ensure there are no Catholic reprisals for the deeds which our kind carried out. Radio Free Belfast [Nationalist Catholic radio channel] threatens us saying that Wilton, Conmore, Sugarfield, and Bellevue Streets will suffer the same fate as Conway and Bombay Streets. All I can say to this is that they will need a very strong force to carry out their threats judging by the number of men we have guarding us.

GLYN CHAMBERS

BELFAST

Seventeen-year-old Glyn Chambers lives in a two-story duplex with his mother, a hospital secretary, and his thirteen-year-old brother in relatively peaceful East Belfast. While the family was not directly exposed to violence during the Troubles, Glyn says that since the cease-fires, it is far more convenient to get to school at the Royal Belfast Academical Institution now that it doesn't take an hour to get through all the police checkpoints en route. "My school is in the city center," Glyn says, "so we've had plenty of bomb scares."

A Unionist [Protestant political party] and a member of the Northern Ireland Young Conservative Party, he says he has learned a lot about Catholics during the Troubles. "You do come round to seeing other people's points of view," he says and, as he conveys in this poem written especially for this book, he does not see why cultural differences should have led to a complete separation of the two communities.

With all its troubles, Glyn is glad to be growing up in Northern Ireland. "I think this country has had a very bad write-up," he says. "I believe that in New York City three thousand people are killed in crimes every year. That's the same as died in twenty-five years of the Troubles."

Two Communities

(Written at age seventeen)

We live in this street, they live in that street,
yet both communities live in Belfast.
We follow this religion, they follow that religion,
yet both communities believe in God.
We vote for these parties, they vote for those parties,
yet both communities recognize each other's mandate.
We feel bound to one country, they feel bound to another
     country,
yet both communities are bound to Northern Ireland.
We think they are troublemakers, they think we are trouble-
     makers,
yet both communities have contributed to the Troubles.
We claim they get too much, they claim we get too much,
yet both communities wish to create a prosperous, equal
society with opportunities for all.
Two communities, but what are the differences?

GEMMA McHENRY

BALLYCASTLE, COUNTY ANTRIM

Twenty-eight-year-old Gemma Mc-Henry, her five sisters, and two brothers began their lives in Woodvale, a mixed area of Belfast, where the children had mostly Protestant friends. "There was some name-calling," she remembers, "but we ignored it. We were happy there."

Then, when Gemma was ten, a neighbor and good friend of her father's answered a knock at his door one day and was shot twice in the stomach by a Protestant paramilitary. "It was time to go," Gemma says, "because Daddy would never feel safe there again." The family moved to Andersonstown, a predominantly Catholic neighborhood, where Gemma's mother and father still live today.

Gemma happened to see an article about this anthology in the newspaper. "I can do that," she said to herself and sat down and wrote this essay about her political awakening while her colicky baby, one of Gemma's and her husband Phillip's three very young children, slept. She says she thought someone was pulling her leg when she received a letter accepting her work.

Children of the Troubles

Being a child of the Troubles in Belfast was normal for me. I didn't know anything else. Just like children in the slums of cities all over the world who know no better, we knew there was a big world out there but this was our world. The love and security we had at home made up for all the madness going on around us.

I was brought up in a mixed area (Protestant and Catholic) and I had mixed friends and thought nothing of it. We were all innocent children. I would be asked by my Protestant friends to say the Hail Mary. To me it was the only difference between us. Sometimes I needed to say it to prove I was a Catholic!

Those were happy days of innocence, but reality hit us with a bang when a Protestant neighbour was shot by Republican paramilitaries for being a member of the Security Forces. And then a Catholic neighbour was shot for being a Catholic.

As a Catholic family it became too dangerous for us to continue living there. After our windows were put in around us twice, it was time to leave. We uprooted and moved to Andersonstown, a Nationalist [Catholic] area of West Belfast. No longer would we shop on the Shankill Road or play with our Protestant friends.

My father, mother, and eight children settled into Andersonstown well. No matter how tough life was, our house was a loving home. Any financial or other problems were kept from us so that we could enjoy growing up. My father worked overtime to keep a car on the road so we could escape every summer to a seaside town called Ballycastle. It was our safe haven away from the troubles. It was a place where my parents didn't have to worry where we were and if we were safe.

Life went on in Andersonstown and so did the Troubles— but it was normal for us children. It was normal to be thought of (by certain groups) as a second-class citizen because you were a Catholic. It was normal to feel that you were not important. It had been this way for so long that people started accepting it. Yes, there had been a few compromises, but the attitude was still the same. It was always one set of rules for the British and another for the Irish. There was too much injustice and things had to change.

For me it changed when the Hunger Strike began. Hunger strikes have been in Irish history for as long as the British have but I had never witnessed one. I couldn't believe that these men were going to be allowed to die. As a teenager I found it shocking that a government who could stop it would not.

So we waited for the sound of bin lids [garbage can lids] banging on the ground. This would mean that a young man had died. At the start of the troubles, the sound of bin lids warned of a nearby British Army patrol. Now it was the sound of DEATH. The whole area was so tense you could smell it. We prayed that someone would step in and stop it—that someone would wake us up from this nightmare—but no one did. When the noise of the bin lids broke out it was deafening. The first Hunger Striker had died. I was afraid. Afraid for every Nationalist and what it would do to us and afraid for my family. The fear was rife. And I was angry at the waste of a human life.

I made the decision to attend the funeral of Bobby Sands. I would usually have stayed away from anything political, but I went as a sign of respect for a young man who had given his life for what he believed in. I did it as a sign of disgust at a government who had let it happen and didn't care about any of us. We were always the stupid Irish to them.

I expected a big funeral but I was stunned at how many people had turned up, many of them for the same reasons as myself. There were thousands walking in silence. It was like a great big river of respect flowing through the streets, a river of emotion. It was packed with heavy hearts. Some were sad, some were angry, and some were terribly afraid of the future.

This was an awakening for me. My usual life of school, boys, and fashion faded away and for once in my life I knew how I felt. This large group of mourners had made me realise that I wasn't a second-class citizen, nor was I unimportant. How could I be when there were thousands just like me? I was an Irish Catholic Nationalist and it was important to me. No longer would I bury my head in the sand. I would be proud of myself as a Catholic and as a human being. I had the right to be the same as anyone else and no less.

PEARSE ELLIOTT

BELFAST

The eldest of seven children and still living at home with his family, Pearse Elliott was born on the strife-torn Falls Road in 1970. When he recently found a class photograph, he was amazed by how many of his pictured school friends are dead or in jail as a result of the Troubles.

Pearse says that hunger striker Bobby Sands's funeral when he was eleven had the most profound effect on him of anything in his childhood. It was the mood of that time in 1981 in the Catholic district of Belfast that he intended to capture in this story, which he wrote in 1995. Until this day he is haunted by images from that painful time: "The great massing, one hundred thousand people being silent, the aura of power, and this coffin phalanxed by the IRA, and the thought of this corpse being responsible for my normally so easygoing mother on her knees in the dirt with all the other women, tears coursing down her face and beating bin lids [garbage can lids] on the ground when he died . . ."

Reminiscent of the way in which children terrified by events often need to describe what happened to them as happening to an imaginary friend, Pearse writes of his own painful and horrifying experience in the third person, as though that were the only way he could manage to get the story told.

Writing since he was a very young child, Pearse won the BBC's Young Playwright Festival award last year and received four hundred pounds for his work.

Pearse entitled this story "The Hurricane's Mane," in order to convey a sense of the storm the country has been in and to indicate that, as with the eye of a hurricane, a peaceful period can be deceptive.

The Hurricane's Mane

1981. It is three o'clock in the morning. Ebony night, no stars, no moon—just big rain on the barren streets. The child is awake. He has been awake since the great pain started. In the distance he hears them come—the war chariot's chimes and the saracen's roars, coughing gear shifts, gaining momentum.

The old mongrel musters a shrill wail, a pathetic rebuke, not much of a deterrent but a gallant sentinel doing his bit. The child bites his gum. He always did this in times of distress but he had never drawn blood like he was doing now. The blood singed his mouth as the war chariots stopped outside, their great noise climaxing in the high-pitched whining of brakes.

The child is aware now, aware of a consequence endemic in his ancestry. He wants to wake them all up, to find some clandestine place, some area where they all could hide, where they all could run, where no one could find or hurt them. But there is no such place.

He hears the percussion of many boots on wet concrete. His heart vaults as the door crumples under the sledgehammer's punch. A thousand foreign roars, screaming intentions, and expletives. The child remains very still until he hears the stairs bend under the heavy tattoos of big boots and he has to get up, for he had never heard his "Da" scream like that before.

Fear burns and the child is ablaze. "Why? Who?" That's what he wanted to know.

"Sure we do no one any harm!" he shouted to deaf ears.

The child didn't know much but he knew this was wrong. "This is fucking wrong, fucking wild, fucking bad!" his mind screamed.

RUC [police] and soldiers, he didn't know how many but more than there were of his family—and bigger too. He stared at their guns, not like cowboys or Starsky and Hutch, but black and sleek and steel. The child knew if they were to spit the result wouldn't be tomato sauce.

"*Why?* Why wreck everything? That's our toilet, you understand? They're my Ma's favorite curtains. Please don't do that! *Why* do you drag everything like roots from the ground? *Why* are all your voices smeared in intimidation?

The child sees the demon who operates them like puppets on strings. The demon is black and it has a forked tail and a split tongue. And it dons a flak jacket. The child also sees his tortured mother, all femininity and sanctuary, raped as the spittle hits her crying face. The child knows where she is for he has been there, lost at night in the dark with the terrible things the mind weaves—only this time the monsters are real.

He was in a car crash when he was a little younger and this was the same. He acknowledged they would be hurt; he just prayed not that bad. "No, that's my Da! You'll break him like a toy!" the child screamed. He rushes into the melee. He wants to grow up quick to sprout big man's arms so he can fight but all he can feel is the kiss of a combat boot.

There are other fears now—the brothers and sisters, the fawns are in the grass and the wolves can scent them. He tries to fight but they wreck him. He tries to scream but nothing comes except heart pain. And do you know what heart pain is? Nothing, nothing but decimation.

The child has an intuition and the rationale to decipher right and wrong. This is wrong.

The child is no longer a child; he is a so-called man now. And when the man reminisces he contemplates this uneasy peace and he can still sense it seething and writhing. He believes Typhon [father of the monsters, in this case signifying the monster of the Troubles] still could be resurrected, if we're not careful, and that is when the man becomes a child again.

ROBIN LIVINGSTONE

BELFAST

Now in his thirties, married, and the father of a five-year-old daughter, Robin Livingstone is the deputy editor of the *Andersonstown News,* a community newspaper in a predominantly Catholic area of Belfast. Although he frequently writes for the paper, this story, written in 1995, is his first work to appear in a book.

Although this is a very tragic story about the tremendous loss sustained by his family from the burning of Dover Street, Robin doesn't discuss any of the emotional reactions one might expect him to have had. This "omission" seems to give the story even greater emotional impact since the reader can well imagine that the pain was more than Robin could bear to fully feel as a child or to write about as an adult.

A very sad footnote to Robin's story of the burning of his family's home in Belfast when he was nine is that his baby sister Julie, whose life his mother saved by clutching her to her breast and carrying her out of the fire, was shot dead by a British soldier twelve years later.

Over the Wall

We moved into the cavernous three-story house at 124 Dover Street in 1966 when I was five years old. Fourteen of us there were: my parents, eight boys, and four girls (and one on the way)—children ranging in age from one to sixteen.

Sharing a bed with a usually indeterminate number of brothers never bothered me much. As long as you weren't lying on pyjama-free summer evenings beside somebody old enough to have started growing hair on his legs (a ticklish night assured if you were), it wasn't a problem. And as long as you weren't on the outside closest to the cupboard where the guy with the hatchet used to hide (big brothers' considerate nightly warning to little brothers), you were fine. Hot, but fine.

Three years in Dover Street went by in a blur of typical boyhood landmarks: I fell off the top of a workman's hut and landed on my head, which wouldn't have been just as bad had the hut not been mounted on the back of a truck. I found a five-pound note on the pavement outside the Arkle Inn one payday and gave it to the first man who came out of the bar (then home to one incredulous mother and seven guffawing brothers). My da [dad] took some of us to see a circus in the Grove Theatre and a rich friend of his drove us home in his Mercedes. We fell asleep wrapped in leather and smoke.

But in there among those reassuringly dull pre-1969 memories, nestling like earwigs in a basket of dried washing, are other, darker recollections which make me uncomfortable solely because they only bother me now; back then they were as natural and accepted as fighting in the playground or pissing in the water at the Falls Baths.

My da, a lorry driver, used to send for lemonade when he got back from work. Ross's Lemonade, he always wanted, sold not in the shop frequented by Catholics at the lower end of Dover Street but in the grocer's further up, across the invisible line that separated the Shankill end from the Falls end. We all took turns at the lemonade run.

Outside that shop groups of Protestant teenagers used to stand, laughing and joking the way teenagers do. Walking into the shop was to run a gauntlet of perfunctory verbal and physical abuse, the "wee Fenian" [little Nationalist Catholic] greetings accompanied by light slaps on the head, sidefoot kicks up the arse. I was never hurt at that shop; I don't think I was ever even afraid. But at six and seven and eight years of age I already knew my place.

We have an aunt in Birmingham [England] and two of my sisters went off to visit her the night they burned Dover Street.

My da took them down to the boat and when the air became thick and the great roar from the Shankill grew louder my mother got us out of bed and sat, alone, with her children in the back room.

We held on longer than just about every other Catholic family in the street. Afraid to go out the front door, unable to go out the back, we crouched together and listened to the yelling and the shooting. The eldest boy, Pat, had earlier taken himself off to do whatever eighteen-year-olds do when balloons go up. Now he arrived home, panting and red-cheeked with excitement, to announce that it was time to get out the back. Our da came home just a few minutes later and he never tires of telling the story of how Pat brought him upstairs and made him peek through a window to see the late Woodvale Member of Parliament, Johnny McQuade, instructing a group of petrol bombers outside our door: "Work to rule, boys," he was telling them. "Work to rule!"

It was as we were leaving by the back door that the first petrol bomb was thrown into the parlour, the sound of breaking glass followed by a gentle whoosh just before the door closed behind us.

The ten-foot brick wall at the back of the yard had broken bottles cemented into its top and the white and green glass sparkled crazily in the bright orange light from the burning Sarsfields Club. Over the other side of the wall was a thirty-foot drop into a corporation depot [grounds of an industrial plant] in Boundary Street. A neighbour, a man called Tohill, ran a set of depot ladders up the wall. It was then a matter of climbing onto the roof of our outside toilet, crawling over a pile of blankets which had been thrown across the glass, and down the ladder into the depot.

The three men took the smaller children, two at a time, over the wall and down the ladder. We had all stayed remarkably quiet and calm throughout, mostly because this all seemed more like some wild adventure than a flight for life. Last over was our mother, clutching two-year-old Julie to her chest. But when she froze at the top of the ladder, terrified of the height and the heat and the noise, shouting at us all to go on without her, the adventure suddenly ended. To the roar of the mob, the crackle of burning houses, and the thud of gunfire was finally added the wailing of youngsters.

After some minutes, my mother was coaxed down by Pat, who got below her, grasping her ankles and placing her feet deliberately and slowly on each rung. It was decided that we should head to the other side of Divis Street, away from the shooting and away from the fires. But as the ragtag procession of half-dressed children and their parents emerged onto the main road, we were attacked with bricks and bottles by a crowd of B-Specials [members of a government reserve militia which has since been disbanded] who were deployed across Divis Street.

As the bricks and bottles bounced and smashed around us, we turned and ran back towards the depot. My father ventured back out onto the road, shouting at the Specials for Christ's sake to let him through with his wife and children. They let up and we filed across the street.

Into Durham Street and we sat down on the pavement to rest. The sound and the light were softer here and as we sat in silence a large estate car pulled up. A man with a camera got out. His name was Mallon and he had come into town to take some pictures. He lived up Saintfield direction where he owned the Ivanhoe Inn as well as some other properties.

After a brief discussion we were piled into the big car for the twenty-minute drive to a small bungalow he owned about half a mile from Purdysburn Hospital. We didn't use the beds in the bungalow, preferring to sleep here and there in the one room, swaddled in the few coats, shirts, and jumpers [sweaters] that we had managed to lug with us.

Breakfast time the next day and a group of women from a nearby factory brought us food: a big catering pot of tea and more sandwiches than even a squad of our size could eat. The women aahed and cooed and patted us on the head as we ate.

Our mother, meantime, who spent four-fifths of her time making sure we were well turned out, was fussing and clucking around, wiping our black-streaked faces and hands with anything that would pass for a facecloth. She never stopped, even when we did.

We stayed there for the rest of that summer and on into the autumn, playing in the small orchard beside the house, reading the cupboardful of old comics that some previous tenant had left behind. Perhaps he or she knew that they would be well used one day.

We even enrolled in the local school for a short while, an intimidating place where they used to crack you over the knuckles with a spoon if you put your hands or elbows on the table at lunch.

My mother took two of us back to Dover Street a few days after we left. The front parlour was badly burned and the whole of the bottom floor was knee-deep in water after the looters had ripped pipes out before leaving. Everything was gone: furniture (beds and all), clothes, ornaments, dishes, cutlery. My mother said she didn't expect to get anything, but later I learned that she was praying she might find a bit of the brass or ruby glass that her mother had left her and which she used to polish at night when we were all upstairs sleeping.

A British soldier came rushing out of the kitchen when he heard us sloshing around. A young woman followed him, doing up the buttons on her floral-print dress. My mother gripped her hands without a word and walked us out the front door. None of us ever went back there again.

We got a flat in Divis where we stayed for about a year before moving up to a big five-bedroom house in Lenadoon in November, 1970. Four of us rode up the Falls Road in the cab of the big furniture van, sitting on the engine casing beside the driver, a heavy horse blanket over our legs.

Twenty-five years later, there are just three brothers left there. My mother died three years ago and she's buried with Julie, the baby she carried over the wall all those years ago.

STEPHEN ROBINSON

BELFAST

Twenty-seven-year-old Stephen Robinson has worked as a plater and welder at Harland and Wolff Shipbuilding for the last ten years. Having read about this anthology in the newspaper, Stephen submitted this story about the way his life was changed when the top of his head was blown away by a terrorist's bullet as he walked home from secondary school.

Now, twenty-two years later, Stephen, the son of an Orangeman [Protestant organization with anti-Catholic sentiments], holds no bitterness toward the man who shot him, and he says that some of his closest friendships are across the sectarian divide.

Shot in the Head

I had just graduated from Blythefield Primary School and I was looking forward to starting my secondary education. My friends who I was with at primary level would be going to the same school. At the time [1973], the Troubles in Northern Ireland were at a very dangerous level. The school which I would go to was very close to an Army base and very often you would see soldiers patrolling. I found it very difficult to concentrate at school and I think that the Troubles could have played a part.

Sometimes you would hear the occasional explosion or maybe some kind of device being thrown at the Army and you were always aware of those kinds of things going on around you.

After school you would get involved in some disturbances with Catholics. It was mainly stone throwing at each other, and I did get caught up in a bit of it now and again, but I tried mostly to keep away from it.

I was finishing my third year and I was getting ready for exams. I can't remember the day that I was shot but I had finished school at approximately 3:30 P.M. and was going home with a few friends. In the distance I could see that there had been some trouble, but I and my friends had not been involved. As I kept on walking, there was this most terrible explosion in my head. I had been shot in the head. At that stage I was in total confusion. I was bleeding very badly and was swaying all over the road. Someone threw a towel over my head. I was later told that a car stopped with two men in it and I was rushed to the nearby Royal Victoria Hospital. I was operated on as soon as I arrived.

I came around about two days later and there was a nurse at my bedside. She asked me if I knew what had happened. I told her I did. She said that I was lucky to be alive.

Something came over me when I was shot and I began to think that I was being croaked by someone who was trying to take me away from all of this. I saw angels. To this day I have not told very many persons about this strange thing.

Later I had to go back to the hospital to get a plate inserted in my forehead because the bullet had done damage when it exited. During my stay in hospital I was to meet a Catholic. He had been shot in the head also and during our brief encounter we got on very well.

He had been working in a nursery school very close to my home as a painter and was shot by a gunman during his lunch break. It was very eye-opening being in the next bed to him and him being shot close to my own home. I have never seen him again ever since that meeting over twenty years ago, but those events make you think.

I was very glad to see a cease-fire and I trust that it will last. There is an awful lot of talking to be done but I see it as new road to better horizons and I trust that we can all continue to make it work for everyone in Northern Ireland.

MARGARET McCRORY

COOKSTOWN, COUNTY TYRONE

Margaret McCrory, now in her thirties, writes and raises her family on a farm seven miles out of Cookstown in County Tyrone. The crisp autumn afternoon that I went to visit her we sat behind closed doors in front of a turf fire in her living room while her teenage daughters made a fancy tea in my honor and her young son played ball with his friends and his dog in the front yard. Occasionally one of the girls would come in to stoke the fire with another piece of peat, which is dug from the earth, dried in rectangular chunks, and used as fuel.

"You must think I'm a fool," Margaret began our conversation. What tumbled out in the half hour we talked privately is that Margaret herself sometimes wonders if she did the right thing in deciding to return to Northern Ireland to marry and raise a family after her own parents had emigrated from Northern Ireland to America when she was thirteen. Her teenage daughter, who visits her grandparents often, is certain that life in the States far outshines life on a farm, seven miles from anywhere, in the middle of Northern Ireland. She is never more certain of this than during lambing season, when she must take her turn staying up all night to await expected births, or when she goes to her job washing dishes at a Cookstown hotel after school—the only part-time job she could find.

Yet for Margaret the importance of the family living in a place they can truly call home outweighs all of the difficulties—even those caused by the Troubles, to which Cookstown is no stranger. After a year of the cease-fires, while most towns were disassembling barricades and relaxing security, I saw soldiers patrolling with rifles aimed and ready to fire near a barbed-wire-covered Cookstown Royal Ulster Constabulary (police) station.

In the following story, Margaret conveys the absolute terror of a child's being trapped in the crossfire in Belfast during the conflagration that resulted from the institution of internment. This policy, which was sanctioned by the government of Great Britain in response to the violence in Northern Ireland, allowed the police to imprison people they deemed suspicious without the necessity of charging them with a crime or producing evidence.

Internment

August 9, 1971, is a day I will remember as long as I live. We were emigrating to America the next day but that's not why I'll remember that date. That was the night of Internment. I was only thirteen at the time, but just thinking about that day still brings back the knotted feelings in my stomach.

I was supposed to feel excited about leaving and also sad to be saying good-bye to our friends and neighbours. But we woke up that morning to a strange silence outside. We found ourselves whispering to each other and sneaking looks out the windows. There was nothing out there at all—no people, no cars, not even the dogs were barking. It was eerie.

We felt something big was about to happen, but when? The waiting was the worst feeling I've ever felt. I don't know if we would have sensed so much tension if my Mum hadn't kept repeating over and over again, "Please, Lord, get us out of here." She looked and acted like she was scared to death and I suppose some of that rubbed off on us. We were very subdued all day. The funny thing was there wasn't a bite in the house, yet no one complained they were hungry.

Late afternoon, and there was still no activity outside. By this time we were all nervous wrecks. We had nothing in the house to occupy us—just a couple of mattresses and our suitcases. Hugh, who was nine, was so nervous that he made himself sick. Mum made him lie down on the mattress in the boys' room on the second floor. Eileen, eleven, was walking around like a zombie, staring straight ahead with huge eyes. She was scary. David, eight, and Maria, seven, were playing quietly on the bare floor, which was really unusual for them. Mum and I took it in turns to peek out of the windows.

Mum had gone into the kitchen to brush [sweep] the floor when the shooting began. We could hear the bullets whizzing over the house and ricocheting off the corrugated iron on the factory wall behind our house. The bullets smashed through the kitchen window. Mum dropped the brush and ran. To this very day she still complains about leaving a pile of dirt on the floor.

Hugh was crying upstairs and Eileen was screaming her head off. Between the deafening noise inside and the explosive noises from outside, we felt like we were in the middle of World War III. All the shooting seemed to be at the back of the house where the boys' room was so we dragged Hugh and the mattress up to the third floor where our room overlooked the front of the house. We all huddled together on the mattresses.

It was very hot but when Mum opened the window a little bit we could feel our throats begin to burn. Which meant that there was tear gas out there, and from past experience we knew what that could do to you. Your throat would begin to burn and your eyes would sting like mad. Then you would feel violently sick. It was a horrible feeling so we quickly shut the window.

The Uzis were going mad out there—the noise was incredible!—and Eileen couldn't stop screaming. I was scared but I also felt excited and very curious. I really wanted to know what was going on out there so every chance I got I would sneak a look outside. I could see men with guns running up our street. They saw me and shooed me in by gesturing with their hands to get down. Mum made me sit with them on the mattresses, but Eileen's screaming was driving me mad so I finally told her that they weren't going to kill her because I was going to do it first. She quieted down to loud whimpering instead.

We could see the orange glow of petrol bombs exploding and hear the bang of plastic bullets being fired. The boys were good at recognizing the sounds because they used to collect spent cartridges after nights of violence. But this was the worst we had ever seen.

Finally Maria, David, and Hugh went to sleep. Mum had to comfort Eileen, who was scared out of her mind. There was too much going on to even think of sleep. Every so often there would be a slight lull and I would run to the window. The sky was really bright now. The barricades were burning so as to keep the soldiers out. I could see men outside shooting their guns up the avenue. They were hiding behind walls, bins, poles—anything at all. It was like watching television. When several bullets hit the wall outside our window Mum made me lie down again.

We heard people shouting for Father Murphy, our parish priest, to come and give someone the Last Rites. Ten minutes later we heard shouts of "They killed Father Murphy!" "They shot him!" "Three bodies on top of each other!" Mum and I could only look at each other in shock. Father Murphy was our friend. He taught Hugh and David how to box. He had been at our house only yesterday—they must be wrong.

They weren't. Ten men died that night, all from our street. Father Murphy had been shot dead while giving a man the Last Rites. And when another man went to help Father Murphy he had been killed as well.

It was very hard lying there listening to the *rat-a-tat* of the gunfire and not think that someone else might be dead. The excitement was gone and fear and deep sadness were left. We lay there until morning when, finally, all noises stopped and we could hear our neighbours outside.

They were clustered together exchanging war stories and talking about Father Murphy. We were next on their agenda. We were never going to get out, they said, and no one was going to risk his life to get us out. I think they were a bit jealous.

Mum didn't give up. She asked everybody until one man with an old post office van said yes.

We had an awful time getting through burnt-out barricades and around overturned lorries—sometimes even human barricades. After many detours we finally reached the airport to find no planes were flying that day. We were bundled into a minibus and driven to Dublin.

We were still in shock from the night before. Even after twenty-four hours with no food none of us complained that we were hungry. Every time we heard Father Murphy's name mentioned on the radio we cried our eyes out but Mum just kept repeating "Thank God we're out!" That's all she would say.

She was dead right though. Thank God we did get out.

MARGARET E. SIMPSON

BELFAST

When I visited Margaret Simpson on an icy, blustery autumn day in Belfast, three generations were awaiting me: Margaret, her husband, her four-year-old daughter Amy, and Margaret's mother, who had obviously been baking all day in anticipation of the Devon tea the family would share with me.

Now thirty-five and living in a sedate neighborhood of detached homes on quiet streets with her husband and two young daughters, Margaret grew up in what she calls a "kitchen house" near the Shankill Road with two rooms up and two rooms down and the toilet in the backyard. She remembers that when street fighting with Catholics would erupt, neighbors would come into her family's house to collect whatever they could find for barricades. One day they took her mother's ironing board.

Margaret has been writing poetry since age seven. The first of her poems that follows was written when she was fifteen. In 1994 she joined a writers' group and really began to take her writing seriously. She has had a number of her poems published in the group's magazine, *Stadium*.

The terrifying events that Margaret writes about in the second poem that follows, "Kneecapped," occurred when she was fifteen, but it wasn't until 1995 that she could bring herself to write about them.

Tragically, kneecapping is a frequent form of "policing" done by paramilitaries of all persuasions in Northern Ireland. Intended to reinforce their power in their own communities, to discourage any possible disclosures to the police or Army, and to frighten people into compliance, maiming a person in this way often means they will never walk or function normally again.

Belfast Boy

(Written at age fifteen)

Look in his eyes,
The lonely stir,
A vacant look
So often there.
His little hands fidget
And his fingers twist,
He is only a number
On a social list.
One of a thousand Belfast boys
With guns and stones for his toys.
What age would you say?
"Almost eleven?"
The child is grown up
And he is only seven.
But he's not your son—
Are you so sure?
He's a son of Ulster
No one wants anymore.

Kneecapped

He came to our door on a Wednesday night
As I was about to leave,
Walk my granny home, at least halfway
Up the back Shankill into Indian territory.
I suppose I thought myself brave at fifteen
To face Ardoyne alone,
Well, almost.
He rang the doorbell, normal enough,
Asked if he might use our phone,
An emergency of sorts, his voice faltered,
He slumped forward, and as though in slow motion
Fell in the hall at my feet.
My mother and her mother dragged him in,
Laid him on our sofa, my dad's leather sofa.
I watched as Granny at his feet,
Ripped his trouser from ankle to knee.
"Went in behind the knee out the foot,"
She said with calm authority.
I brought the basin in, just as I was told,
Crystal clear water turned crimson
When the towel from his leg was rung out.
The ambulance was on its way.
Two men appeared at our door almost from nowhere,
Strangers.
Checked he was getting attention
Then as they had come they vanished.
The police came, they noted his words,
Shot from a passing car.
The ambulance took him.
And we knew he lied.

FRANK HIGGINS

BELFAST

It might be hard for the reader of this black humor account of a childhood experience to imagine how deeply Frank Higgin's life was impacted by the Troubles. But growing up as he did on the lower Shankill Road and going to an entirely Protestant school set in the middle of a Catholic neighborhood, Frank's childhood and teenage years were played out against a Troubles backdrop. "The generation I grew up with," he says, "ended up either in prison or turned against the system. I 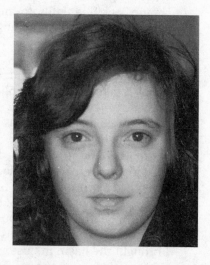 have lost good friends to terrorism and stood by helplessly as more were jailed for what they believed to be 'political' acts. I personally have been shot at, beaten up, and stabbed. . . ."

Now thirty-five, married with two children, and a corrosion engineer in the Belfast Shipyards, Frank attends night school for sociology and Spanish classes and is a member of the same Shankill Creative Writing Group of which Margaret Simpson (page 67) is a member. The group produces a magazine called *Stadium*, in which this short story was first published in 1995.

Innocent Greed

We couldn't get rid of young Bill; no matter where we went, he followed us around like a bad smell. Eventually he blended into the background and stayed there until that unfortunate day. It was the long summer holidays and being off school had lost its lustre. In fact, for the gang and myself boredom had set in. So, to break the monotony, we developed a new ruse.

This was the early 1970s and in various nooks and crannies ammunition was hidden. So what we did was this: when our money ran out or, like on this particular day, we were bored, we would pinch a bullet and take it down to the Army at Brown Square Barracks. When we presented our "find" we were treated like heroes. The soldiers would bring us in, give us tins of Coke, and cram our willing hands with large bars of chocolate. Then, after some relevant questions which we answered with undiluted lies, they would take us in their Land Rovers to the site of our "find." Now, as you can imagine, the last place we took them to was where we'd actually found the bullets, so squads of soldiers plus sniffer dogs would comb various places, all to no avail. This was the greatest scam we ever had and the sight of twenty or thirty soldiers crawling about on their hands and knees sent us into fits of laughter. Unfortunately, we didn't realise that Bill, our silent friend in the background, wanted a larger slice of the action.

Unknown to us, Bill's father was one of the local "boys," and naturally kept various "bits and pieces" hidden around the house. Now Bill wasn't supposed to know about these but, as all boys do, he had found them on one of his rummages through the house. The net result was that Bill decided to use some of these for a scam all of his own.

I happened to be sitting opposite Bill's house when the Army arrived. Using the standard way, which was a sledgehammer to open the door, they stripped the house bare and found nothing. Unbelievably, Bill wasn't having any of this. He took one of the soldiers by the hand and led him up to the toilet. "Up here, mister," he said. And sure enough when the soldier looked, to his delight and Bill's father's horror, he found a sawn-off shotgun and fifty rounds of ammunition. Bill looked pleased with himself, the soldier looked amazed at his discovery, and Bill's father looked uncomfortable in handcuffs. As a reward Bill received the largest bar of chocolate you'll ever see. Bill's father's reward was two years in Long Kesh [maximum security prison not far from Belfast].

There is a moral carefully hidden in this story and it is this:

If you are a terrorist and want to hide guns in your house always keep your kids well stocked in chocolate for, as the saying goes, "a bar in the hand is worth two years in the Kesh."

KEVIN BYERS

PORTAFERRY, COUNTY DOWN

Born and raised in Surrey, which he calls a "leafy" middle-class suburb of London, Kevin Byers's family were immigrants from Ireland. As an English-born Catholic from an Irish family, Kevin considered himself a "mongrel" and was often called upon to defend his Irishness in English secondary school, particularly when Troubles-related events would occur. On the other hand, when he and his family spent summers in Ireland, they were viewed with suspicion by many Irish people for living in a country that was seen  as the enemy. Kevin's internal struggle with his own Irish/English identities can be seen in the following story in which he describes events that occurred when he was sixteen and visiting his grandparents in Belfast.

Following his marriage to his wife, Mary, Kevin moved to Ireland before the birth of their first son. Today he stays home in a Portaferry row house and looks after his three boys, ages six, eight, and ten, while Mary works as a nurse in Belfast. Kevin works from home as a media analyst for a London company via his computer and fax machine. The family is just now getting back on their feet after a period of homelessness and serious illness.

One of the three boys, eight-year-old Eamon, is also a contributor to this anthology. His poem appears on page 244. Two more stories by Kevin Byers appear on pages 207 and 331.

One Night

(Written at age seventeen)

The sound of a door slammed in anger did little to disturb me as I sat in the small cinema. The back row of the balcony, of course, and my arm around the shoulder of a blond-haired girl. We were going steady, or so everyone assumed, including me. I had never really thought about the implications of it but I enjoyed the secure feeling it gave me. Although only sixteen, I felt accepted as an adult because of it.

The film was nearing its end and I began to think about the night air that would hit us in a minute. The lights went up and were responded to by yawns, the shuffling of feet on wooden floorboards, and the nervous coughing of "first daters."

Down the stairs . . . and outside. The realisation that something had happened enveloped us along with the choking, dusty smoke, illumined by the solitary streetlight.

"The bastards have hit the International Bar," a voice in the crowd shouted to nobody in particular. The same sentence was passed between strangers and friends with growing shock and excitement. Before anyone had time to realise the full strength of those words, we had all run the short distance down Portaferry High Street to the town square. On the corner, where the International Bar had stood, was a mountain of smoking rubble and twisted metal.

Before I could think of what to do, I was climbing in it, scarcely stopping to acknowledge familiar faces among my fellow climbers. Automatically, a chain of men formed, passing pieces of wall hand-to-hand until they reached the back of the line. The process continued with machinelike monotony, only disturbed occasionally by an inert face appearing in the stone wreckage. Its owner would be dug out and passed to the back of the chain along with the debris.

A sense of adventure seemed to overtake me. I was beginning to enjoy being part of this group of men united in a great rescue. I pulled at the rock and masonry with a new strength. My hand clasped a cold, tubular steel chair and I hauled it from its rooting. The dampness of my hand didn't seem unusual and I wiped my hand on the leg of my jeans. The red smear of blood on the denim stared back at me. Movement was impossible until a voice slapped me back to reality:

"For Christ's sake, Kevin, if that's all you can do, then bugger off to the back with the rest!"

The adventure was over and all I could feel was shame and resentment towards the man who'd said that. I started pulling frantically at the stonework again. Pray God it may soon be over . . . let nobody be dead. Pull, pull, and strain . . . let nobody be dead. My brain was whirling.

"Get out o' there, ye stupid buggers!!"

All eyes turned to the black uniforms of the firemen scrambling up behind us. "Do ye not realise that there might be another bomb?"

The workers began to jump down, from boulder to boulder. There was something almost routine about the scene. They were like builders at knocking-off time, wiping the dust off their clothes with sharp, slapping motions. Taking their places amongst the onlookers, they were questioned about what they had seen.

The square was as crowded as I had ever seen it. The women stood in groups on High Street as if they were gossiping on a shopping morning. Girls were draped from their boyfriends' necks who, in turn, were nervously playing with a tie or jacket. Beside the two remaining pubs stood the drinkers, pints in hand and smoke billowing from their yellow fingers. I knew they would be swapping stories of how they had been in the International earlier in the evening or had thought about going but had changed their minds, "by the grace of God." Before I realized what I was doing, I was compiling a mental list of the onlookers who had not gone into the rubble at the beginning. A list of those who care more for their Saturday evening suits and of those who had been too drunk to do anything. I hated them all, and realising the unfairness of my hatred, I hated them all the more.

"Cissie Byers's boy is dead."

"Who, young Christopher, you mean?"

"Aye, that's him. They pulled him out with half his stomach gone. He was dead by the time the ambulance got to him."

I could not believe what I was hearing. I had seen Christopher only yesterday. Suddenly I knew that I must get away, away from the square and everyone in it. I had lost sight of my girlfriend at the beginning. Somehow it didn't seem to matter. She would find her own way back home.

Down at the shore it was as if nothing had happened. The gulls swooped down on the bread thrown out for them just as they always did. The water in the lough was calm but my head felt like I was in a fever. Even though Christopher was my cousin, I had never really known him. We would pass each other with a nod and a few words about mutual family but never more than that. It wasn't who was dead that mattered . . . but that anyone was dead. The fact that we shared a surname just brought it closer to home. As I walked, the thoughts in my head flew around like those hungry gulls . . . now settling, now taking off in a different direction.

I knew that this was the end. I couldn't stay here now where people could do this to each other. What had shocked me more than the bomb was the way the people of the town had talked about it, as if it were an ordinary occurrence. I had never agreed with the resigned acceptance of death which was common to my family and friends. Certainly they would cry and build up their remembrance of the latest one to die until he reached the proportion of a saint. But that had never been enough for me.

I hated the wakes and the hypocrisy that went with them and, all the same, I could never accept death for what it was. It was so final when you knew that there was nothing after it. I believed in God, but all that about heaven and hell was a collection of fairy tales for the old ones. They needed it to stay sane. I could not believe in it. The bomb had shown me that death was as near to me as it was to the old ones. And I had no anchor in religion.

Suddenly I realised how often I had thought about leaving but had pushed it out of my mind. After all, I was comfortable here among friends and family. I had a reasonable job in Belfast and a steady girlfriend. But now? Now it was all changed. I didn't love my girl. Look at how easily I'd forgotten about her tonight. I hated the monotony of my job, and my family was choking me, bringing me down with them. I could see my friends with nothing to look forward to but the weekend drink and a place in the family plot when the time came. I could see myself in the same position. I would go to England and see how things were there. And if I didn't like it there, I could always try Canada, Australia—who knows? It didn't matter . . . anywhere was better than this.

When I walked back through the square towards home I felt a new resolution. This time I knew that my mind was set on something and the feeling pleased me. The crowds had drifted away. There was nothing more to see. The drinkers were back in their usual corners in the pubs and the women were standing in smaller groups on doorsteps, talking of the injured and of poor Christopher. Some of the young men, my friends, were huddled on street corners bragging about the revenge they would take, knowing it was only the false bravado of the moment. I passed them by and cursed the futility of their talk. I would leave . . . and as soon as possible.

JEFFREY GLENN

DROMORE, COUNTY DOWN

Jeffrey Glenn, along with his brother and sister, grew up in what he calls the "suburban stronghold" of Holywood, about five miles from Belfast. Now a music librarian, age forty-six, he lives with his wife, Hilary, also a librarian, in the country near Ballynahinch, County Down.

Jeffrey saw my letter requesting submissions for this anthology in the newspaper. "As a compulsive writer I'm always willing to oblige!" he says. "I have been writing all my life. My father gave me the choice of a bicycle or his ancient typewriter as an exam prize when I was aged eleven—I chose the typewriter!"

Jeffrey's story describes in some detail how his young life was impacted by the Troubles even though he lived in a relatively secure suburb of Belfast. Particularly interesting is his assessment of the psychological impact of terrorism. After one experiences bombing after bombing, he says, emotions become "armour-plated" and terrorism no longer leads to terror but to numbing indifference.

Surviving the Troubles:
A View from the Suburbs

As a young child, I used to look carefully under my bed every night before saying my prayers. The Irish Republican Army campaign of the fifties was in full swing and I was checking for bombs. Even if I couldn't see one, I still lay quaking with fear for what seemed like hours every night. Eventually I confessed my fears to my father. I thought I detected a slight chuckle as he reassured me that I wasn't important enough to attract the attention of the IRA. The pangs of terror subsided into a vague unease.

The weeks passed and I didn't get blown up but the ideas of being under siege to the IRA and of being killed by them were among my earliest memories. And, for the last twenty-five years, I have had recurrent nightmares about burning buildings and running along dark streets trying to escape from IRA killers. Far from the gilded existence portrayed by Republicans, ordinary Protestants have been living in fear for a long, long time.

When I try to recall important events in my life, in my mind's eye I always see them taking place before a backdrop of unrest and instability. For example, when I turned up for my first day at Queen's University, Belfast, my tutorial group contained only half a dozen students but no less than three were well-known members of the "People's Democracy" group which had been organising civil rights protest marches all over Northern Ireland. They talked about confronting the police and about bringing down the Stormont government.

To me, it all seemed very alien. I lived about five miles from Belfast city centre and everyday life in Northern Ireland as I knew it seemed quiet and peaceful. I was puzzled. They were talking about the Protestant supremacy and about how Catholics were oppressed. But our neighbours were Catholics—so were half the people on our street—and we all seemed to live the same sorts of lives. We all seemed to get on well together. Politically ignorant, I was ill-equipped to argue and went home from that first day in a state of embarrassment and indignation and with a dawning realisation that there were things going on of which I knew very little. But this was 1967 and my age of innocence was almost over.

Fast-forward two years and I'm actually standing right there on Divis Street the day the Troubles started in earnest. My brother and I had been waiting for my father to finish work and give us a ride home when columns of thick black smoke soaring high into the sky attracted our attention. We walked towards the place where the smoke seemed to be coming from. It was like a scene from Dante's *Inferno*. Buses, trucks, cars, and construction equipment formed blazing barricades and groups of angry-faced men were busy hi-jacking more. Television crews were borne away on a torrent of rage and obscenity. It felt as if war had broken out and the enemy was already in the next street.

And, strangely enough, I was one of the enemy. The barricades were there to stop Protestants from swarming down the series of short streets linking Divis Street with the Shankill Road and, backed up (as the residents firmly believed) by the armed Land Rovers of the Royal Ulster Constabulary [police], attacking Catholic homes. There had been something in the papers one previous evening about violence on Divis Street and about machine-gun fire from the Land Rovers injuring people in the Divis flats. In our suburban stronghold we had found it hard to believe that things could have gone so far. Our street was of mixed religion and, throughout the twenty-five years of the Troubles, it stayed that way. We looked at the panic, rage, and hate on Divis Street and wondered where it had all come from.

It's often said that Protestants and Catholics learn to hate each other "at their mothers' knees." But to middle-class sub-urbanites such as myself sectarianism was an abstract concept. I didn't even find out that there were Catholics and Protestants 'til I was about seven years old. I was walking past a Catholic chapel with a crowd of schoolmates one day when I made to go in. "You can't go in there unless you're a Catholic," I was told. "Well, what am I?" "You're a Praddison," it sounded like. "A what?" "A Praddison!" I still hadn't got it.

I may have been surprised by the animosity driving the Troubles but it was impossible to be untouched by them. One evening, for example, I was stopped by the Army for running through Belfast carrying a bag. It was only a sports bag, and I was running for the bus, but this was 1971 and the streets of the city were deserted after the shops closed. Six rifles were pointed at me. I was spreadeagled against the side of an arm-oured vehicle and questioned. And I thought they were going to call up the Bomb Squad to deal with my sports gear. They soon let me go but I missed the bus. I was more bemused than angry at their intervention. I assured myself that they were only trying to protect law-abiding citizens. But if they had been violent or abusive or had dragged me off for interrogation it would have been a different matter.

Indeed, throughout the Troubles, I was personally more in-convenienced by the Army with their roadblocks, checkpoints, searches, and diversions than by the IRA. But that was just good fortune.

One Saturday afternoon I sat with my brother and parents in the Abercorn Cafe in the centre of Belfast. My parents wanted to sit on and savour their coffee while my brother and I couldn't wait to get off to the music shops. We hadn't gone fifty yards when a bomb exploded. We didn't at first realise what had happened; we had just gone round the corner at the top of Castle Lane. The explosion was so loud and so close that we just ran. We had taken refuge in a shop when somebody said,

"There was a bomb in the Abercorn." We didn't run back. We walked back—slowly—full of dread and sick with fear. When we got to the top of Castle Lane the Abercorn was just a black, smoking hole.

Police and firemen were scurrying about, ambulances were roaring off, bells were ringing, sirens were screaming, and the police wouldn't allow us near. We told them that our parents had been in there and they said that everybody was out now they had all been taken away in the ambulances. Where? They didn't know. We walked away and wandered about Belfast in a stupour for maybe an hour. What were we going to do? How could we find out what had happened to them? We didn't even allow ourselves to think the worst. Eventually we found ourselves at the bus station and we just went home.

Two hours passed and nobody phoned. For most of the time we just stood there, almost catatonic. Then we began pacing—from the front room to the kitchen, from the kitchen to the back room, from the back room to the front room, then a look out of the window. Over and over. Then I remembered that I had arranged to meet some friends and go to the sports club. They'd be waiting for me! I couldn't leave them sitting there! I'd have to go and speak to them. But in case my parents came home while I was away I left them a note. It turned out so emotional that it left my brother white-faced.

I was just opening the front door to leave when my father's car drove up the street. We were so drained that we were beyond words but I still made sure I tore up the note before my parents saw it.

They were high on relief, excited and full of what had happened to them. In the blackness and smoke and confusion my father thought his cigarette lighter had exploded. My mother had realised it was a bomb. Some people were killed; my parents were both injured. When a policeman called at our house a couple of weeks later to take their statements he showed us a plan of the Abercorn and the position of the bomb. My brother and I had been no more than six feet from it. Another fifteen seconds and we would have been killed.

On "Bloody Friday" [January 30, 1972] IRA bombs went off all over Belfast and there were many fatalities. I had arrived in the city centre as usual via Oxford Street bus station and made my way through Bedford Street, Dublin Road, and Botanic Avenue to the main library at Queen's University. As I reached Bedford Street, the Oxford Street bus station was destroyed by a huge no-warning bomb. The victims' bodies were ripped to shreds and had to be shovelled into plastic bin [garbage] bags. As I reached Dublin Road, Bedford Street was devastated by another no-warning bomb. As I reached Botanic Avenue, Dublin Road erupted. And as I took my seat upstairs in the library, a car bomb exploded in Botanic Avenue. Pieces of jagged metal flew over the rooftops and landed in the roadway outside.

That was the day that brought home to me what "terrorism" means because I felt terrorised. My mood was just total black despair. We seemed to be entering some sort of apocalyptic world where your worst nightmares ran for twenty-four hours a day. You couldn't go on a bus or train for wondering if either it or the station would be blown up. You couldn't walk down a street where cars were parked for wondering if one of them contained a bomb. You couldn't leave your car in to be fixed because when you went back to collect it the workshop was probably now a hole in the ground. Every day some landmark that you loved or a favourite store was bombed or burnt.

I remember coming into Belfast one afternoon and finding the giant Co-Op store blazing from end to end. That was the final straw. I put my head in my hands and found tears running down my cheeks.

I remember going home and asking my parents, "Is it going to be like this every day?" But what actually happened was that, although I never saw any light at the end of the tunnel, somehow the tunnel itself gradually became less terrifying.

Maybe it was just like going on the same old fairground ghost train hundreds and hundreds of times. I developed a sense of perspective. I could see that the "war" wasn't going anywhere, though it kept on going just the same. Endlessly repetitive patterns of attrition threw their shadow over everyday life but they brought anger rather than fear. All around me bombs and incendiaries destroyed office blocks, hotels, theatres and shops, city streets, and eventually whole town centres. Bomb hoaxes prevented people from getting to work. Lots of people got shot. Roads were closed. There were Army checkpoints and soldiers everywhere. Car parking was prohibited in town centers and whole towns were cordoned off at night by "security gates." "Civilian searchers" checked your pockets each time you went into a shop. Letter boxes had narrow slots to keep out letter bombs. Yet, after a few years, all this seemed quite unremarkable. I even began to try to persuade friends and relatives from outside Ireland to come over and visit. "It's not that bad," I would say. "It's not like Beirut!"

And now at last we have a cease-fire. How do I feel? Much the same as when my parents came home after the Abercorn explosion. Too numb and traumatised by the fear and tension of the last twenty-five years to feel relief. In the broadest sense, though, there may be a form of peace. John Hume [head of the largest Catholic political party in Northern Ireland, Member of Parliament and key figure in peace negotiations] once said that there was no longer a cause in Ireland worth killing for—and that was about ten years ago. I would guess that a lot more people agree with John Hume now and the tactics of violence may have lost some of their former supporters. In the climate of peace a lot more people seem to have become pragmatists. I could actually imagine some of the leaders sitting down with Sinn Fein [political arm of the Irish Republican Army] and saying "Well, Gerry [Gerry Adams, leader of Sinn Fein], what are we going to do about all this?"

From total despair to cautious optimism has been a long and difficult journey. For me, the line between being killed and surviving has been very thin at times and most of the joy has been drained from years that should have been wonderful.

I have gained experience, however, and learnt something which could be a lesson to those who threaten a return to terrorism: you can see so much devastation that you are no longer moved by it. Another bombing, another murder, another bombing, another murder, another bombing . . . Feelings and emotions become armour-plated. No atrocity can pierce your heart. And this very process makes you increasingly dismissive of the fears, sensitivities, and aspirations of other communities.

On the other hand, after just a year of peace, and despite all that has happened, I find my mind opening to the idea of compromise and I discover that I am even becoming curious as to precisely what an "Agreed Ireland" as proposed by Sinn Fein might be like.

P. J. QUINN

BELFAST

When the Troubles began in 1969, P. J. Quinn was twenty years old and living as he still does in West Belfast, one of the most affected areas of the city. "Some of my neighbours were killed in gun and bomb attacks," he says, "and I saw several shootings at close range as well as discovering the body of a murder victim dumped in an alleyway."

In his story, P.J. captures the intense feelings of terror that could come over anyone in the Troubles, particularly a young man home alone while parents are away for a weekend.

Today P.J. is a librarian and he is working on a screenplay. No stranger to publishing, he had an epic-length poem published in *The Irish Review,* a prestigious literary journal, in 1989.

Clutch of Fear

I can still recall those dark, fear-filled days of 1975. There were various theories about how and why the bitter and bloody feud between the Official and Provisional wings of the Republican movement [IRA] began but the one that I thought most reliable was that the seeds of it were sown during the summer when the Secretary of State for Northern Ireland started releasing internees [prisoners] who belonged to the Provisionals. This goodwill gesture, it was hoped, would be reciprocated by the Provo leadership in terms of a scaling-down of their terrorist campaign. If memory serves me right it made little difference to the bombing and killing except that in one respect—largely unforeseen even by senior intelligence experts—it made it worse:

When the Provo prisoners were returned to their communities they found that the Official (Marxist-oriented) IRA had taken advantage of their absence to increase their influence in Provo-controlled areas by muscling in on their lucrative empire of bars, nightclubs, illegal shebeens [alcohol outlets], one-armed bandit joints, and other places of entertainment. Naturally the Provos resented this and they held meetings to discuss what to do about it. The course of action they decided upon was characteristic of their thinking as a whole—they decided to exterminate the Officials and their sympathisers. And the emphasis should be placed on "sympathisers," for very few of the Provos' victims during this brutal vendetta could have been described as "activists." The Official IRA had been on permanent cease-fire since 1972 when their leaders renounced violence in favour of political action. Officials and their supporters organised themselves into "Republican Clubs" which concentrated on working-class nonsectarian politics. It was these Republican Club members, many of whom had never held a gun in their lives, who bore the brunt of the Provo purge. While the bloodletting was not confined to Belfast, it was most intense there.

I don't know what the first incident was that actually sparked the feud. Numerous stories, put about by both sides, circulated in the streets and in the newspapers. Consensus on such matters is always difficult, but the Republican feud, like most feuds, began in "little" things and quickly spiralled out of control. And I definitely do recall that, whoever struck the first blow, the merciless and cold-blooded nature of the murders chilled all decent people to the bone and brought real terror to thousands of homes throughout Northern Ireland.

Among the more ominous developments was the spraying of homes belonging to the Officials and their supporters with red "death crosses," allowing the Provo killer squads to identify their targets with ease. They bombed each other's bars and clubs; Provos hurled petrol bombs into Official business premises; Officials drove to Provo nightspots with rifles strapped to their motorcycles and raked everyone inside with gunfire; workers were forced to flee their jobs; families were intimidated out of their homes by means of threatening phone calls, black bereavement bows tied to gateposts, bullets dropped through letter boxes. Fear spread from one side of Belfast to the other. Doors were locked and bolted after dark and furniture was piled up against them to slow down killers who might try to sledgehammer their way in. The women of the Republican areas, whose sons, husbands, and brothers were the targets, came onto the streets in impromptu demonstrations, chanting, "End the feud, end the feud!" But more lives were to be lost before they got their wish.

I was alone when the doorbell rang in the early hours—my parents were away on autumn break [vacation]. I woke up instantly because my thoughts were choked with the horror of the latest feud killing the previous night. A Provo with a machine gun had shot his way into a house just a hundred yards from my own and opened fire on the tenant—a Republican Club member or sympathiser, I'm not sure which. Not one of the hail of bullets hit him, but two hit his young daughter and killed her. I had been sickened when I heard it on the news and now I went cold with fright. I didn't know precisely what time it was because it was too dark to see the bedside clock without turning on the light. But the silence outside told me it must be after midnight. That really scared me; we got very few social calls and none after nine P.M.

I leapt out of bed like I had found a corpse beside me. I doubt a corpse could have been much colder than I was just then. "Cold with fear" was a phrase I had read in thrillers but for the first time I was experiencing it from the inside. It wasn't the first time that the Troubles had touched me. When I was walking home from school one day the man in front of me had been shot dead by soldiers. When Internment was introduced in 1971 I had come under Loyalist [Protestant] sniper fire while standing beside a barricade. Our home was raided by the Brits four, five, six times. A land mine meant for a passing Army patrol had blown out our windows, brought soot down the chimney, and plunged the lights out all over the neighbourhood. We lost our windows again when a huge car bomb exploded a few feet from our front door, seriously injuring some people standing in the street. I had been stopped, questioned, and searched by soldiers and policemen more times than I could remember.

But this was different. It was the wee small hours; it was me alone in the house and someone outside with his finger on the bell. Northern Ireland in general and Belfast in particular was in the grip of a ruthless gang war. Now I knew real fear. I was as cold as if I had just stepped from an icebox and my heart was churning blood through me at a rate I had never thought possible.

The first thing I did was tear off my pyjamas in the dark and pull on my trousers and shirt. I thought to myself that if I got shot I didn't want to be found in my pyjamas. Incredible the things you can think of at such moments. Fastening my shirt buttons, I stepped into my shoes, darted out of the bedroom, along the landing and down the stairs, swiftly but silently, for I didn't want to let on to the caller that there was anyone inside. I was already in the hallway before the bell rang a second time—*dingdong*, like millions of doorbells all over the world but the fear it struck into me was something the like of which I had never known before and have never known since. My knees were shaking like jelly, my pulse was running like an express train, and that little heart of mine—an organ of which I had scarcely ever been aware before—was beating in my ears like a punchball. Quickly and quietly like a cat—for I was always very nimble—I unlocked the parlour door and ran to the front window, hoping, praying that I would see British soldiers and/or policemen outside. Then I would have gone to the door at once. I'm not saying I adore the security forces and I know that some members of them have been responsible for some of the worst atrocities of the Troubles, but I feel much safer opening the door to them in the dead of night than to an unknown civilian. Sure they might search the house, throw things about, ask loads of questions. The nasty ones can be very nasty and the nice ones can be very nice but nasty or nice at least you can be reasonably sure they won't shoot you dead at point-blank range. In any case, I wasn't wanted for anything so I had little to fear from them. It's the unfamiliar civilians who cause the real fear.

And my fear mounted when I slid into the chair by the window and peered through the net curtain and the space in the slats of the venetian blind. The caller was indeed an unfamiliar civilian. Although the lamp across the street was out—vandalism, I think—and the position I was sitting in afforded only restricted vision, I could make out enough of him to say with confidence that I didn't know him. Average height and weight, curly hair receding at the front—and he seemed to have a light moustache. This I detected from his profile when he turned his head to look up the street. He wore a nylon parka jacket with a fur-trimmed hood, the kind that was very much in during the seventies. Nothing sinister about that as such. I wore one myself. But I knew that it was a good coat within which to conceal a weapon, whether a handgun or an Armalite rifle with the butt broken down. Age? I'm a bad judge of ages, even in daylight, but he was somewhere between thirty and fifty.

There was a car parked at the kerb—his, I was pretty certain, because I knew it wasn't any of those which regularly parked there. It was too dark to be sure if there was someone else in it but somehow I felt there was not. This, I thought, so far as I could still think clearly, was a good sign. The killers very seldom operated alone. Or maybe that was part of his plan—to make me think he was alone. He would know that with the feud going on nobody would answer their door without checking things out first. So maybe two or three other hoods were lying down inside the car and when I opened the door to the caller, thinking he was alone, he would dive for cover and they would spring up and open fire at me. Or maybe they were already hiding around the corner out of sight. Or maybe this caller was a diversion and the rest of his gang were already trying to break in by the back. Or maybe he was a maverick Loyalist [pro-British Protestant] gunman just looking for any Catholic victim at random. Or maybe he was just an ordinary thug intent on breaking in and ransacking the house. Or maybe he was a perfectly decent guy who had just come to the wrong door by mistake. There was no way of knowing for sure without opening the door to him and I wasn't brave enough or stupid enough, depending on how you look at it, to do that.

I was sorry I hadn't barricaded the door with tables and chairs like I knew other people were doing. It doesn't stop determined killers from getting in but it gives you a little more time to get out by the back unless, of course, they have the back covered just in case you try that. But barricading your doors has a down side too for if they lob a few petrol bombs into the back and set the whole place on fire you have to break through your own furniture before you can get out by the front.

But what was I worried about anyway? I didn't belong to the Officials or the Provos, I wasn't on any death list, I wasn't wanted by the security forces. I was just one of the many citizens who were not involved in military, paramilitary, or political activity of any kind and who just went through every day minding their own business and doing nobody any harm.

On reflection, this didn't guarantee me immunity. Lots of people had been shot for nothing except their religion—and some not even for that—some were just mistaken identities.

That was one of the saddest aspects of the conflict—the many victims who took no part in violence but got snuffed out anyway. Sometimes the death dealers just got the wrong house. Malachy McGurran, I suddenly recalled—Chairman or something of the Republican Clubs—had recently issued a warning that the Provo killer squads were using outdated intelligence and were quite liable to shoot the wrong people. That had happened once already during the feud. The victim had been unfortunate enough to move into a flat vacated some weeks previously by a prominent member of the Officials. The Provos were unaware of this and shot the wrong man. The last I heard of him he was critically ill and not expected to live. Just another statistic, another few column inches in the paper but now, as every joint in me quaked with fear, I had a lot of sympathy for him. I began to gain insight into how other people, including the locally recruited security forces, must feel when a knock comes to their door in the small hours. They too must feel the clutch of fear that I now felt.

One thing for sure, though I only thought about it later, if he was a gunman he was a very patient one. His two rings had been unhurried and well spaced out—even polite—and that's not what you expect from a would-be murderer. Or was this too part of his deception? Perhaps he reckoned that if he rang persistently and aggressively he would earn my suspicion immediately and would then have to get in the hard way.

Suppose I went back to the hall and phoned the police? I would have to do it without light. I remembered police leaflets advising people how to ring the emergency services in the dark if they felt it wasn't safe to turn on their lights. That's how bad the violence was then. But we had paid the leaflets scant attention. Some people just stumble on, hoping they will never meet that kind of situation, like all those who never bother to fit a smoke alarm, thinking it will never happen to them.

I said to myself: index finger across the top row of buttons to the last, then straight down to the last—that should be 9—

then press it three times and ask for the police and implore them to get here fast. Then I thought it might not be a good idea. The police had been ambushed in the past on their way to what turned out to be false alarms and they would likely think twice before driving into the heart of a Republican [Catholic] area at this hour just because somebody rang to say there was a stranger at his door.

Besides, it didn't seem very masculine. If a woman rings the police to say a stranger is at her door she might get a sympathetic hearing but a twenty-year-old guy—they might laugh at me for bringing them out for something like that. And even if I did phone them and they came promptly—which was doubtful—it would take some minutes and if the caller really was bent on murder he wasn't going to stand there much longer.

In fact, why hadn't he made his move already? Maybe I was right about him being a diversion. Maybe the real danger was developing at the rear of the house. I had better get back there and check, I thought. But wait—if I left the window I wouldn't know what the guy at the front was doing. Some people I know tell me I think too deeply about things and perhaps they are right. Maybe thinking too deeply can cause mental paralysis and leave you so you can't decide what to do. On the other hand, maybe it helps you to stay alive. The record of civil strife in Northern Ireland is not lacking in stories about people who answered knocks on their doors without a moment's hesitation and got their brains blown out.

While I was thinking all this the caller rang the bell a third time—*dingdong*, gently, quietly, with no overt hostility or menace or antagonism—but to me it was a sound that packed more fear than a thousand-pound bomb going off. I always liked peace and quiet and shunned noisy gatherings—that's one reason I grew up a loner. But just then I would have welcomed all the noises I usually detested—the drunks shouting curses on their way home from the bars, the corner boys mouthing at one another across the width of the street, the filthy joyriders screaming around in stolen cars. I would have welcomed a riot, a gun battle, or a full-scale war. Anything seemed preferable to that nerve-destroying silence of the dead hours with that stranger outside and me alone inside and that gentle *dingdong* echoing up the hall like a seductive voice beckoning me to my death.

I knew I had to do something—even if it was only run out the back and keep running—or fear would make me freeze, almost literally, on the chair where I sat. I sprang up and made for the kitchen where I pulled open the top drawer and drew out a large carving knife, sharp as a lance. I lifted the venetian blind across the kitchen window and glanced into the dark yard. So far as I could see there was no one in it and I was thankful for that. Then I went to the fireplace in the living room, lifted the poker, and ran back to the hall. Knife in one hand, poker in the other—I was well armed for an ordinary civilian who didn't have a gun and didn't want one. But who was I trying to kid? If the caller had a gun this domestic hardware wouldn't count. Still, I was pleased with myself for even having the courage to finally go to the door.

But I was still cautious and so I stole silently into the parlour again and slid once more into the chair beside the window. I was relieved—and that's an understatement—to see the stranger turning away and going back to his car. He actually closed the gate behind him—and the ill-mannered callers don't do that. Then he looked at the upstairs windows and, seeing no sign that anyone was in, got back behind his wheel. As he did so the roof light went on and I saw that he was indeed alone as I had thought. I heard his engine start up and watched him drive away.

My heart was still pounding like a steam piston out of control but I felt that the worst was over and I started breathing again. I had been short of breath many times before for I'm a keep-fit enthusiast but healthy physical exertion bears no comparison to a few minutes of concentrated fear. It took a little while for my heart to get back to anything like its normal beat and, if no other good came from that incident, at least I would never again take my heart for granted.

I went from the parlour back to the living room and from there to the kitchen where I peeked through the venetian blind again to make sure there was still no intruder in the yard.

Then I went back to the parlour again just in case the caller was pulling a fast one, driving away to throw me off guard and then returning. But, no, he was gone and the street was deserted and as quiet as a morgue. I returned to the living room once again and, feeling fairly sure that he was gone for good, turned on the light. The clock on the mantelpiece read 1:52 A.M. What in God's holy name was anybody ringing our doorbell for at 1:52 in the morning? The simplest explanation was that he was a stranger in the area and just rang the wrong door. Or maybe he was a seldom-seen relative with bad news about some member of the family circle—that would certainly account for his calling at such an hour. And it might also account for the fact that I didn't recognise him for, with one or two exceptions, I saw my relatives so infrequently that I wouldn't know them if they dropped dead in front of me. Certainly he hadn't behaved like a typical killer for the murder gangs were seldom put off by unanswered rings.

Knife still in one hand, poker in the other, I went to the inner door in the hall, unlocked it, then undid the three bolts on the outer door and unlocked it too. Warily I opened it and peeped into the street. The cool air that broke upon my face was very agreeable, just the right thing after so much tension within a confined space. I looked right, left, right, left, then laid my weapons against the doorframe and ventured as far as the gate where I looked right and left again. Not a sinner in sight. All was quiet, so quiet it might have been some other city in some other part of the world where there are no late-night killers to worry about. And it was a lovely night with the exquisite scent of late autumn in the air.

Then up the street at his usual slow crawl came a neighbour from further along the block with his little terrier on a leash—Mr . . . Mr . . . I never did know his name.

"Hello, young fella," he said. "Nice evening, isn't it?"

"Lovely," I replied. "Out for a walk, are you?"

"I walk to keep my blood pressure down."

"Just watch where you go at this time of night," I cautioned, "or you might get shot."

"You're right, you're right." He laughed as he disappeared into the darkness.

A little snatch of light conversation works wonders after so much fear. I felt myself returning to normal and then came the feelings of shame and embarrassment which I suspect most of us encounter after an unnerving experience. What had I been so worried about anyway? There was Mr. Whatever-you-call-him, three times my age, out for his constitutional, feud or no feud. It was only a stranger ringing the bell after all. I should have gone straight to the door, asked him what did he think he was playing at, knocking people up out of bed at this hour? Get lost! Clear off!

And what if he was a gunman? I would have bent the poker over his head and buried the knife in his ribs before he got off his first shot. Most of us play John Wayne in our imagination some time or other; it compensates for lost divinity. But when the evil moment is actually upon you it can be very different. Or maybe what really scared me so much was being alone. Maybe if I had had a girl to protect I would have been brave. Perhaps when there's just yourself to care about you suffer a sense that you aren't worth fighting for. Perhaps somebody else being there can make all the difference. Being such a loner I've never been sure about that and maybe I never will be.

With my heartbeat back to normal, I withdrew inside, taking the knife and poker with me. I bolted and locked the doors, poured myself a glass of pineapple juice from the fridge, and sat down to drink it. I wondered and wondered and wondered who that caller had been and what was his business in the dead of night but I couldn't figure it. I never did find out who he was. My parents were just as baffled as I was about him when they got home.

It was a solid hour after he rang the bell before I went back to bed again and another hour before I fell back into a fitful sleep. And, although I like darkness, I can't remember a night when I was more glad to see the dawn.

While my night of anxiety had ended, not so the anxiety of others for the Republican feud was fated to send yet more people to untimely graves. Its final victim was the reputed Provo Intelligence Officer who directed the murders. Officials, who when pushed to it could match the Provos for ruthlessness all the way, walked into his favourite place of entertainment, singled him out, held him down on the floor, and pumped eight bullets into his head from three inches away.

After this, mediators were brought in to hammer out a peace deal as it was clear that neither side was winning or gaining much from the slaughter. In broadstroke, it sounds similar to what was to happen twenty years later on a bigger scale [i.e., the current peace process].

AINE DA SILVA

GLENGORMLEY, NEWTOWNABBEY, COUNTY ANTRIM

Belfast-born, twenty-one-year-old Aine da Silva remembers being torn as a child, unable to fit into either community. Although her mother was "quite Republican [Nationalist Catholic]," Aine says, her father's clientele for the pony club he ran in Hannahstown was mostly British and Protestant and she played with their children.

In her poem, Aine emphasizes the uncanny alertness that children had to develop to survive in high-conflict areas. "My senses were always magnified," she says, "because since primary school I have always been in fear for my life." Six people in her family have been killed in the Troubles.

Today Aine is studying psychology at the Open University in Belfast and working at the National Schizophrenic Fellowship in Ballyclare. She is committed to feminism and works on *Women's News* magazine in Belfast. Describing herself as "a pacifist," she tells me that, in the political climate of Northern Ireland, this is "radical."

Aine has been writing since primary school and has had quite a few of her poems published in anthologies.

Self-Preservation

(Written at age eighteen)

Self-preservation.

The silent terror
controls our words
our voices
our hearing
our seeing
our understanding
and our thoughts.

We know where we are not supposed to walk.
Our Christian names and surnames betray us
across enemy lines.

But we have learned the hard way
we know the time and place for lies.

We are the experts of self-preservation.
Children of the cold war.
Children of the Troubles.
Our bombs are close but they are not quite nuclear
although they steal our families from us.

We know the art of self-preservation—
we were born into it.

We watch with our ears
and hear with our eyes.
We know what the abandoned car might mean.
We know what the crowded car might mean.
We know because we've had to live it.

JOHN DELANEY

VENTNOR, NEW JERSEY,
UNITED STATES OF AMERICA

John Delaney, the seventh and youngest child of a lawyer and a schoolteacher, was born in Belfast in 1960. Today he lives near Atlantic City, New Jersey, where he is a desk clerk in a noncasino motel.

Finding this a rather amazing contrast, I asked John what lay behind his emigration and, in particular, why New Jersey? "When I left Ireland in 1985 I had pretty much given up on the country," he said. Several of his older friends had gone to America and discovered that there were so many jobs surrounding the casinos in Atlantic City that even illegals could easily find employment. "Within a few years," he said, "there was a sizable Irish community in the area."

Although John had told many of the stories that follow to various people, he did not begin writing them down until November of 1995, when he saw my letter about this anthology in *The Irish Echo*. As an editor, I found his work interesting for many reasons, but one in particular was his amalgam of Irish and American spellings and syntax that seems to me to indicate just how much he is a citizen of both countries.

John's use of humor as well as his insights about the futility of sectarian violence convinced me to include almost all of what turned out to be the longest story in this book.

Just Another Day in Belfast

PROLOGUE

Saturday morning, March 1980, and I've got a stinking hangover. The incessant drone of Army helicopters above doesn't bother me—their presence is reassuring that all is normal. More worrisome is the clatter of plates, pots, and pans in the kitchen below as mother does the dishes, and the sound of my father coughing his lungs out in the bathroom. I'm definitely not in the mood to see them today—I've a funny feeling that I may have knocked something over when I came home last night—and hope that the feeling is mutual. I lie back and wait for them to go out shopping and my thoughts turn to the pilots of those helicopters. What do they think about? Their wives, girlfriends, or when they get home to England? It must be tedious up there.

Eventually I heard the car pull out of the drive which is my cue to get going. This is a big day. Tottenham Hotspurs (my team) play Liverpool in a cup tie so I'll have to don my best gear, i.e., a Spurs shirt and jeans! The weather is glorious for early spring, so I load up the radio with new batteries, purloin some ten-pence pieces from my brother's room, and I'm off. As usual, I'm broke but my best mate Sam works the bar today so there'll be no problem.

The street I live on is quite unusual for Andersonstown, what with its hedges, trees, and shrubbery which, although pretty, have their disadvantages. They make excellent camouflage to both the so-called forces of law and order and those waging an urban guerilla war in Northern Ireland. No sooner have I left the house when, seemingly from nowhere, a British Army foot patrol jumps out in front of me, and before I know it, I'm pushed up against the wall for the customary P-check (personal check). I have to make a quick decision—is this lot in a good mood or a bad one? I go for the former which is a mistake.

"What's your name, mate?" I rattle off my reply as quickly as possible, knowing the young squaddie won't have a clue what I'm saying. After three or four attempts he finally gets it right and radios in to Lisburn Army Headquarters. "Where you coming from?" This seems stupid as I just came out of my own front door but that doesn't seem to appease the lad, so I go through the whole address, again at high speed.

"Where you going to, Paddy?" This is when things started to go wrong. Wearing full combat gear on a warm and sunny day (and constantly on the lookout for IRA snipers), he wasn't amused when I explained I was going to the pub to listen to the game over a few pints. It only gets worse when Lisburn reports back that I had no record and, unbelievably for someone from West Belfast, I had a good job. This seemed to amaze and frustrate him and for that the penalty was quite simple. After a rigourous and largely pointless search (considering my light attire), I was ordered to stay against the wall for another hour for my own good health. "If we can't have a good day, you can't either."

Coincidentally a couple of my friends passed by and weren't stopped. They just nodded towards me and went on their way. One was involved with the IRA!

And that was it. I missed the game and the Spurs lost. But it was just another day in Belfast.

Andersonstown, West Belfast, a nice quiet neighborhood where I was born in 1960 and grew up unaware that in a few years the lives of everyone around us would forever be changed. Strange enough, as the conflagration that engulfed the Lower Falls of Belfast and Derry City to the west appeared nightly on the BBC News, our area was referred to as "Silent Valley." One very crucial event would turn what we called "A'Town" upside down. On January 30th, 1972, British Paratroopers shot and killed thirteen unarmed civilians engaged in a civil rights march in Derry, claiming that they had been fired upon by the IRA. This was nonsense and everyone knew it. Anger, rage, and hatred swelled the support for the Provisional IRA and led to an explosion of riots and civil disobedience. "Silent Valley" was about to wake up.

From then on, every summer my parents would whisk me off to County Donegal on the west coast of the Republic of Ireland, hoping to extricate me from what was by now known as "the Troubles." This was obviously a futile exercise considering my access to TV, radio, books, and newspapers. Also, there was the fact that I lived in Belfast for ten months of the year.

Some people got involved in the Troubles, many just coped with it, while others just ignored the whole thing if they could. There were those, however, who lost family and friends and I do not want to make light of their losses. But I took a different path in dealing with life in Andersonstown. I tried to laugh at it when I could. These are my stories and, unfortunately, they're all true.

Greater Andersonstown is a huge sprawl of housing projects set in the foothills of the Black Mountain on the west side of Belfast. Built mostly to provide cheap homes for badly needed Catholic labour (which had outstretched the bounds of the Falls Road after the Second World War), it was also a convenient way to keep the Fenians [nationalist Catholics] confined. Stuck in the middle of this urban mess was Fruithill Park. It was to here that some of the more wealthy (and I use that term loosely) among the Catholic population set down our roots.

Just a stone's throw from our street was the "estate" where we were treated as snobs who didn't understand the true effects of British rule. We lived in "bought houses." As kids even a short walk home through the area was, if we were lucky, met with insults and threats. Football games were basically a war between "us and them," with the most injuries inflicted on the other side often deciding the winner.

As the seventies wore on, the Troubles escalating with each day, I soon gained some semblance of acceptability with the estate crowd. They still regarded me as being privileged but conceded that I was as opposed to British rule as the next person. I was never fully allowed to enter their inner circle, even though we could all laugh, joke, and drink with the best of them. But our street was still part of the ghetto and to say the war didn't touch us would be plain wrong. Having the IRA fire off a volley of rounds at an Army unit, totally missing, and hitting my bedroom wasn't exactly my idea of fun. I was only about twelve at the time. Luckily I'd been allowed to stay up late that night to watch a movie.

One afternoon the Army wasn't so lucky. What was normally a fifteen-minute stroll home from school, on this day took almost two hours. I was P-checked five times, even by patrols who were within speaking distance of the last one. When I finally got home my mother was clearly upset. Two of my brothers had been "lifted" [picked up by soldiers] and taken to Fort Monagh for interrogation. The Provos [members of the Provisional IRA] had shot dead a soldier behind our house just as Brian was on the roof fixing the TV aerial and Kevin was up a tree cutting branches. They were almost shot on sight!

Actually it turned out that the sniper had a pretty good aim. One shot had done the job from almost one hundred yards away, through hedges and trees. Anyway, our tranquil little street made it onto the front pages the next day. So what? I had to make my own dinner that evening as the Royal Ulster Constabulary [RUC] conducted their investigation. Once again it was so annoying. Another life had been lost as a consequence of the war but it really didn't matter at the time. He was in the wrong country.

Indifference to such acts was now widespread but, one evening while we were watching the news, my mother stunned me. Just days after an innocent Catholic had been killed in Belfast by the Army, four RUC were blown to pieces while on patrol in south Armagh County. At the conclusion of the report, and without even turning to me, she simply said: "Serves them right." In silence I contemplated this remark. It was a natural reaction to what we knew was retaliation for a terrible crime committed by the Crown Forces. What made it worse was that we knew the soldier would never stand trial for his actions.

The turmoil that followed that Bloody Sunday in January 1972, along with a major snowfall, closed down schools and businesses all over the North. Within the Catholic areas of Belfast and Derry almost complete anarchy prevailed and our Fruithill assumed its own role in securing the newly established "no-go" areas. With the law having been taken in the peoples' own hands, barricades were erected at vital points to prevent unwanted intrusions by the British. As our street led to the "estates" entrance, and was adjacent to the outside world, it became a natural location for lookouts and obstructions of almost any kind. I say almost—when the local brewery sent out its trucks on delivery runs they were inevitably hi-jacked and the contents mysteriously vanished!

As all semblance of order broke down, we spent three or four days hanging around the streets waiting for petrol tanks to explode after another car had been torched. But the best was yet to come. A huge articulated lorry had been taken up on the Glen Road and the driver forced to drive it down Fruithill to block off the entrance to the estate. Unfortunately, with the snow and ice, it slipped and skidded past its intended spot, jack-knifed, and ended up squarely in the middle of the road. Everyone just stood around wondering how this marvelous prize could be rescued.

I can't remember whether I was astonished or just plain embarrassed as I saw "me da" marching up the street with a set of garden hedge clippers. Without a word, he set about cutting the cables which joined the truck and the driver's cab. The two were parted and, with much pushing and shoving, the mission was finally accomplished. As he made his way back to the house, people were clapping and cheering. I'll never forget the look on his face—he'd done his bit.

From then on such incidents become commonplace and it was never a surprise when there was a knock on the door, a few of the lads asking for "your mammy's car." It usually would turn up a day or two later, after a search by family and friends but not by the police. Not only did they not care but they were afraid to approach the vehicle for fear of a booby trap.

The relationship between the Army and the local population was peculiar at times. Considering that there was what amounted to a war going on—riots, nail bomb attacks, and shootings occurred on an almost daily basis—one would be forgiven for thinking that having a laugh with the British would be inconceivable. But we always felt that, as much as ourselves, they were stuck in a lousy situation doing what was probably the only job available to them. (The RUC [police] and UDR [Ulster Defense Regiment—a government militia] were different. We hated them because, in the final analysis, they were Irish born yet allied to a foreign country.)

The game we played with the soldiers on the street was a delicate affair. If they went too far an "incident" might result while we could easily get "lifted" if we pushed our luck. Many times either of the above did transpire but mostly each side followed the rules.

One winter's night, with little prospect of excitement in sight, Paddy called to say he had raided his father's money jar and, with a little help from me, we could afford a six-pack. I duly obliged by offering up my next day's school dinner money and sent him on his way.

As he made his way back, the ubiquitous foot patrol made its appearance and demanded to know the contents of his bag. On seeing the beer the unit's eyes lit up and their point man made a simple offer: "Give the beer to us and you'll not be P-checked. If not, and we discover that you're underage, we'll call in the RUC and have the store's owner in big trouble for selling alcohol to a minor." The deal was made and Paddy came back empty-handed and we stared at the walls for the rest of the night. It was a trivial incident but one that reinforced our mistrust of authority.

It's fair to say that I was incensed by this "daylight" robbery and, on the following Saturday night, my dole check in hand, the opportunity for revenge presented itself. As I stood at the packed bar waiting for service a sudden hush fell over the Whitefort Inn crowd. An eight-man foot patrol had just entered and cautiously made their way around the pub for no apparent reason. If they were looking for someone he would have been long gone, alerted by the doorman.

One Brit took up an observation position beside my place and I immediately changed my order to two pints. This guy was about eighteen, just over five feet tall, and looked ready to piss his pants. He was terrified! Even his rifle looked taller than he was.

Anyway, I decided to P-check him, asking his name, where he was from, and if he had a girl waiting for him at home. The pints arrived and he froze in total amazement when I offered the extra one to him. At first the crowd looking on wondered what Delaney was doing, giving away a precious pint to the enemy who was physically (he had a gun clasped in his hands) and duty bound unable to accept. But the roars of laughter soon erupted, as I continued to insist that he accept my gift, and everyone realised who the joke was on.

Not content with having totally humiliated the youngster, I

then did one of the most stupid things in my life. Shoulder to shoulder with the unfortunate, I grabbed the nozzle of his SLR [self-loading rifle] and tried to whistle a tune by blowing over the top of his gun as if it were a Coke bottle. By now the place was in hysterics, seeing this fully equipped member of the Crown Forces being made to look like a fool by a drunken Fenian.

Soon enough the commander of the patrol saw from the end of the bar that his smart, highly trained unit was now the laughing stock of the Whitefort. Frantically waving to his squad, he motioned them to leave in as dignified manner as possible. But as my friend left he turned to me and said, "Thanks, mate, maybe some other time."

I'll always remember the look on his face and the thought that he was probably about to receive one of the worst tongue lashings of his life. Sadly, he was just another human being caught up in something none of us could understand. Still, if he was punished, I've no regrets. He deserved it.

The strange thing about Belfast was that, under abnormal circumstances, life just went on. The only way to keep going, at times, was to totally disregard events that would create fear and panic.

One afternoon in Belfast's city center, I was dragged into a shopping trip by my girlfriend who had a particular store to visit. Without any warning, a massive explosion went off just about five hundred yards away from our destination. As people fled the area we looked at each other and quickly agreed to try somewhere else. It was no big deal. I don't even remember whether anyone was killed or injured, only that we'd been inconvenienced.

Bomb blasts were always a matter of great debate at home. Was it a large one in town or a small one close by? We had our Richter scale which was based on how vigorously the windows shook, although an attack on the local police barracks often confused us. It was often large and, of course, close by. The same logic applied to gunfire, so we were able to determine whether it was the IRA, the British Army, or both who were engaged. If the two sides were involved in a gun battle we couldn't go out to play on the street or, in later years, go to the pub. Such a nuisance.

Many studies have been undertaken over the years by various independent and governmental groups in an effort to assess the impact upon the life of the people (particularly the young) of living in what at times is a war zone. Needless to say, none of their findings ever conclusively proved that behavior had been affected by the Troubles. Well, one Saturday night in the winter of 1979, a bizarre incident floored me!

The lads and I were going home, in a total state of intoxication, after a very late and extremely wild house party when an RUC patrol pulled up beside us. This was quite unusual—they were on foreign soil—but at two A.M. they must have reasoned it was worth the risk to venture outside the station. We whispered to each other to cooperate and be friendly. There was no point getting into trouble outside our own front doors, especially in our conditions.

Three or four officers dismounted their Land Rovers, put us up against the wall, and went through the usual name and address routine. When it came to me, the cop asked: "Aren't you Fred's son, the solicitor?" I replied in the affirmative and he called in the guard, explained that these boys were OK, and let us all go. With that they disappeared and sped off down the road.

We got back to our house to finish off the few beers we'd managed to steal from the party when "Fra" started pacing the room mumbling that something was wrong. We tried to get him to sit down, shut up, and drink his beer but it was no use. He hadn't been pushed around, verbally abused or even P-checked. It was unfair treatment, as far as he was concerned, just because the cop knew my "auld fella." He then tried to talk us into collecting the empty milk bottles down along the street to launch a surprise attack on the barracks to prove that we had as much right to be harassed as everyone else. Obviously we told him to fuck up and go to bed but when I woke up the next day it struck me: he was right! British military rule had created a mind-set that we were, and expected to be treated as, third-class citizens. Anything else was an aberration. But it was just another day in Belfast.

Call them what you will, Nationalists or Republicans, they all have one common goal—the end of British rule in Ireland, ultimately leading to the creation of one unified country with its own laws based on the democratic wishes of all the people, regardless of their race or religion.

Just as with many other conflicts around the world (most notably in the Middle East) even those with the same agendas invariably found ways to clash with anyone with a different ideological approach to achieving their aims. Moribund as it was in 1969, the IRA seemed powerless to protect the Catholic population from a "Protestant Parliament for a Protestant people," backed by a sectarian security apparatus which appeared to be on the verge of carrying out one of the greatest pogroms of the century.

Over the next couple of years a schism occurred in the Republican movement which led to the emergence of the Provisional IRA, who argued that the British and Ulster Unionists would listen to nothing but violence. The days of peaceful sit-ins and protests were over—this was war! Those who regarded this strategy as folly remained with the old guard who practiced a more limited armed campaign, along with preaching a socialist doctrine, as a cure to the six counties' problems. They would now be known as the Officials.

This brought on a climate that was strikingly similar to that which came about after the signing of the Treaty which created Northern Ireland back in 1921, when families were torn apart by allegiance to a certain wing of the movement. It was quite simple—those involved wanted the British out but couldn't agree on how best to achieve it.

Throughout the seventies, beatings, punishment shootings, and sometimes murder, were prevalent in West Belfast as feuds suddenly erupted between supposed allies. Many prominent activists were executed while, on the street level, a beating could result simply from being on the wrong side of the bar—one side for the "Stickies" (Officials) and one for the "Pinheads" (Provisionals). Things got worse when Dominic McGlinchey formed the INLA [Irish National Liberation Army] who reasoned that even the Provos' campaign wasn't enough. The Provisionals, who feared that their image as freedom fighters would be put in jeopardy by a purely sectarian war, loathed the INLA and did everything to distance themselves from that group. Meanwhile the police and Army sat back, not interfering, letting the feuds continue. It saved them a lot of time and trouble.

One fellow I knew named Sean supported the Officials while I personally believed that Britain could only be brought to the bargaining table by the use, not only of protest, but also an all-out military struggle. We were still good friends and often had lively and heated arguments as to the way the "cause" should be fought for.

One such evening as we were having our usual disagreements on the way back from the pub, a crowd of about twenty suddenly surrounded us. They were Provos. Very quietly two of them took me aside and told me not to move until their business was complete. From the other side of the street I watched an argument develop which eventually turned out to be quite one-sided. They beat the living daylights out of Sean and, just for laughs, took turns jumping on his back as they left.

Somehow Sean was back on his feet within a few minutes but, to my amazement, he refused to let me clean him up at home. Instead, he warned me to go indoors for my own safety and to have no association with him for the next couple of weeks. The following nights brought forth tit-for-tat beatings in the area culminating in a serious shooting of one of the Stickies who was lucky to live. (The rumour at the time was that he was set up by his brother.)

Following this feud, things were relatively calm. The Officials had been vanquished and neither the Army or the RUC were particularly interested in day-to-day policing. Into this vacuum stepped the Provos who established their own form of law enforcement in the ghetto. Basically there was no one else capable of or willing to do it.

Northern Ireland during the seventies has often been compared to other trouble spots around the world, especially Beirut. In actual fact, life went on with little disruption in most parts of the country except in times of extreme tension. For those who inhabited those parts of Belfast, Derry, and County Armagh where the effects of the conflict were felt every day, the opportunity to get away, if only for a short break, was one that could not be passed over. Unfortunately, the Troubles had a curious habit of following one around, like a ball and chain that could not be unshackled. A short trip across the Irish Sea was an obvious choice for many, offering the chance of work and a quiet life but when the IRA brought their campaign to the British mainland the same racial slurs, distrust, and discrimination found at home raised their ugly heads in England. It was worse for those Protestants "across the water" who in vain tried to argue that they were as British as the English themselves. But everyone was branded with the same iron—we were all murdering bastards. "Go home, Paddy!"

For me, though, the Irish Republic was much more preferable because of its proximity to the North and its natural beauty. At every opportunity, during school holidays or later when I was on the dole, I'd pack a bag, hitch about ten rides, and finally end up on the west coast of Donegal. Since we had a house there and knew the locals, I was treated reasonably well but I was still an outsider from the "Black North" [derogatory term for the six counties of Northern Ireland]. Those who visited maybe just once a year, however, were usually blamed for barroom brawls, paying for it with at least a broken nose.

Each summer our quiet retreat was allocated for two weeks at the time to the older members of the clan who were by now married with children. (That's one advantage of being the youngest and single—I was there for the whole two months!) For example, Colm and Ann had just spent a wonderful fortnight with their first, newly born son and sadly packed the car with all their worldly possessions for the trip back home. As they began their three-hour return journey, little did they realize that on the other side of Donegal's most famous landmark, Errigal Mountain, events were unfolding that would bring the Troubles crashing into their lives in a most unexpected way.

A renegade IRA unit had earlier in the day carried out a botched robbery on a Letterkenny bank office, the end result being a wild chase over the hills and valleys of Donegal, the Army and police in hot pursuit. At the foot of Errigal the gang came upon a group of German tourists who had pulled over to enjoy the view and the gang seized the chance to switch cars. Holding the tourists at gunpoint, they jumped into the car and then discovered to their dismay that it was a foreign, diesel-run car. They didn't know how to start it!

As the security forces approached and with everyone now in a panic, who should happen along but Colm and the family. Again, with a rifle pushed in their faces, their car was this time successfully taken and the fugitives sped off leaving six bewildered tourists (and a crying baby) behind them.

Using sign language Colm was able to persuade their newfound German friends to go back to the house to report the incident, which was no easy task, considering the state of the Irish phone system and the fact that mother thought the whole thing was a practical joke being played by her son. "Sit down, have a wee cup of tea, and stop fooling around!"

Over the next few days a massive search was conducted all over the west coast which, although not catching up with the gang, eventually uncovered the car. It had been driven into a secluded nearby lake, its roof smashed down to delay discovery, and everything inside totally ruined.

As it turned out, the hijackers were led by Dominic McGlinchey, one of the most notorious and sought-after men in the British Isles. Many years later he would be gunned down in the streets of Drogheda (halfway between Belfast and Dublin) possibly by family members whose wrath he had incurred over the years. During his reign he had succeeded in spreading his form of terror across the country, including our safe and secure haven of Donegal. The realities of the war were never far away.

Funnily enough, it was in Drogheda that I came closest to being arrested in all my years living in Ireland. Our English teacher coaxed the Christian Brothers, who ran the school, into allowing him to take his class of nine to Dublin to see a screening of one of James Joyce's finest works which would never be shown in a Belfast movie theatre.

Naturally the minibus wouldn't start after we had taken a short break in the pub in town and the local repairman said he would need about two hours before he could help us. After a couple more pints we decided to see what the town centre was like, leaving our tutor to await help. Around this time Protestant paramilitaries had, just like the IRA, decided to take the war to their enemies' homeland [the Republic of Ireland], causing death and destruction unlike anything witnessed before, even in the North.

The closer we got to the main street the clearer it was that something was going on—the road was being sealed off and police and ambulance vehicles were everywhere. This was quite normal to us so we continued on our way until a guard [policeman] stopped us and explained that one of the department stores had just received a bomb threat. When we inquired further as to the situation he recognized our accents, and yes, put us up against the wall!

Without the technical capability available to his Northern counterparts to check our IDs he chose to leave us there, threatening to throw us in jail if we tried to move. After a long wait, the rest of the lads came along and, considering the general state of intoxication of us all, it became obvious to the officer that we were hardly most-wanted terrorists and he let us go. But it was a nice, nostalgic (though very ironic) incident which reminded me of home!

Back in Belfast the war continued at its usual pace. IRA bomb attacks ravaged the city center business districts on an almost daily basis, coinciding with murderous attacks on police and prison staff. Even civilian workers involved in construction projects for the security forces were, regardless of religion, seen as legitimate targets. (This was a deliberate ploy to show the world that the cause was purely political, not sectarian.) The response to all of this from Loyalist paramilitaries was as predictable as it was savage. It seemed as if the evening newscasts always carried a report of the most recent slaying of an innocent Catholic who had strayed away from safe territory. This was especially true in North Belfast which, unlike Andersonstown, had no clear dividing line separating the opposing sides, often making a normal walk home a frightening experience. Nor were things helped by the fact that, in our opinion, the RUC were, at the very least, turning a blind eye to what was going on.

Meanwhile the Northern Ireland Office, under the auspices of the British government, attempted to create the illusion that life in the six counties was as normal as in any other part of the United Kingdom. By pumping millions of pounds into the province, an excellent road system was created and industrial sites built and a leisure center was constructed in each major population area. This was a great idea—giving access to the people of the more deprived areas to a variety of sports and a much needed boost to the local economy as well.

In Andersonstown, though, things are never quite as they seem. By day everything was placid. But as darkness fell our leisure center became a rallying point for almost nightly attacks on Army and police patrols by large numbers of teenagers with nothing better to do. Eventually the whole thing turned into a ridiculous cat-and-mouse game, with the Crown Forces not even bothering to enter the area, leaving scores of frustrated youth with little else to do but to build makeshift barricades and, maybe on a good night, hi-jack someone's car and set it alight. It was just a bit of crack [fun] to relieve the boredom of life in West Belfast. Unfortunately for me, the center was placed smack in the middle of my route home and I was almost always forced to make alternative travel plans unless, of course, it was a better than usual show. In that case I'd take a grandstand seat to view, well out of harm's way, the action.

Actually the locals were as adept as the British in their use of propaganda (which is all their good deeds amounted to) and one event stands out above all others. The Northern Ireland Office launched a province-wide media blitz in 1976 stating simply that "Seven years was enough." This was sure to grab the people's attention and for one wag on the Falls Road it certainly did. Within hours of the announcement on the news, a slogan appeared on a wall in the Beechmount area which read "Seven years is enough. Seven hundred is too much!" [Referring to what some say has been eight hundred years of British occupation.] That, for us, was the end of what was such a glorious campaign!

Nothing they did could change the reality—the British were occupying our country and we wanted them out. But thanks for the leisure centers!

The conditions that had evolved following the escalation of the conflict eventually pervaded every aspect of life in Belfast, including our favourite pastimes. Even a football match pitting two of the city's teams against each other turned into a tribal confrontation based solely on the supporters' religious backgrounds.

As much as I loved the sport, the thought of actually attending a highly charged fixture [well established sports event] terrified me, especially when it was being played at Windsor Park set deep in the heart of Protestant South Belfast. Cliftonville versus Linfield—Catholic versus Protestant—after a few pints the lads persuaded me to go and within minutes of reaching the grounds my worst fears were confirmed. Outside the stadium on the Falls Road [Catholic] side the RUC presence was overwhelming and made worse by the constant goading and taunting from our crowd. It seemed clear that both sides were looking for a violent clash. Once inside, the atmosphere was frightening. The Catholic supporters, having been penned into one end of the ground, found themselves almost outnumbered by fully equipped riot police, complete with vicious attack dogs.

It's doubtful whether the majority of the crowd even remembers the game as the whole ninety minutes turned into a contest by the "fans" to outsing the opposition with such gems as "You Dirty Fenian Bastards" to which we replied, "You Dirty Orange [Protestant] Bastards." Songwriters we were not!

At one point, one of the lads in our section produced a British Union Jack flag, set it on fire, and was promptly surrounded by a horde of RUC men who "escorted" him from the terraces and threw him in jail for the night. Not to be outdone, an Irish Tricolour was dealt with in the same manner by those in the opposing stand. The perpetrator was led away . . . and minutes later we witnessed him regaining admittance through a side entrance.

The walk home was no better as the Protestant fans, relishing their victories both on and off the field, fired off a volley of stones and bottles at us, secure in the knowledge that the police would not interfere.

Back in the safety of Andersonstown I made a vow that this would be the first and last game I would attend in Belfast. And it was.

By now it must be clear that the Whitefort Inn was not only just the local watering hole but also an establishment that was a microcosm of the world in which we lived. Christmas, New Year's, St. Patrick's Day—you name it—we were in the "Fort." Everyone knew who you were (most important!), the fish and chip shop was next door, and it was close to home. In a way, the British and their Unionist allies had created a monster by isolating such a large, and at times, rebellious population in one place. In the Fort, the IRA were free to operate in any way they chose, sure in the knowledge that their activities were unlikely to be reported to the authorities. Even if you didn't support them, you would turn a blind eye. It was the occupying Army who were the enemy.

I always felt very secure in that bar—though no one liked to sit with his back to the door—and one Saturday afternoon, when the Army came in to evacuate the place, we ignored them. They had apparently received information that the Provos were in the process of transferring a bomb, via the pub, when the operation turned sour. Needless to say, we treated this with scorn—another excuse to harass our people. However, the manager took it seriously enough and finally convinced everyone to leave, except for me and Gerry. It was only after the promise of free drinks to take outside that he was able to get us off the premises.

Across the street we drank our pints, amused by the British bomb squad going about their futile business but annoyed that our night would be ruined. Eventually we called it a day and stayed home that evening with our girlfriends. This was sacrilege!

Came the next day, I dutifully went off down the road to get the Sunday papers. Just as I got home the phone was ringing—it was Gerry. A short article in the paper described how an explosive device had been found and defused the day before in the Whitefort. I still mistrust the British Army, but . . .

The war changed over the years and the days of random, unorganized attacks were over. Information from informers—there were many—resulted in large-scale arrests, botched ambushes, and volunteers being killed in action. So the IRA abandoned its traditional function as an army of a people risen [in rebellion], and studied the craft of guerilla warfare, setting up small cells of dedicated and well-trained soldiers, acting within a complex chain of command. The fewer people you knew and who knew you were in the IRA the better. Also long gone were the days when "I'm ready to die for Ireland" meant automatic acceptance to the movement.

The British, with their long experience in colonial wars, soon adapted and progressively built up an astounding intelligence network in the North. For example, now if you were P-checked the soldier didn't have to ask you much more, once he had your name. He already had all the answers within a minute of calling in.

As the IRA became a smaller, more elite organization, the Army felt safer patrolling the streets, monitoring those who attended funerals for the war dead, and even doing what was once unthinkable—checking out the Whitefort on a Saturday night.

That was not the only time that I "dodged a bullet" [had a lucky escape] at the Whitefort. As I got older, more summer weekends were spent at home in the "Fort." On one occasion in the late seventies, however, a sudden urge took me to Donegal during August. This was a deserved break from the marching season during which both sides and the security forces were on full alert. Ostentatious displays were the order of the day, proving one's allegiance to whichever ideological camp you belonged.

None of this impacted the lives of those in Donegal and, as usual, a few of us were getting ready for an evening down in the poolroom when we got a call from Belfast. The public bar of the Whitefort, filled with punters [spectators who sometimes bet or gamble] watching the afternoon horse racing, had been blown up by a lone Loyalist paramilitary member. One person was killed and numerous seriously injured. It sent a major shiver down my spine. I undoubtedly would have been there had I not left town.

Again the abnormality of life in Belfast rose to the surface. Within an hour of the explosion those only slightly injured lined up outside our family's law office (directly across the street), their unfinished pints in hand, waiting to submit claims against the Northern Ireland Office for their physical and mental harm. May as well get some money out of it, right? I supposed I would have done the same.

One of the most common misconceptions about life in Northern Ireland is that the Troubles are a religious war, with the British acting as peacekeepers, separating two warring factions intent on wiping each other out. The television and print media have often been willing conspirators in propagating this lie and I'm frequently asked in America a simple question: "Are you lot still killing each other over there?" My reply to this is always the same, and one that is often heard among the people I grew up with: "Some of my best friends are Protestants." And it's true.

One evening I ventured into the city center to attend a stag night for a colleague from work in the private members club run by the Ulster Bank. The groom-to-be had been to Donegal a few times with me and even had the audacity to visit the Whitefort a couple of times. (We had to call him Paul as his real name would have been a dead giveaway as to his religion.) As the night wore on, one of the crowd began to make blatant remarks about where I was from and the fact that I didn't belong with those of the true faith. I was totally outnumbered and unsure whether some of the others of the crowd felt the same way. "Paul" tried to calm things down but, in his condition, it only made matters worse. "Why are you defending the Fenian from Andersonstown?"

I was about to take my leave when I felt a hand on my shoulder and I was told to sit down and enjoy the rest of the evening. James—definitely not his real name—was a member of the UDR [Ulster Defense Regiment] and I knew for a fact that he carried a licensed gun, even when off duty. He looked my adversary straight in the eye and simply explained that I was a friend of Paul's and that was good enough for him . . . and everyone else in the bar. Religion meant nothing. Eventually our bigot for the night left and later the lads escorted me to the Falls Road taxi stand, quite a risk for them. So much for the sectarian divide.

However, as much as we were friends in social situations, the reality of the conditions in Belfast dictated that these occasions were few and far between. When James pulled on the uniform of a British Army regiment he was, as much as we liked him, once again the enemy.

April 6, 1981, marked my twenty-first birthday. Little did I know that one month later a series of events [hunger striker Bobby Sands died on May 5th, followed by the deaths of nine more hunger strikers] would unfold that would ultimately change the course of Irish history forever. Nor did the thought enter my mind that I would, four years later, pack my bags and cross the Atlantic for a new life. This was my day and I was going to enjoy it. Down to the Whitefort for a few pints with the girlfriend and the lads, back to her place, and finally make my way home, trying to avoid Army patrols on the way.

After all, it was just another day in Belfast.

NATASHA RITCHIE

BELFAST

Eighteen-year-old Natasha Ritchie expresses a disinterest in the Troubles that she thinks others of her generation may share. When I talked with her in Belfast and asked her how her life had been impacted by the Troubles, she said, "I pretty much ignore the whole thing," although in her poem she reveals that her disinterest is a studied attempt to decrease the pain she feels about the violence.

Natasha says she couldn't hate anyone just because of their religion. "I just don't see how it can matter. I'd like it if everybody'd forget about religion," she says. As a matter of principle she does not specify which religious community she belongs to.

Natasha has used writing to express her feelings for as long as she can remember. She wrote this particular poem as a response to my request for poetry in the *Belfast Telegraph.*

Pain or Peace?

(Written at age eighteen)

Lying in bed you hear a bomb in the distance
Close your eyes and forget, try to keep your innocence
Watching the news, there's twelve more dead
Maybe a sigh or a shake of your head.
There's nothing you can do, there's nothing you can say
You can't stop the pain, make the hurt go away.
So you go out to your friends and play your games
You're only young, you can't make it change
You learn to ignore, pretend it never happened
When you let it get to you that's when childhood ends.

And now there's a cease-fire, now we have peace
How long will it last? A few months? A few weeks?
You don't know what to think, a whole new way of life
You're just not sure, but the other way wasn't right.
There's always been trouble, since before you were born
People fighting, people killing, families forlorn
Now there's a new way to live where nobody dies
But should we believe it, or is it all just more lies?
Will we have a new life where there's no need to grieve
It's going to take time before I can believe.

BRENDA MURPHY

BELFAST

Now in her forties, the mother of twelve-year-old Bridie Murphy, whose contribution to this anthology appears on page 31, Brenda is also "Mammy" to a seventeen-year-old daughter named Lorraine. The family, including the children's aunt Lorraine, live next to the "peace wall" alongside the Springfield Road in West Belfast, where they have seen a tremendous amount of violence over the years.

It was the sectarian murder of a relative that drove Brenda, at seventeen years of age, to try to help the Republican [Catholic] cause by transporting an illegal weapon, an effort for which she was arrested and jailed. Her story tells in excruciating detail what it was like for a teenager to face years in prison—an adult prison where no allowances were made for first-time or juvenile offenders.

After paying her debt for a crime she openly acknowledges having committed, Brenda was arrested again when she was in her twenties and accused of being a member of the IRA. She served several years in prison for the "crime" of membership in this organization, although she swears to this day that she most definitely was not a member of the IRA.

While most people would hold tremendous bitterness for the

loss of so much of their youth, Brenda Murphy is undoubtedly one of the most upbeat, industrious, charming, and humorous people I've ever met. Very dedicated to her community and the fight for justice in Northern Ireland, Brenda is well known in Belfast as a political activist who rarely takes "no" for an answer when she is trying to help someone in need. She and three members of Equality, a group to which she belongs that works to stop discrimination, were honored to be invited to personally meet with America's President Clinton when he visited Belfast in November of 1995.

In addition to her community work, Brenda is a writer of some renown. Several of her stories have been published by the highly respected Blackstaff Press in Belfast, several others have appeared in various anthologies, and she has a collection of short stories that she hopes will soon be published as well.

Condemned

I was escorted to the holding cells, after my brief court appearance, by two female prison officers. Flanked on either side, each holding one of my arms, I felt like meat in a sandwich. They told me it would be several hours before the police had arranged an escort for the prison van. I settled down into the corner of the cell to wait, not speaking. I studied these two women from head to toe. Their uniforms were royal blue. On their heads sat three-cornered hats which had an odd, almost Napoleonic, look to them. Their thick legs and ankles were covered by beige tights and their feet were encased in what looked like remarkably heavy, black lace-up shoes.

Their faces, like their tights, were also beige. The smaller of the women in blue had a sharp pointed face with high bony cheeks. Her eyes were very small and seemed to be set far too widely apart. Her lips were too thin and just a slightly darker shade of beige than her face. Something about her face would have reminded you of a bird, an annoying twittering, twitching bird. Not a bird who would fly gracefully, but one who would flap madly, as if it were trying to beat the air with its wings.

Her colleague in blue, although possessing the same facial colouring, looked nothing like her. Underneath the three-cornered hat was a large face, not fat, just large. Her forehead was wide, her nose was not big, but strong. Her cheek bones were broad and her eyes were normal-sized. It was her mouth which would make you look at her. Her lips were closed but the top lip sat out, well in front of her bottom lip. It gave the impression that she had a receding chin but this was not the case. When you looked closer at her mouth you could see that, although her mouth was closed, her lips met only at the corners. They were prevented from meeting by her top teeth. They were so prominent, particularly the front two, that they overshot her bottom teeth and rested on her bottom lip even while her mouth was closed. It was sad that this should be so because without those teeth she would have been a handsome woman. Not beautiful ever, but a handsome, solid woman.

For six hours we sat waiting for the police to arrange a security escort. Finally a voice shouted that we were ready to go. We walked in single file out into the open courtyard and into the prison transit. In front and behind the van I was travelling in sat police Land Rovers. They would accompany us from the police station to the prison. The windows of the van were made of smoked glass. I could see out but no one on the outside could see in. It was six o'clock in the evening—a bitterly cold evening in Belfast. Workers and last-minute shoppers hurried along streets I would probably not walk along again for many years. Their coat collars were turned up against swirling snow flurries. All these people were oblivious to the small procession of vehicles in which I was travelling. A great surge of sadness overwhelmed me. I closed my eyes and thought about the last four days and what I had been through.

I had been arrested about this time on a Monday night

under the Special Powers Act.* It is an old law used only in Northern Ireland. Under these Special Powers anyone arrested can be held for up to seventy-two hours without a lawyer. The interrogations with the police are neither audio- nor video-taped. If you are charged at the end of this time you will appear in a court which has no jury. There will only be a judge to decide whether the police or the accused are telling the truth about what occurred during the interrogations.

I had heard about the beatings that were carried out in these interrogation centres. But I had never been arrested in my life and really had no idea of what actually went on after being arrested. As I had been caught with a rifle, I presumed that the need to interrogate me would be minimal. After all, I had reasoned, they had all the evidence they needed to charge me.

For the first twelve hours after my arrest I was seen by three different sets of detectives from Special Branch [for the investigation of terrorism]. These detectives asked only the questions I expected and behaved in a civil manner towards me. I admitted that the rifle was mine but refused to tell them where I got it. I gave my name and address and asked that my parents be informed of my arrest as I was seventeen years old and they would be worried if I did not return home. I asked to see a lawyer even though I knew that was not permitted. I was very nervous and more than a little frightened but this interrogation wasn't too bad. I thought that the stories that I had heard about interrogation centres must have been exaggerated.

The interrogation rooms that I had been brought to were all exactly the same. The rooms were fourteen feet square, windowless, with bright fluorescent lights burning day and night from the low ceilings. Each room had one table in the middle

---

*The Prevention of Terrorism act, enacted in 1974, further extends police power so that a person can be held in jail for up to seven days with no access to a lawyer. This law is still in effect today in Northern Ireland.

and three chairs. The fourth time I was brought to the interrogation room I was left alone for a few moments. Then two new detectives entered the room. One was a youngish man of about thirty-five. He was smartly dressed in a dark suit with a white shirt and a tie. He was tall and slim. Behind him came an older man who was in his middle to late forties. He was also wearing a suit but it was an old suit. The knees of the trousers sagged and the jacket had a shine to it. I could not see the waistband of his trousers because a large beer belly hung down over it. This older man was bald and combed some of the hair from the side of his head across the top in an attempt to hide his bald patch. His face was meaty and his jawline was slack and hung in jowls. He carried a folder which he slapped down onto the table. Then he sat down and started to read what was in it, totally ignoring me.

The younger detective walked around behind me and I turned my head to follow his movements when he slapped me hard with his open hand across the back of the head. I jumped up off the chair and he grabbed me by the hair and screamed as loudly as he could that I was to sit down and under no circumstances was I to move unless he said so. I was not to look around at him and I was to answer all his questions.

Someone screaming into your ear is very painful. As he screamed his questions into me I sat silent. Every time he got no reply I got slapped on the back of the head again. Then he would scream for me to stand up and when I did he would jam his fingers, which he held out stiffly, into my back or ribs. If I bent over or put my hand instinctively up to where he had hurt me he would slap me on the head again. Then he would ask in a bewildered and angry voice what I thought I was doing standing up. When I tried to tell him that he had told me to stand up he would smack me again.

Then he decided that he would ask me questions while pushing his fingers into the bone of my chest. He used his fingers to underline each word he said. The whole time this was happening the older detective sat with his head down at the table reading the folder he had brought in with him. He could have been sitting in a quiet library on a Sunday afternoon.

This abuse from the younger detective continued for about two hours. At this stage I had taken to saying over and over again, like a mantra, "I have nothing to say, I have nothing to say."

Then there was a cough from the older man at the table. He stood up and brought his chair round to where I was seated. He put the chair right down in front of me with its back touching my knees and the seat of the chair facing out towards him. He removed his jacket and put it on the table. He rolled up the sleeves of his shirt and loosened his tie. I thought to myself, "Dear God, please don't let him start hitting me as well." He straddled the chair, throwing his leg over it the way you would sit on a horse. Then he pushed the chair tightly against my knees, forcing me to push my legs in under the chair. He put his forearms across the back of the chair and then put his face really close to mine. His nose was less than a quarter of an inch from my nose.

This intimate closeness was embarrassing to me and made me feel uncomfortable. I pulled my face away but he took my face in his meaty hand and said, "My colleague would not think it polite if you turned your face away from me, Brenda." His voice was quite beautiful. A dark brown, well-modulated voice that sounded like liquid silk. He sprayed when he spoke; a fine mist of his spittle speckled my face and lips. His breath smelled strongly of peppermint and beneath it something else. A smell of rotting meat, foul and fetid. I imagined some debris of a long-ago eaten meal stuck between his teeth and putrifying there. I felt sick.

With his beautiful voice he told me that I would tell him everything that he wanted to know. He went on to tell me that he knew that I was responsible for a catalogue of bombings and shootings. This was totally untrue and I told him so. He looked away and his friend smacked me hard across the back of the head. I was to learn that when I denied anything to this man he would look away and I would be hit. After a while I simply refused to answer every question and every allegation. Then he started to ask if I had had sex with all the IRA men in my area. From his mouth came the most awful filth that I have ever heard in my life. His tone never changed as he described what he believed I did sexually with IRA men. I was a virgin and hearing this from a man older than my father humiliated and frightened me. I felt totally naked. I looked forward to the breaks between interviews, only to lie in the cell and dread the next interview. On the third day I was very close to breaking down. I wanted to say, "Right, okay, what do you want me to say? I'll admit to anything. Just leave me alone."

The detectives were like some sick Abbott and Costello routine, with one hitting me and the other pouring out his foul words from his foul-smelling mouth hour after hour. Of the two methods they used I could handle the violence better. I felt sexually threatened by the older man. His closeness, his spittle, his body odour totally intimidated me. When it was over and I was charged I was relieved and glad even though I knew I was going to prison.

Persistent humming broke into my train of thought. The prison officer with the prominent teeth was humming irritating snatches of hymns like "Jesus Loves the Little Children," then "Jesus Wants Me for a Moonbeam." I wondered if humming like that made vibrations run down those two enormous front teeth and did it make her bottom lip feel tingly like it did when you blew on a piece of paper over a comb. The woman with the buck teeth was tall and well built. I thought of how it would feel to be bit by those teeth. The very idea made me feel ill.

We finally arrived at the prison and I stepped stiffly down from the van. The women prison officers took an arm each and walked me across the reception yard. The walls of this yard were various shades of grey and made of enormous masonic bricks, each about two feet long. The walls were about eighteen feet high and were strung with coils of barbed wire. Bright security lights ran along the top and cameras were placed at ten-feet intervals along the walls. One camera was pointed in towards me; the other outwards. It was dark already at six in the evening and I was freezing.

We reached a thick iron door and the prison officer pressed a bell. Feet and the jangling of keys could be heard behind the door. It was opened and we stepped in. The warden who opened the door spoke to my two escorts. "Freezing, isn't it, Miss McClelland," she said.

The woman with the buck teeth replied, "It is, indeed, Miss Smith. Myself and Miss Holland will be glad of a cup of tea in the Mess."

The warden called Smith walked in front. McClelland and Holland guided me after her into a room with red tiles on the floor and pale, dirty yellow walls. On one side of the room were bath stalls with half doors on them. They walked me past these and stopped at a scrubbed wooden table. Facing the table were three small cubicles like changing rooms. These also had wooden half doors. The room was warm and smelled of carbolic and disinfectant.

"Right, who have we here?" asked the warden called Smith. The bucktoothed woman called McClelland said, "This prisoner is called Brenda Murphy," as she searched in her handbag and handed documents over to Smith. "We will leave her in your capable hands, Miss Smith, and go to get that tea. We will see you in the wing tomorrow then, Brenda," McClelland said. But Brenda did not answer.

They left and I stood looking at the warden called Smith who was looking at the documents which McClelland had handed to her. She read them for a few moments, then lifted her head and addressed me. "Well, now. You go into that cubicle behind you, close the half door, and take off your clothes. All of them, mind. I will give you a sheet to wrap around you. Just take your clothes off and throw them over the door."

I could feel my heart hammering in my chest. "Jesus Christ, these other two will probably come back and give me a kicking."

The Warden Smith interrupted these thoughts. "Look, Brenda, nothing is going to happen to you. I write down a list of everything which you enter the prison with. You undress, put the sheet round you, and when you come out with the sheet around you, you go over and have a bath. All inmates must have a bath. When you come out of the bath I will have a fresh set of clothes ready for you."

I did not reply, nor did I move.

"Now look here, if you will not undress of your own accord I can call help down here and we will strip and bathe you by force. You don't want that, do you? Now, here's the sheet. In you go and undress." She held out a white bed sheet.

I reached slowly out and took it from her and walked to the changing cubicle. I slowly undressed. Taking off my sweater and jeans first, then wrapping the sheet around me, I wriggled out of my underwear underneath the sheet, the way you would undress at the beach. All the while my eyes never left the top of the cubicle door in case the warden would look over. When I was naked except for the sheet I sat on the built-in, slatted wooden seat that was attached to the wall behind me.

I was sure that, as a Republican [advocate of a united Ireland free of British rule], I was probably supposed to refuse to take my clothes off. But I couldn't bear the thought of being held down and stripped naked. I was too sore to bear being dragged into a bath and washed and humiliated by strangers.

"Right you are," I heard the warden say as she walked towards the cubicle. My hands were clenched into fists, holding like grim death to the sheet around me. "In you go and have a bath. I'll write a list of your clothes into the property book while you do that. And be quick now."

I walked from the cubicle to the bath stall, watching the warden over my shoulder all the time. I went in and found a large, old-fashioned bathtub which stood on claw feet. I put the plug in the bath and ran the taps. I was looking about for shampoo and soap but could see none.

The warden was at the top of the door. "Here you are," she said, handing over a towel and what looked like a two-inch-thick piece of ivory-coloured wood about three feet long.

I took both from her. "What's this for?" I asked, uttering my first words since my court appearance.

"That's soap. The male prisoners make it for us. Just break a bit off that. And you're only allowed two inches of bath water, so turn the taps off now please." As she walked away I said, "Could I have some shampoo—my hair is really greasy."

"Shampoo. You can have shampoo when your parents bring it for you. We don't supply it so just use the soap." And with that she walked away.

I tried to break a piece of soap off the long bar but I couldn't do it. In the end, still wearing the sheet, I stepped into the bath. I took the sheet off and hung it over the bath taps so that I could grab it in a hurry. I sat with my back to the door and put the large bar of soap into the water. It was lukewarm so I turned the hot tap on.

Smith's voice rang out. "I told you, only two inches of water. Turn that tap off."

I turned it off and rubbed the face cloth vigorously along the enormous bar of soap. At last it started to give a lather. I washed my body. The carbolic soap stung my shins where the skin had been broken from the kicks I had received. My ribs hurt and there were black-and-blue finger marks on the top of both my arms.

There was a plastic jug on the corner of the bathtub which I used to scoop up the water and pour it over my hair and face.

I lifted the huge bar of soap and rubbed it up and down my head. I lifted my long hair in one hand, pulled it over my shoulder, and rubbed it against the soap in an attempt to create some suds. I got very few suds but I scrubbed at my hair as hard and as quickly as I could. I called out, "I need to rinse my hair. Can I turn the water on to fill the jug?"

"No. You use what's in the bath," Smith shouted back.

"But that water's dirty," I replied.

"Just use it or don't, as you wish, but no more water!"

So I scooped up the water and poured it over my hair. I heard the warden approach so I jumped up, grabbed the sheet, and pulled it round my body just as Smith looked over the top of the stall. "Good, you're finished. Let's go," she said abruptly.

"I'm not dried yet," I said, "and I have to wash the bathtub."

"Just hurry up. I'm due my break soon. Never mind washing the bathtub. A prisoner will wash it tomorrow morning," Smith snapped.

I half dried my body. Then, wrapping the sheet tightly round me, I walked from the bath stall across the tiled floor.

I stood uncertainly in the centre of the room, hair dripping onto my shoulder.

The warden said, "Right, I have all your dirty clothing marked in the book. Do you have rings, chains, or anything like that?"

"No," I replied.

Smith continued. "Do you have any scars, bruises, or injuries?"

I said, "Yes. I'd like to see a doctor. The police beat me."

"You will see the doctor and the prison governor first thing tomorrow morning. Meanwhile, I will take note of your injuries. Have you taken, or do you take, any medication?"

"No," I replied.

Having filled in the brief medical history, Warden Smith said, "Right, come on over here and step on these scales."

"Why?" I asked. Like all fat girls, my weight embarrassed me.

"We take everyone's weight and height," Smith replied.

The scales were not the household type that you step onto and then your weight is displayed. This was an upright one where you have to move a bar along until you come to the correct weight. "About what weight are you?" Smith asked as I stepped onto the scales.

"I'm not sure, maybe nine stone," I lied, knowing I was at least a stone and a half more. Smith moved the bar to nine and kept on moving it until it rested at ten and a half stone. I flushed red. I stepped off the scales and asked, "Could I have my clothes now please—I'm really cold."

"We supply you with clothes until you can wash your own or clean ones are sent in on your visit," Smith answered.

"Okay, can I have them please?" I asked again.

"Just one more thing and you can get dressed," Smith said as she walked towards me. "Just open up the sheet."

"What?" I asked, alarmed.

"Come on now," Smith said sternly, "it must be done. Everyone who comes in here must be seen."

"No," I said, "I don't see why I have to do that."

"Because the rules say you must. Now open up that sheet! It's like this—if you don't it will be removed," said Smith.

I opened the sheet and stood naked. I stared at the dirty yellow wall, my face and neck burning a bright red as this woman took a look at my naked body. Then she said, "Drop the sheet please."

I did as I was told, feeling the tears sting my eyes. This was worse than being hit and yelled at. I was seventeen, I was fat, and I felt dirty, humiliated and degraded. No one had ever seen me naked since I had reached puberty. I was ashamed of my body but I knew that even if I were as thin as Twiggy I would still feel as I did at that moment.

"Right, that's fine, you can wrap up again. Just lift each foot now, so I can see the soles," said Smith. I did so. After this Smith looked through my wet hair the way a nit nurse [a nurse who treats people for lice infestations] would and for the same reason. "Right, that wasn't so bad now, was it," said Smith.

I just looked at her. I hated this woman for what she had just done to me. I would always hate this woman. I felt that I would like another bath, a proper bath with scalding water and lots of soap.

"Right. Take these," said Smith, going to the scrubbed table and lifting a bundle of clothing from it. "What size bra are you?" she asked.

"Size thirty-eight," I said, going red again.

"Right, I'll get you one now. You go into one of those cubicles and get dressed."

I took the clothing in one arm and held the sheet tightly closed with the other. I walked into the cubicle and put down the clothes. There was a blue blouse with white spots on it and a blue cardigan. There was a pair of dark brown stockings that had been darned with red thread in about a dozen places. The skirt was of dark brown wool with an elasticized waist. There was a vest and girdle with suspenders attached to it. The girdle was something I had only seen in films. It was a ghastly pink which people called "flesh coloured" for some reason.

Then I saw the knickers. They were thick white cotton with thick elastic at the waistband. These were enormous and there was no elastic at the legs . . . just a thick hem around each leg hole. But worse than all this was the fact that, although they had been washed and were clean, they were not new. These had been worn by someone else. I called out, "Excuse me."

"Yes, just coming. This is the only thirty-eight I can find," said Smith, handing over the bra.

"Look at these knickers. You've given me someone else's. They have been worn. Anyway they wouldn't fit me. They are far too big and there's a girdle thing here with hooks up the back. What's that for?" I asked.

"Well, now, those knickers have been boil-washed in bleach. They are perfectly clean. You don't expect to be issued with new ones, do you? New knickers are only issued when the old ones are beyond repair and have been condemned. It's the same with any other part of the prison uniform."

"Condemned," I said and went on with genuine surprise. "You condemn clothes . . . what to? The gas chamber, to be hung . . . what?"

"No, to the bin. If it can't be repaired it is condemned and thrown out. We enter it in the book. That's how we keep a check on the prison uniforms," Smith told me. "What for?" I asked. "No one is going to steal these things."

"You'd be surprised," Smith said.

"I'd be fucking astounded," I said quietly to myself. I pulled on the used, but clean, knickers. I was glad they swung between my legs like a hammock and didn't actually touch my skin. The bra was amazing—I had never seen one like it. The cups were made of what looked like small pieces of cloth sewed in ever-decreasing circles, ending in a huge point that would put your eye out. The cup on the left had been ripped off at some stage and had been sewn back in. No doubt it had been reprieved from being condemned. But, as a result of this repair, one cup was actually smaller than the other. I didn't bother complaining about it. I just squashed my left breast into it and pulled on the rest of the revolting attire.

I felt utterly ridiculous. The skirt hung on me and fell almost to my ankles and the blue spotted blouse was too tight. I took a size two in a shoe and they had none in that size so I had been given a size three which my heels slid in and out of with every step I took. I felt as if I had gone back a century . . . that it really must be 1871 instead of 1971. The clothes were so Victorian.

I shuffled behind Smith, through gates that had male officers opening and closing them. Keys jangled, hanging from skirts and trousers of the prison staff on chain-link sorts of belts.

We eventually arrived on "A" wing. It looked exactly like the picture in the poetry book, *The Ballad of Reading Gaol.* There was a slate black floor and on each side, at eight-foot intervals, set into deep doorways, were the cell doors. On the second story, which you reached by climbing a steep set of wooden stairs supported by a wrought iron frame, the layout was exactly the same. There was a catwalk right around the second story with a bridge across the centre of it. Wire had been stretched across the gap between the catwalks. It looked like heavy chicken or fencing wire.

"What's the wire for?" I asked.

Smith said, "It's called 'suicide wire.' It's to prevent prisoners throwing—"

"—I understand the word 'suicide,' " I interrupted her. I followed Smith halfway up the wing and went into what I would later discover was called "the guard room."

"One on, Miss Daly," Smith said to another warden who was sitting at a desk. I would learn that when a prisoner entered or left a wing that "one on" or "one off" would be shouted.

"New arrival, Miss Daley. All shipshape. Here's her documentation. I'll be off as I'm overdue my break," said Smith, handing the documents to the warden called Daly.

"Right you are, Miss Smith," Daly said.

"I'll see you tomorrow and no doubt for many years to come," Smith said to me over her departing shoulder.

"I'll look forward to it, pervert," I called back.

Daly stepped in between us. "Now, now, we'll have none of that. I'll take you to your cell," she said, steering me further up the wing.

She showed me into a cell which had an arched ceiling about fifteen feet high. A small, also arched window was in the thick wall close to the ceiling on the wall directly facing the door. A single bed was dead centre of the cell. Piled on the bed were a grey and black, army style blanket trimmed with red stitching, a pair of white sheets, and pillow cases. There was a white enamel basin and jug, edged with blue, and a white enamel "Po," [chamber pot] also edged in blue. A plastic, half-pint mug, a knife and fork and spoon. To the left of the bed was a small white-painted wooden locker. On it was a Bible and a stand-up cardboard thing with the prison rules written on it.

"As you are a new prisoner, you have to be locked right away. But tomorrow night you will be allowed to have associa-tion with the other prisoners until eight o'clock." Daly chat-tered in a friendly manner. Then she lowered her voice. "The other girls are expecting you. It was on the news that you'd been charged. They will see you at breakfast tomorrow." She meant the other Republican prisoners, but I gave no indication that I knew what she meant.

"You have had a beating," Daly went on. "I can get the medic to bring you some painkillers." I did not respond. "I'm a Catholic," she whispered. "The others will tell you I'm okay. My boyfriend's father was interned in the fifties."

"That must have been nice for him," I replied deadpan.

Seeing that she was not getting the response she had hoped for, Daly said, "I'll get the cookhouse to send you up something to eat. I know you are a little wary but you'll see I'm okay. You make up your bed and I'll be back with some food, alright?"

"Right, thank you," I replied. That seemed to please Daly who smiled and went out the door, locking it behind her.

I sat on the bed and looked around the cell. I felt like crying. I knew that bitch, Warden Smith, was right. I would be here for many years to come.

ALISON ROY

BELFAST

Partly perhaps because she was raised in the sedate Belmont District of Belfast, Alison Roy has not suffered the kind of loss that she describes in her poem. But she has always been aware of and sensitive to the pain the Troubles have brought to others in Northern Ireland. This particular poem, written in 1992, was inspired by a book by Martin Dillon called *The Shankill Butchers* and was first published in Women Together's *Poems for Peace* in 1993.

Although she truly appreciated the different atmosphere in Belfast during the 1994–1996 cease-fires, Alison wants people to know that the paramilitary punishment beatings and racketeering continued as before.

The Clock Ticks, Echoing Round the Walls

(Written at age seventeen)

The clock ticks, echoing round the walls.
They clink china cups and saucers, make polite apologies,
Then move to leave.
I sit there, motionless; watching them, clad in black, move
Like spiders throughout the room.
Searching, scrabbling for something that belongs to them.
I scream suddenly.
They look up startled: caught in the act, they move hurriedly
toward the door

On their spindly, hairy legs.
Then they are gone.

The clock ticks: I begin to cry.
Deep, rocking sobs that shake my whole body.
Don't you realize what you have done, you murderers?
Upstairs there sleeps a baby, beside me lies a bloodstained
carpet,
And six feet under in an oblong box is my husband.
No apology, no hypocritical sewage that will leak from your
    mouth
Will ever make this aching hole disappear.

I try to clear away the funeral feast which surrounds me,
To escape from the cloying perfume which still hangs thick in
    the air.
But my shaking hand knocks over the tea,
And it spreads through the carpet,
Until I hear it squelch beneath my feet.
It can be removed, unlike the blood which will continue
To bathe my dreams and colour my life.

Why did you do it?
What gave you the right to take away someone I love?
He did not suffer, but the family left behind
Will continue to be haunted.
You are not sorry, you are cowards,
You came masked in the night.
You have no cause;
For it has long been buried amongst the corpses of your vic-
    tims.
I want nothing more than this to stop,
So that another door is not opened to faceless strangers
Who fill the room with gunfire and blood.

But I, like you, am lying to myself,
For there will be no peace
Only the eternal sound of bombs and gunfire.

MYRA V. VENNARD

BANGOR, COUNTY DOWN

Born in the 1930s, Myra Vennard grew up in North Belfast in a working-class Protestant family. Her father worked in the Harland and Wolff shipyard. She married and began a family in Belfast but moved to Bangor, which she calls a "bedroom community" of the city, because of her fears for her children's safety during the Troubles. Widowed now for seventeen years and her children grown and gone, she lives on her own in a small apartment in Bangor and devotes much of her time to writing.

Myra was sensitive to the undercurrents of religious segregation even as a child; she says she always felt that the tensions would have to be worked out in some way. That way, as it turned out, was violence, and the deaths of over 3,100 people since the Troubles began in 1969. But Myra believes that those people did not die in vain because it seems to have taken that much loss to finally bring people in Northern Ireland to a readiness for peace.

The other force for peace in which Myra firmly believes is the emigration and return of Ireland's young people. Having left in great numbers because of the Troubles, young people are returning now with a vastly expanded perspective.

"Ulster Rain" was one of the first poems Myra wrote and one of a very few she has written about the Troubles. "Writing about the Troubles is painful," she says, "and you've got to be very careful about what you say."

A personal essay by Myra Vennard appears on page 349.

Ulster Rain

Here—
You can smell the rain
Before it comes.

Only Ulster knows its own rain
And its relentlessness—
Threatening first
Down the coast
Over the sea
Behind the mountain—
Rolling inaudible
From blackening yonder—
A slow drag of cloud
Like massive pillows
Smothering the sun.

Ah!
—That we had smelled the rain
Before our birth—
Before it seeped into our blood
And sprung an unfathomed well
Behind our eyes.

PART II

THROUGHOUT THE DIVIDED COUNTRY

While Belfast has received much international attention for the many acts of violence committed there, the media have perhaps not been as diligent in conveying the impact of the Troubles on other areas of Northern Ireland. In this, the second part of this anthology, those who are growing up or who have grown up in towns, cities, and rural areas throughout the six counties of Northern Ireland describe how the division of the two traditions and sectarian violence shaped their youth.

REVEREND COLM
O'DOHERTY

DERRY, COUNTY DERRY

Born in Derry in 1961, Reverend Colm O'Doherty has been a Catholic priest in that city for the last nine years. His father was a salesman who, because of the difficulty in finding work in Northern Ireland, often had to live in England. His mother cared for the family's five children and worked in a shirt factory as well.

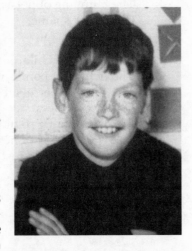

"My childhood was the Troubles," says Reverend O'Doherty. "Many of my school friends ended up in prison or their brothers or fathers did. I saw people killed or injured; I saw our town being blown to bits by bombs." He was arrested one day, he says, because he didn't have any identification.

The strongest childhood memory Reverend O'Doherty has of the Troubles is of January 30, 1972, known throughout Northern Ireland as Bloody Sunday. That day the British Army Parachute Regiment gunned down thirteen civil rights marchers on the streets of Derry. "They were innocent people and I knew many of them," he says. "That was the worst moment for all of us, and we cannot forget."

In this poem, written as a homework assignment when he was only ten years old, young Colm recorded the terrifying sights and sounds surrounding children caught up in a street riot.

Riots!

(Written at age ten)

There's riots! There's riots!
Oh what a shame,
It's children like us who get all the blame,
The banging of bullets,
The bumping of horns,
Oh what a shame,
The riots are on.

The crying of children filled with gas,
The ticking of bombs which mostly come last.
The smell of petrol all over the ground
Oh my goodness!
My head's going round.
The whizzing of stones flying through the air,
This is one thing I just can't bear.

MARTIN McCLURG

CARRICKFERGUS, COUNTY ANTRIM

Until the cease-fire began in 1994, Martin McClurg was not allowed to go into Belfast on his own even though he and his family lived only twenty miles north of the city. "I remember one Christmas when I was little, my mum, sister, and I were in Belfast shopping for presents when there were bomb scares," Martin says. "Seven bombs were discovered that day in Belfast. It was very frightening as our car was stuck in the multistory car park and we couldn't get home. Everywhere Mum took us to try and get a bus or train we were stopped by the Army as all the streets were being sealed off because there were so many bombs. Mum says it was a nightmare."

Now in his mid-teens, Martin McClurg wrote this poem for a literary competition when he was ten years old.

Our Street

(Written at age ten)

The men arrived to build a wall
It grew and grew it was so tall
It divided our wee street in two
Now I don't know what to do.

I'm not allowed to speak to Paddy
Because he's a mickey says my daddy
He's been my best pal since I was four
And I can't play with him no more.

There's bombs and bullets every day
They throw their stones down our way
I'd like the troubles here to cease
And we can all live in peace.

JOYCE CATHCART

BALLYMENA, COUNTY ANTRIM

Joyce Cathcart invited me to have Sunday dinner with her at her parents' house near her own home in the Ballymena countryside where she lives with her husband and two-and-a-half-year-old daughter Ashley. The family has lived in this largely Protestant area about twenty-five miles north of Belfast throughout the Troubles.

As her story reveals, Joyce's mother and father were direct targets of paramilitaries when she was a child. Now in her thirties and only weeks from delivering her second child when I met her, she says she still feels very vulnerable, particularly living out in the country with few neighbors around. "Anybody can bundle Daddy into the car and take him out and shoot him and there'd be nobody to hear it," she said. Her father, an auto mechanic with his own business, has received threatening warnings not to repair police cars. A milkman was shot dead in their area for delivering milk to the police.

A response to my call for contributions to this anthology, Joyce's story was written during the cease-fires, which, she says, were responsible for a cessation in recurring nightmares about the Troubles that she has had ever since her parents were attacked when she was ten years old. One can only hope that such violence will not return to Ballymena and that Joyce's new baby will not have to dream the same frightening dreams. As Joyce concludes her story, "The nightmare has gone on long enough."

A Normal Childhood?

I grew up in a very close family unit consisting of my father, mother, and older brother. I was a clingy child, very much devoted to my parents and elder sibling. Whereas most children eventually get bored of the long school holidays, I dreaded the return to school as I missed my mother's company so much— even as a teenager!

My father had worked all the hours God sent to convert two old ruined houses in rural County Antrim into a reasonable habitation for us all. As he had grown up in the countryside, he wanted the same for his children. He worked as hard as physically possible to provide for us. Money was tight but we never wanted for anything. I loved our home and the river that ran alongside us. If ever I needed to think about anything I headed down the river with my dog, enjoying the beautiful scenery and the smell of freshly cut grass. It was truly a country idyll in a country torn apart.

I can vividly recall when I first realised that the world was far from the happy, loving environment my parents had created for us in our home. It happened in school whilst awaiting the start of a school's programme on the television. The programme was preceded by a news report about a war in some African country. As a sensitive child, disturbed even by pictures of Snow White's wicked stepmother in a fairy tale book, I took what I had seen to heart. I couldn't believe that one person would intentionally inflict such pain on another. When I questioned my father about such devastation ever happening where we lived he made reassuring noises as any concerned father would. The pictures of death and destruction stayed with me, although I thought it was something that happened to other people in other countries. Little did I know that my own country would soon have its own "war" making headlines across the world.

I was seven years old when the Troubles broke out. My family had just returned from our first holiday together to the Isle of Man. Although young, I was immediately struck by the deserted Belfast streets where formerly all had been alive with hustle and bustle. As my family didn't live in Belfast, the Troubles left me mainly untouched for the first few years. As far as I was concerned Belfast was a war zone up the road, exciting but out of bounds as far as shopping trips, etc., were concerned. Although I didn't understand much of what was going on, I do recall asking my parents if Bernadette Devlin [Nationalist Catholic leader] and Ian Paisley [Protestant leader] had started the war simply because theirs were the names which I heard over and over again when the news came on.

As a special treat one Christmas my brother and I were to be allowed a trip into Belfast to see Santa Claus at one of the large department stores. I was both thrilled and nervous at the prospect. I was on the edge of my seat on the way in and out, ready to dive to the floor should our car be sprayed with bullet-fire.

My parents frequently made trips to Belfast throughout these years. Each time I waved them off I wondered if it would be the last time I would see them. Would they be caught in a bomb and blown to pieces? I treated each goodbye like a last goodbye and could not settle to games or toys until they returned safely. Often they would be delayed due to bomb scares which made the extended wait even more agonising.

As we lived in the country many of our friends were farmers. At a certain stage of the Troubles many of them sold up and moved to Scotland or England. "Sanity just across the water," my father called the mainland. He was very tempted to get out himself. Family holidays for several years were spent in Devon [a county in southwest England], staying with best friends of my parents who had started up a Bed and Breakfast business there. My father thought it was an ideal place to raise a family. I was worried by the tales of witchcraft in this English county. Snakes were another worry—a sight never seen in Northern Ireland, apart from in captivity.

Attempts to move away from our native land did not materialize, although at one stage we nearly emigrated to Australia where both my parents had secured jobs. At the last moment, just before the contracts were exchanged to sell the house, they simultaneously changed their minds and decided to stay. Later events, however, led to my parents regretting this decision. At the time, it suited me fine not to leave as my main concern about emigrating was having to leave my Alsatian dog behind.

My grandmother and stepgrandfather lived on a farm in a quiet country area not far from us. My grandfather often walked to the local pub just down the road to enjoy the camaraderie of the locals and the crack [amusing talk] as much as his pint of stout. My uncle also frequented this local [pub]. One night the phone rang very late—always a sign of bad news. The pub had been blown up and both my grandfather and uncle were missing. My father immediately jumped into the car and drove to the site of the destruction. We waited at home fearing the worst. Luckily my grandfather escaped with only cuts and bruises but there was no sign of my uncle. My father and his stepbrothers searched through the rubble most of that night. Fortunately my uncle had left the pub early and had gone on elsewhere, oblivious to all the concern his actions had caused.

Sheer relief that no harm had come to my relatives was tempered with disbelief that quiet country areas were also to be targeted by the men of violence. There were to be no safe havens in a land saturated with hatred and bitterness.

I was ten when events hit even closer to home. My father had always been an avid gun collector. His collection of rifles was his pride and joy. Inlaid with silver and engraved, they were objects of aesthetic value as much as anything. On a bright September morning I left for primary school as usual. My father had slipped a disc in his back and had been ordered by the doctor to lie on a board on the floor. As I kissed him and my mother goodbye it seemed like any other day. It was only when I got home from school that I realised the ordeal my parents had gone through.

Masked gunmen had ransacked the house, taken my father's guns (as well as an antique gun which was the only possession my grandfather had left him when he died), tied and gagged my parents, and threatened to shoot them. The ordeal lasted several hours. As they left, they warned my parents that they knew the schools my brother and I attended and, should they prove too helpful to the police, we would suffer.

Our home had been violated and was never again the safe childhood haven it had been. That's when my nightmares started—all variations on the theme of gunmen bundling my father into a car and murdering him down some isolated country road. Amazingly the nightmares have only recently stopped with the declaration of the cease-fire, but I'm sure they will resume again with the violence.

Waves of unease came and went through my teenage years as events blew up and then calmed down again. "Normal" is a comparative term when you've lived with the Troubles longer than you've known peace. Bomb scares and door searches became a way of life.

I always had friends on both sides of the religious divide,

but with every new atrocity I wondered if I could really trust those of a different persuasion.

I treated the announcement of the cease-fire with a large dollop of scepticism. At the time, I never would have envisioned it lasting as long as it has. But I still don't take it for granted. Each day without a life being taken is a bonus. I now have a two-and-a-half-year-old daughter and another baby on the way. For their sake I want peace. No principle is worth spilling another drop of Ulster blood for. Life is precious; the nightmare has gone on long enough.

PASQUALINA JOHNSTON

NEWTOWNSTEWART, COUNTY TYRONE

Pasqualina Johnston came to my attention when her childhood poetry was featured on the American TV news magazine *60 Minutes*. As a young girl she lived in the village of Victoria Bridge, just outside Newtownstewart. Although they were from different traditions, the village children all played together and the families helped each other in times of need. Pasqualina grew very close to a little Protestant girl to whom she refers in "The Other Side," written at age fourteen.

Eventually her friend's family chose to leave the bombings and threats of violence around Newtownstewart and the two girls, who had been so close in childhood, have not seen each other since.

Now in her thirties, Pasqualina leads a busy life as a nurse, wife, and mother of three boys. She was very, very grateful for the ceasefire. Having married a Protestant man seventeen years ago and been subject to hard feelings from both sides, she is well-acquainted with the emotional toll of the sectarian divide.

The Other Side

(Written at age fourteen)

I've played with them in the street,
I've shared my younger years with one.
We stayed together and shared our treats
We sang and skipped and had lots of fun.
Then alas we grew older
The war began
And we grew bolder.
Now when we meet
We never speak
For fear of the boys in the street
Because she's of the "other side."

JOHN McCANN

LISBURN, COUNTY ANTRIM

Since adolescence John McCann has known that his beliefs did not fit the mold in Lisburn, where he grew up. "I was very aware of how strong the Unionist tradition was there and how anti-Catholic the sentiments were," he says, "but I kept my mouth shut. If you said anything different than your community you'd be considered a turncoat."

A bank employee approaching forty, John is not normally given to writing, but he says he saw an article in the newspaper about this book and thought he had as much of a story to tell as anyone. "I just sat down and blathered away at the keyboard," he says, "and before I knew it I had ten pages. I loved doing it!"

John is very aware of the changes the cease-fires have made and grateful for them. "Only five or six years ago if you saw a tourist in Belfast your eyes would follow after them. You'd think, 'What are they doing here—they must be lost!' And now they're coming in droves."

Personal Memories of the Troubles

I was born in a country district in 1957 but my family moved to an area just outside Belfast when I was three years old.

My childhood memories were of the economically good 1960s. As the political storm clouds gathered, I played barefoot in our hay field, oblivious to events elsewhere, and watched the neighbouring farmer gather the hay my father had sold to him from our field. By the time I was nine or ten, the Civil Rights protest marches were beginning to take place. I remember seeing these images on our newly acquired television—marchers with banners and placards about "Democracy In" and such-and-such "out." In the eyes of a nine-year-old brought up in a semirural area, this was a fantasy scene of crowds marching around the city. The nearest equivalent I knew was the crowd every Tuesday at the local open-air market in the town nearby. The reality was that the Catholic population had had enough of fifty years of the Northern Ireland government's apartheid-style rule and were protesting against it—with good cause.

There was a delivery man in our area who brought his bread van round once a week and I remember him lecturing my mother about what he saw as the dirty, dishonest Catholics "dictating" to the Protestant majority. This type of view is occasionally encountered today and seems very naive, extreme, and dated. But it was common then.

In my school, which like all schools was almost totally, if not 100 percent, of one religious group or the other, there were about three Catholics among a thousand pupils, the others all Protestant. Many schools have the obligatory "loud-mouth" or bully but with political feelings running so high on all sides, a lad I knew picked on one of the Catholics who was in his class. He gathered a gang and before we knew it a trap had been set for the Catholic as he walked home from school. He was set upon and savagely beaten with sticks and iron bars and was nearly blinded as a result. The perpetrator, as much a victim of the troubles as *his* victim, realised in the cold light of day what he had done; threatened by his father and with expulsion from school hanging over him, he shot himself dead. I always felt that people like him were the unrecorded, unnoticed victims of the Troubles.

Once I was sitting with my friends in school having our lunch-time sandwiches. It was a hot summer day (don't adolescent school days always seem such!) and we were sitting at the top of a fire escape stairs at the back of one of the school buildings. This vantage point afforded an excellent view over the town which, despite its Protestant majority, is dominated by the tall spire of St. Patrick's Catholic Church. One of my friends had just commented, in characteristically uncomplimentary style, on that building and Catholicism in general, when there was a huge explosion—a deep rumbling boom which reverberated through the ground where we were some half mile away. In front of my eyes, a large furniture warehouse near the Church seemed to lift into the air, then disintegrate with further explosions into a confetti-like cascade of roof rafters and slabs of masonry which showered the surrounding area. In the school yard below us there was eerie silence. And then in an almost surrealistic way the school bell rang for the end of our lunch break and children started running—from the explosion or to get to class? I never quite knew.

In 1972 I was sitting in class when our teacher, a normally conservative character who would not interrupt a lesson for anything, told us all to sit still and listen. To our surprise he produced a radio and switched on the news. We heard the dramatic announcement that the Northern Ireland Parliament at Stormont was to be abolished and direct rule from London imposed. Our teacher listened thoughtfully, silently, staring out of the window. At the end of the bulletin he said, "No Surrender!" the Loyalist [Protestant] slogan of resistance to a united Ireland.

One of the aspects of my upbringing which was untypical for a Protestant was that my father and myself would often go to Dublin at weekends to stay with my aunt there. She was having a new house built and my father was heavily involved with this. It occurred to me that much, if not all, of what I was told by the "experts" among my contemporaries and their parents about the Republic and southern people was absolute nonsense. I was being lectured at school by people who had never set foot in the Republic and who had never met a Catholic but who claimed to know all about both. Among the more memorable stories I was told was that Protestants' Bibles would be burnt if they "went down there" and that Southerners "burnt everything British." Not only did I have many relatives in the Republic, all of them Protestants and very happy with it, but my aunt in Dublin was very openly pro-British! Not one of my relatives or friends in the South ever complained of discrimination against them, let alone anyone trying to burn them or their Bibles! The truth was that the area which became the Republic NEVER had a large number of Protestants living there anyway so they have always been so thinly spread that the (vast) Catholic majority have never seen them as a threat and, therefore, do not discriminate against them.

In the final years at school, aged sixteen to eighteen, I became involved with a youth movement organised by local sixth-formers. This was the "InterSchools Movement," designed to bring people together from all social backgrounds and all religious and political backgrounds. It was a brave and positive movement with some seven schools involved and it flourished for a few years before the hostility of two headmasters, one from each side of the "divide," precipitated its collapse. But not before, at age eighteen, I met and spoke to Catholics for the first time—and this in a land where almost 40 percent of the population are such! Even now, there are many people who have never (knowingly) spoken to somebody from "the other side" and have no intention of doing so.

With the experiences I had had in the Republic and the contact with Catholics through the InterSchools Movement, I formed the impression that, while Unionists [Protestants] were not necessarily the narrow-minded ogres the outside world portrays them as, their ideology was seriously flawed in many ways.

LARAGH CULLEN

DUNGANNON, COUNTY TYRONE

Even during the cease-fires, six-teen-year-old Laragh Cullen's life was still impacted by the Troubles in much the same way she describes in this poem that she wrote when she was eleven. An Army base was built next to her school, St. Patrick's Girls' Academy in Dungannon, and Laragh says, "Every time a helicopter takes off or lands classes have to stop as nothing can be heard above the noise." In 1988, her school was extensively damaged when rockets, aimed at the Army base, exploded on the school grounds.

Laragh is the youngest of four daughters raised by her mother, a community nurse, after Laragh's father died when she was two. She began her writing career when this poem, which she wrote when she was fourteen, was selected for an anthology published by Women Together for Peace in Belfast. Nobel Prize poet Seamus Heaney attended the book launching festivities. Now Laragh writes poems regularly as part of her leisure activities.

A Dream of Peace

(Written at age eleven)

Peace in our country,
A truce in our land,
Harmony in our world,
All war banned.

I live in Dungannon,
I've never known peace,
I'm tired of the choppers,
Soldiers and police.

I'm tired of the sirens
The town's like a cage,
I wish there was peace,
I'm eleven years of age.

NEIL SOUTHERN

BANGOR, COUNTY DOWN

A married mature student at
Queen's University, Belfast, when
he wrote this essay in response to
a notice in the *North Down Spec-
tator,* Neil Southern says that, as a
Protestant at a university that now
has a Catholic majority student
body, he often feels isolated and
alienated from those around him.
His identity, he says, is very much
comprised of his Protestant religion and politics, of which he is
very proud, and at this juncture he
thinks that Protestant identity is
under siege. "Our only friends are
ourselves," he says, and he de-
scribes the current state of affairs for Ulster Protestants as "total
isolation."

When I met with Neil in Belfast he tried very hard to give me a
feeling for what his Protestant identity meant to him as a child and
to explain why it remains a central focus for him now in adulthood.
As an outsider, coming from a country where religious sectarian differences are not the ones we most often are in conflict about, I
struggled to comprehend the central role of Protestantism and the
sectarian divide in Neil's life. "We are two distinct nations in Ireland," he told me, explaining that he views Protestants as a completely different ethnic group from Catholics. He says that his
greatest fear is of having to live in a country that is not "Protestant

orientated" and where his children will not know what their Protestant identity is.

My Recollections of the Troubles

When the Troubles began in October, 1968, I was three and a half years old. My family had in the August of that year moved from Belfast to Bangor, a middle-class area which, much to the distaste of the indigenous Bangorians, had taped to its prestigious periphery a number of working-class housing estates. These estates facilitated the overspill of working-class Protestants from Belfast, many of whom, although wishing to escape from the conflict, had failed to shake off the militancy which had been fueled by the perceived insurrection of the Nationalist [Catholics wanting reunification with Ireland] community. It was in such a social environment, namely Kilcooley Estate [housing project]—often considered to be the most militant—that I grew up.

In 1970 my father joined the Royal Ulster Constabulary [police] Reserve. As was true for so many other men, the impulse which motivated my father to such action was derived from a sense of patriotism. He wanted to defend not only the state but the deeper abstract values of Protestantism.

Despite the initial approval for my father's joining the Police, there were unperceived ramifications which had irrevocable detrimental effects on our family. With policemen being targeted at their homes by the IRA, security became of paramount importance and my freedom as a child to innocently respond to a knock at the door was utterly curtailed. In the dark days of the 1970s I can recall being harshly rebuked by my mother for having answered a knock at the door. Although the person knocking could well have been a terrorist, thankfully it was no more than a Pakistani salesman "armed" with an innocuous suitcase and its saleable contents. It was situations such as this that, coupled with my father's dedication to RUC duty, precipitated my mother having a nervous breakdown. My mother, like so many others, became an indirect victim of the Troubles.

Terrorism has taken its most depraved form in the killing and maiming of people within their own homes. How could one even begin to conceptualise how many young children must have felt at the moment that the sanctity of their homes was shattered by the thunder of evil men only to be followed by the sight of the sickly stillness and motionlessness of their fathers' bodies. Equally so, it is beyond the comprehension of normal individuals to conceive how men who had just inflicted such devastation upon a family could take their exit in a state of rejoicing and euphoria. The father's death and the lifelong pain of a child could never be justified by some abstract political rationale.

My earliest memories of media reports concerning the Troubles were newspaper articles about the extensive bombing of Bangor's Main Street in the early seventies. I was approximately seven years old and at that time Bangor's atmosphere was electrified. The chaos generated by such unprecedented destruction had an impact on the total community, regardless of social class or religious persuasion. Perhaps as a memorial to something that I did not fully understand, I sustained the memory of the bombing of Bangor by cutting out the exciting newspaper pictures that had so captivated the community's attention.

In the five years that I attended Protestant secondary school I never came into personal contact with a Roman Catholic. Yet contact was made. The daily bus journey to school often gave vent to the expression of our young Loyalism. One particular bus shelter "housed" a number of Roman Catholics awaiting their transport to school. The habitual practice was not only the issuing of a myriad of verbal assaults, rude gestures, and spit; one specific bus driver actually slowed the bus down and pressed the door release, thereby facilitating the launching of a barrage of eggs aimed at the Catholics. This policy was finally halted when the exasperated Catholics contacted the police. The bus driver was disciplined and the school bus assigned a police escort for a number of days.

Given the fact that most of the students at our school were from working-class backgrounds, the Troubles did not have the impact one might have expected. My only memory of the Troubles during secondary school was the death of the hunger striker Bobby Sands—an incident which evoked no sympathy within the corridors of our school.

Perhaps the most potent sentiment embracing what it meant to be a Protestant was fashioned on the anvil of industry. Upon leaving secondary school I commenced an apprenticeship with Harland and Wolff shipbuilders in Belfast. I can recall the feeling of absorption as, at the age of sixteen, I was aware that I was entering the "heartland" of industrialised Protestantism.

Particularly among the manual employees, there was no separating the world of work from the world of politics. The symbols which represented aspects of Protestant culture were displayed with veneration throughout the various workshops. The individuals who materialised their Protestantism in this fashion gained both recognition and respect and were viewed as being active guardians of our religious heritage.

Interwoven into the fabric of Harland and Wolff was a belligerent intolerance of anything which stood for political nationalism or Catholicism. Certainly there were Catholic employees but their opinions and political aspirations remained unexpressed.

Throughout its history the shipyard has served as a bastion

of the Protestant political culture. The shipyard is probably the only surviving workplace wherein it is still possible to observe the unfettered flying of the "Ulster" flag. Many Protestants feel that the flying of their flag ought to be an inalienable right which should not be liable to proscription either in the workplace or elsewhere.

PETER SJ MERRIGAN

DERRY, COUNTY DERRY

Eighteen-year-old Peter Merrigan grew up in Derry housing projects along with his two sisters and a brother. His father, currently unemployed, was a truck driver and a garment worker and his mother stayed home to raise the children.

Certainly unusual for his age, Peter is already very clear that writing is his vocation. "I'm on my third novel now," he told me. He attends a media course five days a week in hopes of a career in journalism, which he says he hopes will eventually lead to being a novelist. This is his first work to be published outside of school magazines and newspapers.

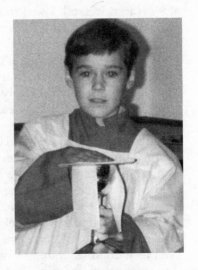

In this story Peter sets out to show how he understood the Troubles as a preschool child, but it soon becomes clear that by using the young child's point of view he is casting a humorous and ironic light on the ways adults in the two communities exacerbate the sectarian divide. Like Natasha Ritchie, another eighteen-year-old author in this collection, Peter seems a bit disdainful and even bored with his forebears' ways of dealing with what he calls a "tired argument."

Troubles on the Homefront

(Written at age eighteen)

I woke to what was going to be another normal day as a citizen of Northern Ireland. I was four, maybe five years old—I can't remember exactly and it doesn't really matter, to be honest. This story doesn't concern my age.

Breakfast? Who knows. It's not the kind of thing a guy remembers fourteen years later. Heck, I can't even remember what I was wearing. (Probably those green corduroy jeans that all children were forced to wear at that particular stage of their lives.)

That was around 1981 and by then the Troubles were in full bloom, standing tall, and even had an uppercase letter at the beginning of the word. At the innocent age of four, however, I didn't have a clue what the Troubles were. If anything, I thought trouble was what you caused when you hit your little sister or fed bugs to your neighbour's cat—those little things in life in which children were not allowed to participate. But even as a child as young as two, I suspect I could feel something wrong in the air. That good old Derry air must have seemed a little stale.

As I grew up I was surrounded by spray-painted walls with large white letters on them saying things like "Up the IRA" and "Long Live the Queen." Well, whoever the queen was, shouldn't everyone want her to have a long life? Not too long, of course. Imagine living 'til you were a hundred. Wow! I'd have another ninety-six years to go.

There was one thing I couldn't work out though—what was this "IRA" I saw on every other wall? *I Ran Away?* That *is* what the older kids told us but, somehow, I didn't quite believe them. I mean, if someone ran away, why would they be telling the world? Sympathy?

I doubt it. I don't think anyone at that age really knew what the Troubles were all about except for little Billy down the road, whose older brother was usually the one with the empty spray-paint canisters under his bed. But Billy wasn't about to tell because his brother twisted his arm and told him not to—or else! Even Billy didn't fully understand, I'm sure. We were all led to believe that young people were living on the streets [as runaways] and were telling everyone by painting "IRA" on walls and that some people feared for the Queen's life and didn't want her to die in the near future.

It was shortly after this that I learned the difference between "Derry" and "Londonderry." Being a Catholic, I had to call the maiden city [a walled city, unbreached by England's attempted sieges] "Derry" while the people on the other side of the bridge called it "Londonderry." (Up until now, being a Catholic simply meant you could call "Prod!" and such other names at people and they would call names back at you.) Learning these differences was as easy (!) as learning to play chess when you couldn't tell the rook and the bishop apart.

Derry was the name that the native Irish people called this wondrous city—when I say "native" I don't mean caves and bear-skin clothes. And Londonderry was the name given to us by the British settlers—those people on the other side of the bridge. (Bishops move diagonally, don't they? Or is that the rooks?)

If you are slightly confused by now, don't worry—you're not the only one.

The Army, I now noticed, seemed to be on every street corner in the city—the *British* Army, everyone seemed to stress. They were the men with funny accents and mud on their faces who let you look through the telescopic sight on their rifles. This Army had been here all my life but it wasn't until I was around six or seven that I became totally aware of them. It was not long after this that the Troubles really began to make sense to me.

It seemed that some people wanted a united Ireland. They were the IRA (which, unlike what I thought, were the initials of the Irish Republican Army). Some other people didn't want this. They kept singing "God Save the Queen" (yes, she was still alive) and we weren't supposed to sing it. It was a catchy tune, though.

As the years ticked by, I got a further understanding of what a Catholic should do with his life (this law according to big brother Catholics): Fill a bottle with paint or petrol—whatever you can get your little Catholic hands on first. Then wait for the "Brit" jeeps to pass by on their clockwork schedule and throw the filled bottle at them. If it is petrol it should be lit by using a piece of cloth tucked neatly into the neck of the bottle. (A section of your father's best shirt will suffice.)

But, on the other hand (this law according to parents and priests): A good Catholic and Christian will offer to make peace with the Protestants and won't annoy the British soldiers who are merely doing their job.

As I dragged my unimportant life through secondary education, important things began to happen. It seemed that the word "peace" was on almost everyone's lips. As yet, however, the political war game continued and wives still lost their husbands, children still lost their fathers, and a cease-fire seemed more than impossible.

After I got out of secondary school, a man with a beard, Gerry Adams, wanted peace talks and the British government, now headed by a man in a grey suit, decided to do something about this Irish thing that lingered at the bottom of the paperwork, covered in coffee stains and dust. Troops of soldiers were taken back to England, posts were left unmanned, and the Strand Road security barriers here in Derry were taken down.

Things were different now. A cease-fire on both sides had begun and people prayed that it would only last. A peaceful Ireland would be good—good for publicity, good for holiday seekers, and, most of all, good for us. We would not have to worry about the shooting of friends or relatives and a harmony would settle over the land.

But a united Ireland is not essential for this kind of happy future. Many people say that these two communities can, and someday will, live together under one roof. I'm inclined to agree. I believe that a person should live for themselves, not their country. Their home is Ireland—but it's only a place, not a being. If the rocks could talk, I'm sure they wouldn't mind what they were called. They would only want people to live happily.

I hope, one day, that people will see the damage they have caused. We don't need to play war to settle a tired argument. Sit down, talk it over. Throw down your gun, take the hand of the enemy and shake it, for this may be the only chance of true peace in our time. Let the people of your generation be the ones to accomplish something that previous generations could not.

ANN McCALLION

In her fifties now and a home-maker with three grown children and a granddaughter, Ann Mc-Callion lives with her husband, Manus, in the Creggan Estate in Derry where she has lived for forty-four years. In this story, "Over the Border," Ann describes the very personal ways that the Troubles impacted her life as a girl and a young wife and mother.

For Ann, one of the most difficult hardships caused by the Troubles was having to raise a family in the house she describes in her story, a house that at least by American standards would hardly be large enough for a couple without children. The end unit in a brick row house that sits on a hill just above downtown Derry, Ann's home is identical to hundreds surrounding it, most of them home to families with children who are crammed into about 750 square feet of living space.

What would it do to a person, I wondered as I visited with Ann in her tiny living room, to live with such intense overcrowding? What would it do to a marriage and a family to have absolutely no private space? Little wonder, I thought, that Ann's fondest dream has been to have a real house of her own. And how tragic it is that she has been denied that modest dream all these years as a result of the Troubles.

Ann's very poignant account of coming of age and beginning a family in the Troubles won first prize in a literary competition sponsored by the Derry City Council and British Telecom.

Over the Border

This story is dedicated with much, much love to my father, Pearse Doherty, who showed me the beauty and tragedy of Ireland.

For all of my adult life I have held a dream so very close to my heart—yet it has been so very often denied. As the "For Sale" sign outside my house squeaks and sways in the breeze, I still dare to dream.

My dream is that of a new house in which no one has ever lived—a new house that would be mine, with the stamp of my personality on it. It just had to be new because I was discontented trying to make other people's houses and flats my own when really I always felt they belonged to someone else. Looking back now it all seemed so simple in 1968. Just get married, put my name down for a new house in Carnhill, and in time my dream would be reality. After all, plenty of houses were being built in Carnhill and all I had to do was wait my turn. Simple!

As simple as the time when I was fourteen and my father tried to explain what going over the border meant. It was 1960 and I was still at St. Mary's School in Creggan when my father bought a car. It was a Vauxhall Cresta with blue and silver paint work. The shape of the car reminded me of a huge rhinoceros. The excitement in the family was great because this meant we could go to other places for holidays than Buncrana [an undeveloped strip of beach just across the border in the

Republic of Ireland] or Portrush [a nearby seaside resort town in Northern Ireland]. Now, with a new car, my imagination was working overtime. On our first trip my father said we would be going over the border.

"OVER THE BORDER": I said those words slowly. "OVER-THE-BORDER." What did they mean? I never thought to ask him, though I couldn't figure out the words. I just hoped there would be slot machines, bumper cars, sea, and sand. Anyway, Sunday afternoon arrived and my mother and father organised us into the back seat of the "rhinoceros." I was putting up a good fight with my brothers and sisters to sit at the window, because if I was going over the border, I needed to make sure I had the best view as I didn't want to miss a thing. I couldn't wait until Monday morning to gleefully tell my school friend Margaret Thompson that *I* was "over the border."

I was so happy and impatient to get going. Settled at last, we drove off and eventually the car stopped at a square building at Brigend. This didn't seem unusual as the bus always stopped here on the way to Buncrana. What was unusual was that my father took a little thin book from the glove compartment and asked me to get it stamped for going over the border. I was filled with excitement. The man in the dark uniform with a spotlessly white shirt stamped the book with a resounding thump, like the way the girl in the post office stamps my mother's family allowance book [government assistance]. He then slid the book over the well-worn countertop. I looked at the mark he had made and it annoyed me that he didn't keep the stamp within the squares outlined on the page. Also I noticed the writing. It was different from what I was used to—the letters were beautifully shaped and sloped—but I didn't understand the words. Suddenly I realised where we were going.

Exhilarated, handing the book back to my father, and full of my own importance, I asked, "Daddy, are we going to Mexico?"

His blue eyes looked in askance at me.

"Don't you know rightly we're going to Buncrana? Now what made you ask a question like that?" he asked impatiently.

Buncrana! God, what a letdown. How was I going to face Margaret? In my most accusing tone I answered him, "Well, because you're always singing about 'South of the Border Down Mexico Way.'"

I felt like an idiot and fell into a sullen silence. How was I to know Buncrana was "over-the-border"? As far as I was concerned going to Buncrana was the same as going to Portrush. What had a border got to do with it? A border, as far as I knew, was a dividing line to show where one thing started and another ended, which was clear and visible to the eye and therefore easily understood—like the flower border on a garden or even the plain navy border around my mother's apron distinguishing it from the floral pattern. But a border between Buncrana and Derry I just couldn't take in.

Of course my curiosity got the better of me and I wanted my father to show me exactly where this border was so I could understand better. Needless to say he couldn't show me anything tangible. He tried his best to explain that as we lived in the North of Ireland we had a different government than the people "over the border," who lived in the South. But I wanted to know what would happen if we took a wrong road, crossed the border and didn't go through a Customs post.

I tentatively inquired: "How would we know what part of Ireland we are in, North or South, if we didn't have a map?"

He gave a very simple explanation. "Well, Ann, if you look at the telephone boxes in the South they are green and in the North they are red."

And there was me, thinking they were different colours because that was the only colour paint they could afford! Within me, however, I felt the stirrings of a deep sadness. Somehow it seemed as if a shadow had been cast on the future. Yet, at fourteen, to my mind people were people, Ireland was Ireland, and that was that.

Of course "that was not that," as I was about to find out. I was sixteen years old. It was Friday night and Eileen Reid and the Cadets were playing in Borderland. I was allowed to go. I was thrilled and felt really grown up. Now this was a big thing in my life. At that time I was working as an apprentice hairdresser and a Friday was usually busy with the girls having their latest hairstyles done for the weekend dances. Usually the talk would centre on which band played, the time the bus would leave, which dress was to be worn, or which boys in particular would be there. And now it was my turn. I felt my hair would never dry. All day I worried that I'd miss my friends and they would go on without me. I was anxious too that I'd be kept late at work and miss the bus. Everything was a mixture of worry and excitement.

When I eventually got home I demented my mother, "Mum, where's my make-up? Mum, where's my slip? Did our Nuala borrow my skirt? Mum, did you see my bag? Have you change for the bus?" Everything was duly handed over with a silent knowing look. Naturally before I got out the door I was told a list of Do's and Don'ts. It was like the Ten Commandments only with more added on.

I wailed at her impatiently, "Ach, Mum, I'm going to enjoy myself. It's Eileen Reid and the Cadets playing. I'll miss the bus if I don't hurry." I was out the door like a frenzied whirlwind.

Settled on the bus with my friends—Maura, Ann, Jo, and Tallas—we moved off to the dance. Borderland was in a village called Muff, just five miles from Derry. As the bus travelled along I noticed it slowing down on the outskirts of town. I wondered what was wrong. "Do you think there's an accident up ahead?" I asked Jo, worried more that we wouldn't get to the dance.

She peered out the window, then looked at me puzzled and elbowed me in the ribs. "Ach, Ann, you're daft. Sure it's the border—it's only the stupid oul Customs Post. Here, did you see my new lipstick? It's Strawberry Meringue. Want to try it?"

I felt like the "brainless wonder." Something in my splendid rush of excitement was marred. I was saddened and angry with myself because I hadn't even the wit to connect "Borderland" with going over the border. Once again I was disappointed, but this time I was shocked into a greater awareness that my beautiful country was divided. I could feel a sense of injustice growing within me which grew all the more into resentment every time I crossed the border. I went to the dance, but again there was a shadow on my heart. Something was lost—or maybe I was just growing up. Would the "border" ever go away?

To go over the border was quite a normal thing to do—going on camping trips, dances, or for walks on the beach at Lisfannon in County Donegal. Also it was just as normal to stay in the North and go to Portrush at holiday times. As I got older my parents gave me more freedom and sixteen soon became eighteen.

At eighteen going over the border had its moments for us. There are many hilarious stories of smuggling butter and cigarettes and various other items from the South to the North. One night my brother, Michael, his girlfriend, Rosemary, my boyfriend, Manus, and I borrowed father's car and decided to go for a walk on the beach at Lisfannon. Before we crossed the border we bought soft whipped ice cream at a nearby garage. At the Irish Customs Post, as we were about to get the little thin book stamped, the big, burly, crisply uniformed Customs Man stepped out in front of the car in a very authoritative fashion, and with a very definite raise of his hand he commanded us to stop. This was significant and in stark contrast to the return journey when the British Customs man usually asked in a bored tone, "Anything to declare?" In a booming voice he said, "You can't come through here with that!"

We hadn't a clue what he was talking about. He kept pointing to the ice cream. "Ach, sure don't you know there's foot and

mouth disease and you can't bring milky products through."
His brow was thick with frustration. "Sure can you not see the
mats out for you to disinfect your feet?"

It must have shown on our poor innocent city faces that we
were confused beyond redemption, very obviously not from an
agricultural background, and had no understanding of the seriousness of Anthrax. Somehow his attitude softened as he
next suggested we pull over to the side of the road and eat our
dripping ice cream. We were all trying to stifle the giggles, and
I thought I would explode, when Rosemary called out to him,
"Hi, mister, do you want a lick?"

"No, thank you," was his pleasant reply. "I don't think that
would be appropriate!"

As we finished our ice creams we wiped our mouths with
our undisinfected tissues and then dutifully wiped our feet on
his disinfected sodden mats and drove merrily on our way with
the hysterical hormonal laughter privileged only to youth. We
must be the only four people in the history of the long-
lamented border to "smuggle" anything into the South with the
unwitting aid of a customs officer.

This incident made me think all the more of the absurdity
of the border. Would it ever go away? To my eighteen-year-
old earnest heart Ireland was Ireland—still one country. But
shadow days were looming.

In 1968, I was approaching twenty and settling down with my
boyfriend, Manus. We set the wedding date for the fifth of August. It was about this time that the seeds of my dream of a
new house started to grow within me. With my heart full of
love and hope for the future my wedding day arrived. And
within two short months "the border" came forcefully into my
life. Shadow days had arrived.

In 1968 there were ominous sounds and buzzing talk. "One
man, one vote!" "Build more houses!" "SS RUC!" [Referring to

the Royal Ulster Constabulary—the police—as the Nazi elite guard, *Schutzstaffel*] "Justice!" "Civil Rights!"

Warning bells went off in my head. I knew instinctively that these cries were going to affect my future, maybe even my dream of a new house.

There was rioting on our streets and as 1968 turned into 1969 the promise of more riots became apparent. What started out as people voicing their discontent with the government and the RUC's policing methods turned into a vicious battle between the protestors and the RUC. With their bare hands the people tore down parts of the city and flung it at the RUC with all the might their built-up anger could muster.

Men, women—even children—throwing stones and building barricades to keep the police out. Exhausted and humiliated policemen lying on the ground. What good now their symbols of power—uniform, riot shield, guns, and water cannons—against a risen people.

I was numb with sorrow. In my mind's eye the spectre of "the border" came to the fore. Sackville Street, where the RUC lay, was the North, and Rosville Street, where the people stood up against injustice, was the South.

My first son was born on 26 July 1969 and wasn't it just great that in this particular week the first men had landed on the moon? Indeed, what a giant step for mankind. In my hospital bed I wondered if anyone told the police and the rioters of what was going on in the outside world. Apparently not, as the riots went on unabated throughout all of the North of Ireland.

But I had a responsibility now; my new baby son needed my attention. As I carried him up the stairs to our flat I whispered to him that I was sorry it wasn't a new house, but that I would do my best for him in the future. Delighted as I was with my new son, there was a fear in me about his future. What would I tell him about all this trouble? What was the Christian thing to say? What was Christian nowadays? So many values were crumbling away, respect for people seemed to be hard hit, never mind "love thy neighbour."

In my head I heard echoes of words whispered to myself many years before—"Over-the-border." As I looked at the torn-up footpaths used to strengthen the barricades or stone the RUC, the empty burned-out buildings with missing windows gaping like big, black, toothless, smoke-stained mouths, my soul cried with anguish at this legacy of suffering created when spiteful people divided my country.

We all seemed to be viciously punishing each other. The RUC battered and gassed us because they believed we all wanted a united Ireland when what people wanted was a decent home to live in, a job, and to be treated as equals in the voting system, with one vote each. We stoned them because they were seen as the armed force controlled by a corrupt Unionist government.

I thought of the empty burned-out arguments for retaining the border and I finally faced the truth of the injustices people do to each other. I was so angry that something so invisible as "the border" could make its presence felt in such a horrific manner. It was easy for politicians to blame "the border," to point to "the border" as the cause of all our ills.

In the distance, as I nursed my baby, the riots continued.

In the midst of all the insanity, my dream tugged at the roots of my heart. If only I could just get my new house! Every Thursday I'd put Dermot in his pram and visit the Housing Office. I had to scoot around and over many barricades, be stopped and searched by the RUC, and avoid the rioters to get to the Housing Executive Offices at Fahan Street. The strength of my dream made me unafraid. Each week the kind lady at the Housing Office pleaded with me to have a bit more patience. Mrs. McLaughlin knew my story so well, I didn't even have to introduce myself. Yet on this particular Thursday she told me that as soon as the builder handed in the keys I'd be allocated a new house.

My imagination went wild! I was thrilled! At last I could have the home I always wanted. I could picture myself hanging new curtains, getting measured up for carpets. Getting the dinner ready in the new kitchen, furnishing the new bedrooms and bathroom of the new house—my new house which no one ever lived in before. I promised myself that when I was given the key I would be the first through the front door and first into all the rooms. Then after that, everyone was welcome. At last my dream was about to come true!

However, serious things were happening on the streets. The violence was getting worse. With no sign of it stopping, there was talk of bringing in the Troops "to keep the peace." I knew that logically there was something dangerously wrong if an army had to be brought in to "keep the peace." Shadows from my past caught up with me and in my heart I knew it would be fatal.

The following week a letter arrived from the Housing Executive. I knew what the letter contained. With trembling hand I fingered the slim brown envelope and I felt sick. The dark print, in contrast to the white notepaper, jumped out at me. I couldn't believe my eyes. We had been allocated a re-let, three-bedroomed flat in Creggan Estate! The hot tears of disappointment slid down my face, burning two lines into my cheeks. Manus held me close to him and we both cried as we looked at our sleeping baby. When at last I settled myself, I rang Mrs. McLaughlin and in a very sympathetic voice she explained: "You see, Mrs. McCallion, a family was burned out of their home at the weekend and immediately went onto the emergency housing list. Unfortunately for you, we had to allocate them your house in Carnhill."

I gripped the telephone handle tightly. I could hardly breathe. I felt my heart pounding in my ears. Slowly tears of realisation slipped down my face as I wept bitterly for myself and my denied dream. I wept also for the woman who had lost her home and, although it was hard, I wished her well in the house in Carnhill.

I wept too for the people who divided our country and our city. But most of all I wept for the people who divided us as a people, leaving smouldering consequences to their hatred. Consoling myself that at least I still had a roof over my head and all my possessions, I made arrangements to move into the flat on the fourteenth of August, 1969. On that fateful day, the British Army moved into Derry.

The guns and bombs are silent now. Even if the politicians are still arguing, as is their nature, at least now they are listening to each other.

Although it took a little time for me to believe there was a cease-fire, my first conscious awareness of it came to me when I realised I could walk the streets of my beloved Derry with my shoulders relaxed and my breathing more even—and even with a lighter step. There is time to stand and talk, laugh and shop, without automatically hunching one's shoulders in fear of a bomb or a shooting.

Instead of the cruel noise of bombing and gunfire there is the noise of development. There are traffic jams now, not created deliberately as they used to be by the Army and RUC, but by lorryloads of building materials. The new buildings with their sparkling windows, glinting and gleaming, reflect hope for us all.

The shadow days are gone. The border has gone, the Army has gone, the bloodshed and violence have stopped, and I still have the nerve to dream my dream. I still have hope that maybe in peace time my dream will come true.

ANNE McEVOY

NEWRY, COUNTY DOWN

Still living in the house in the Derrybeg Estate [housing project] that she describes in her story, thirty-two-year-old Anne McEvoy, a school cafeteria worker, is married to a carpenter and has two children, a nine-year-old boy and a six-year-old girl. She told me that it is for them that she put her childhood memories on paper about a year before she learned of this book.

As a little girl, Anne was more amused by what she saw of the Troubles than upset. Cat-and-mouse games with British troops and the police provided entertainment for her and other Catholic children, who, because of security risks, were often confined to their own housing project.

In her teens Anne came to understand the seriousness of the conflict between Catholics and Protestants and became politically active, as she tells us in her essay. Today, after twenty-five years of the Troubles, she says that all she really wants is for her children to grow up in peace.

My Memories of Life in Derrybeg

Derrybeg was an estate [housing project] of 360 dwellings in the town of Newry, all of which were lived in by Catholics.

Most of the residents were the first tenants, since the houses were all built between 1960 and 1965. It was a close-knit community. The women of the estate reared their families together and the same families still remain, with our generation still getting married, living here and rearing our children here.

When the Army first came to Newry I was about seven. We greeted them with excitement and the women of the estate made them tea. After a few short months this had changed. This was when the shooting and stoning started and Derrybeg became a no-go area for the policy and Army. I cannot remember all the events which took place here but a few do stand out in my memory. The biggest was the time that Derrybeg was the venue for the largest civil rights march in the history of Northern Ireland. Thousands of people came from all over and were fed and housed by the people of Newry.

Other memories were of young victims who I knew personally and so they had a greater effect on me. One was a boy of thirteen who was shot by an Army foot patrol while he was sitting on a wall. Another was shot during a hi-jacking on the Camlough Road. The third was an eighteen-year-old who was blown up by his own bomb in a local pub on Christmas Eve. These events all happened when I was between eleven and fourteen years old and, although I was shocked because I knew these boys, I still did not realise the significance of what had happened.

I lived on Second Avenue at this time with my mother, father, and my sister Catherine. Our house was situated in what was known as the middle entry, which was a crossroads with four openings into different areas of the estate. This was the most used entry in the estate as it was closed in by tall hedges on all sides and if you were running from the Army or police you could get away much quicker here. It also became a hiding place, like a safe deposit box, for guns or anything else that had to be disposed of in a hurry.

This was exciting for me as I used to quite enjoy watching

the boys getting chased down our entry. But I suppose it caused problems for my parents since quite frequently our house would be raided because of guns or ammunition found in the hedge. My father was an ex-Navy man and I supposed this was the only thing that stopped his getting arrested on a number of occasions. He was a quiet man and had retired from the Navy with heart trouble when we were very young. He never really got involved with any conflict on the streets but he had heated discussions with his friends about political affairs.

My mother was also a quiet person and not the slightest bit interested in politics. She would never allow any talk about the IRA or Army, Protestants or Catholics to go on in front of us. As she was in the habit of saying, "Young minds are easily swayed." She did, however, take us up to the Camlough Road to see the civil rights march and also welcomed people who attended into our home for food and shelter, as did all the people of the estate. As soon as we were old enough to vote she made sure that we did and said, "People fought for Catholics to get votes, so we should use them."

When Derrybeg first became a trouble area my sister and I were kept at home while our cousins and school friends from other areas of the town were able to go to youth clubs. The children from Derrybeg were excluded, not because we were not welcome, but because it was not safe for us to be out of the estate. We may not have gotten home safely if there was trouble. So we grew up only meeting children from other areas of the town at school.

None of the people who lived in our row of houses were directly involved with the Troubles; none of our fathers were ever arrested, and our house was the only one of this corner ever to be raided. At this time everyone had a black-and-white television which had quite a lot of interference when the Army was about so it became the pastime at night to tune the TV into the Army radios. This way most people knew when the Army was entering the estate. But as our father was in the Navy we had a ship-to-shore radio in our house. It wasn't a transmitter but it could pick up the Army and police quite clearly and our father could fix it in minutes to appear harmless. Although the Army had their suspicions, they could prove nothing and so with each new battalion which entered the estate we got raided. Most times we were raided we actually were waiting for the knock at the door.

Once the Army decided to raid our house without mentioning my father's name on their radio. So on that night we were sitting as usual listening to the radio when we heard a voice giving orders to go to a man's house and investigate. It did not give a name or address and so when mother said, "That sounds very close, P.J., maybe you would be better turning it off," he replied, "I will now, but I want to find out who's getting raided." Suddenly there was a knock at the window. Now the Army did not go about tapping windows! So the door was opened immediately and there was the Army, two jeeps of them, who dismantled the radio. And that was the end of the raids on our house.

This was a peculiar way to bring up children, I suppose, but to us it seemed perfectly normal. As far as our parents were concerned we were safe on the streets. There were not many cars in Derrybeg at that time since a large proportion of the male residents were unemployed. Therefore we had the run of the estate, apart from the main road which ran from the Camlough road to the Meadow.

At an early age we knew to lie flat on the ground at the sound of gunfire, which in those days could come from any quarter. At any given time the Provos (Provisional IRA) and the Stickies (Official IRA) would begin shooting at one another, or either of these organisations would be shooting at the Army. There was also the threat that the Unionist B Specials [particularly aggressive members of the security forces] or the UVF (Ulster Volunteer Force) [Protestant paramilitary organization] would enter the estate. Although this threat never became a reality, it led to the forming of the Vigilantes. This was a group of men from the estate who patrolled the avenues at night to help the residents feel safe in their homes.

The Vigilantes did chase down some suspicious characters as it turned out. During this period the street lighting was controlled by the Army so that when a patrol would be passing through at night the lights would be off to act as a camouflage for their darkened faces. This led to a lot of confusion amongst the Vigilantes, who in the dark were known to pounce on members of their own patrol, convinced that they had caught an intruder in the estate. In fact, the Vigilantes caught more Vigilantes than anything else. This was a great source of entertainment to the women of the estate when they gathered for their daily chats at the corners.

Through all of this we were considered safe and, indeed, felt safe and played quite happily amongst the alleyways and avenues of the estate, only stopping to lie down when the shooting began. Of course, when it stopped there was a treasure hunt to find the empty bullet cases or rubber bullets. These rubber bullets were considered a prized possession and many mantlepieces bore them like precious ornaments. We did not stop to think that many people had been killed or injured by them. In fact, Derrybeg had the greatest number of casualties and deaths due to the Troubles of anywhere in Newry at that time.

The only time the shooting ever frightened our family was the night my mother got caught in the crossfire between the Provos and the Army. This was during the week the annual mission for women was on. All the women of the estate attended this, so word was sent around for everyone to be home at ten, straight after the mission.

My mother kept herself to herself in those days. She was friendly with the neighbours but she would not have been one of the women standing on the corner watching the conflict. She was also very trusting and wholeheartedly believed that no one would shoot at the Army when civilians were about, even though this had happened on numerous occasions. So she took it upon herself to ignore the warning to be in by ten o'clock.

When the mission was over and all the women safely home except our mother, we sat worrying about what was keeping her. She had decided to visit our Aunt Mary Catherine at the bottom of the hill for a cup of tea. When she left at eleven o'clock she saw an Army foot patrol. Instead of staying in Aunt Mary's house, she thought she would get safely up the hill and home by walking between the soldiers. We were listening like most of the neighbours to the Army coming over the TV when the shooting began. In my mind it was the worst shooting I ever heard. How many bullets were fired that night we will never know. We were crying at our door, convinced our mother was shot, maybe even dying . . . What my father was feeling I don't know, but my sister and I had to be held back from running out to find our mother.

When the shooting finally subsided, our mother made her way back to Aunt Mary's by crawling on her hands and knees. It was nearly an hour later when she was brought home very much shaken but unhurt. After the initial relief of seeing her safe, my father proceeded to yell at her about ignoring the warning. This was the only time I can remember my father really shouting at my mother—for it was always the other way about. And this was also the only time when she conceded that he was right.

During all these troubles I attended St. Joseph's Primary School for Girls along with most of the other girls in the estate. The school was run by nuns whom we dreaded. They, in turn, seemed to have a distinct disliking for anyone from Derrybeg—or so it seemed to us. This largely came about due to the fact that we disrupted the routine of the school just by living where we did. We travelled to school on a bus which was regularly stoned, burned, or stopped by the Army. This would lead us to be late most days and we rarely arrived in time to take part in the assembly for morning prayers.

We sometimes didn't get to school at all during times of rioting because the bus service would be cancelled by the bus depot. To add to the nuns' annoyance, we would come into the class and everyone would want to know what happened. So we would boast about the goings on over the weekend and thus, to the nuns' dismay, we would be the envy of our classmates. We added to this envy by being sent for anytime the estate was surrounded so that we would get safely home.

There was a lot of political activity in the estate around the early seventies after Internment [jailing of suspected terrorists without trial] had taken place and each house was in some way sympathetic to either the Provos or the Stickies. This reflected on the children as parents of either persuasion did not allow them to mix. We formed our various groups and began to be known as the Sticky children or the Provo children and each one of us knew someone whose father, brother, cousin or friend was in Long Kesh [maximum security prison, also called The Maze].

By the time I was thirteen I had moved away from playing about my own door and was now one of the teenagers who hung about the shops and street corners. I was quite a contrast to my sister Catherine who was quiet and gave my parents no cause for concern. I, with some of my friends, became politically sympathetic to Sinn Fein [political arm of the Irish Republican Army]. These friends belonged to families who had all been touched in some way by the Troubles. One friend, whose father was living on the run in the south of Ireland, also had two brothers in Long Kesh at the same time. Another friend had a sister in Armagh Gaol [jail] for Women. Through these girls I met lots of others who had brothers or fathers in prison.

This led to an acute absence of men in the estate during this period. Every week, two buses—one from each organization—

left the estate to visit the imprisoned men. If by chance you got your name on a prison pass you felt very privileged.

At this time my friends and I started attending political meetings and marches for the release of the internees. I caused my mother and father a lot of concern and was the cause of rows in the house. I was a very stubborn teenager and when told not to do something I deliberately went out and did it. I was smoking at fourteen years of age and I had no fear of the Troubles. I felt I could go where I wanted and no one was going to stop me.

The fact that I had gotten into Grammar School annoyed me when it should have been something to be proud of. All of my friends had failed the eleven-plus [an exam to determine the course of one's education] and attended Secondary School. I was determined to be expelled from school and I behaved quite badly. I did homework when I wanted to, attended classes when it suited me, and when it was time to sit the junior exam to qualify for another three years at the Grammar School I was convinced I would fail. But, to my horror and my parents' delight, I managed to pass once again without even trying.

By this time I was fifteen. I decided I had had enough of this school and refused to go back. My parents let me have my own way and took me out of the Grammar School and put me into the Secondary School.

Once there, I promised them faithfully I would work hard, but of course I didn't. I got worse if possible. Many times I saw my mother crying over me and my involvement with political activities.

By the time we were in our late teens most of the men arrested during Internment were released, so it seemed that Derrybeg was once again full of men and boys. Everyone had to join in the celebration of the anniversary of Internment just to show all these men they were missed. We all went to bed early on the 8th of August so that we would wake in time to rattle our bin lids [garbage can lids] and light the bonfire at four A.M. The noise could be heard for miles. We rattled the bin lids because this was always the signal to let people know that the Army was raiding someone's house. It seemed appropriate that it signalled the anniversary of Internment.

From our point of view, the 9th of August was the highlight of the year, challenged by nothing but Christmas. We would wait patiently to see if there would be any hi-jacking—and if there was, was it a bread van, sweet lorry, or toy lorry? Or, to our utter dismay, was it a lorry full of beer, cigarettes, whisky, or other food stuff which we had absolutely no interest in. The worst memory I have of this is when they hi-jacked a butter lorry. I can remember going up to the Camlough Road and seeing all the melting butter running down the road. The smell was disgusting. If we were lucky enough that Markey's Shop was getting a supply of sweets, ice cream or cakes that day the lorry was sure to be hi-jacked by the older boys.

When a lorry was hi-jacked it was stopped—we were never interested in how this was done. In later years we knew that quite a bit of force was used on occasions. The lorry would then be emptied of its load. This was where we came in. It would suddenly appear that every young boy and girl from Derrybeg was on the Camlough Road. We would run in all directions carrying as much as we could manage through the entries and into the back gardens, out of sight of our parents. None of us were ever officially allowed on the Camlough Road on these occasions for our parents could not be seen to condone these activities.

So, we would eat our prizes in secrecy and quite often end up being sick—which happened to myself and a girl called Janet one day when we had to eat a box of forty-eight ice pops before they melted and went to waste. To us that would have been a bigger crime than our having them in the first place.

Sometimes coal lorries or foodstuff lorries were taken. This was of no interest to us. But as Derrybeg was a close community the content of these lorries was shared equally throughout the estate. My parents would not allow their children to eat a sweet from a hi-jacked lorry, but it seemed that on quite a few Christmases our father would climb up into the attic and come down with bottles of whiskey, tins of meat, and other nonperishable foodstuff that just happened to have been stored there.

To a child, growing up in this environment all seemed perfectly normal. In fact, we were the envy of children who grew up in quieter neighbourhoods. Our cousins would come for holidays on the 8th and 9th of August and, if there happened to be no shooting, they would leave feeling quite disappointed.

In 1980, we saw the start of the hunger strikes in the H-Blocks of Long Kesh and I no longer saw the Troubles as fun. I felt that the men had no choice but to take a stand against the British government. I was now as hostile towards the Army and the police as most of my friends were. I knew a lot of people who were arrested in riots and such and I attended all the Hunger Strike marches and rallies in Dublin. As the men continued to die, I joined in with the new wave of hijacking—this time realising what was happening and why. By the time I was in my late teens life had changed a lot. We no longer knew all there was to know. People who were involved with organisations kept it to themselves and it would be a shock to us when we heard who was arrested. There was no more shooting in the streets, very few attacks on the Army and literally no hi-jacking. The Stickies seemed to disappear altogether and the Provos were spoken of in whispers. Derrybeg had gone from being notorious for trouble to being one of the quieter estates in the town.

I am now married with two children, still living in Derrybeg at the grand age of thirty-one. My children have never heard gunshots or seen the Army getting stoned and would not know what the word hi-jack means. Our town is still known as a Nationalist town and being close to the border there is still some trouble now and then, but not to the extent that there was. My eldest child is a boy who was born on the 27th of November, 1986, the day the Newry police barracks was hit by mortar bombs. He is now seven and heard his first bomb and realised what it meant two weeks ago when, once again, the Newry barracks came under mortar attack. Unlike me, this had a devastating effect on him and his sister. At their age, my friends and I would have been running through the fields to see the damage.

The dangers facing children now are different. I do not consider the avenues safe for my children as we are now a main traffic route to the town. Our children play in their gardens [yards] and they are brought in if there is the slightest sign of trouble. The passage of time has mellowed us all. What we once viewed as an everyday occurrence now fills us with dread.

The above essay was written in August, 1994, when there was a lot of talk about a cease-fire. The explosion which I referred to was the last to be heard in Newry as the cease-fire was called three weeks later.

It is now the 4th of July, 1995, and once again there is hi-jacking on the Camlough Road. Yesterday Private Lee Clegg [British Army] was released from prison after serving only four years of a life sentence for the murder of Karen Reilly who was a passenger in a stolen car which drove through a checkpoint that he and his comrades had set up.

July, 1995—The cease-fire is ten months old and up to a few months ago it looked set to continue. But now we are not so sure. Like most people I know, I welcomed the cease-fire since for us it meant that our children might not know the bitterness that we grew up with. I, myself, believe that nothing could make our parents' generation forget the Troubles and the resentment of their time. The Protestants and Catholics of their era will never live side by side. They will always live in the past with their memories and they will still feel the hatred.

When they look back on it they do not see it as fun. They reared us during all of the Troubles and, although we as children thought the shooting and rioting were normal, they knew it wasn't. The men I remember being in prison were their friends and families. To us they were grown-ups who had no effect on us at the time. They were the ones with the worries of where we were and who we were with. Ours was not the innocent childhood they wanted for us.

I now want that innocent childhood for my children. I want them to play in the streets without seeing Army foot patrols. I want them to look to the police for what they were meant to be . . . simply a police force to deal with ordinary crimes and traffic duties. I do not want them growing up in the midst of the Troubles and I do not want the worries that my parents had.

Up to now my children have had a peaceful life here in Derrybeg. They are not familiar with the sound of shooting and, like my own mother, I do not talk politics in front of them so they are still innocent. But will it remain this way? These past few weeks the main subject on the news here was the impending release of Private Clegg. Because of the cease-fire, his release brought about cries for the early release of all political prisoners, of which he is considered one, no different in our eyes from an IRA man or a Loyalist [Protestant] who has committed murder. Private Clegg's early release has taken place and with it has come a fresh wave of rioting and hijacking which is reminiscent of the early seventies.

According to Downing Street [residence of the Prime Minister of Great Britain], this will have no effect on the cease-fire. To us, this is utter nonsense. We are the people living with this and, although I have no relations in prison, I can understand the bitterness of families who do have. Why should Private

Clegg be freed? There are men from Ulster—both Protestants and Catholics—who are currently serving life for murders they have committed without hope of a review. Are they not in the same position as Private Clegg?

We are now into the third day of rioting here and it has spread throughout the province. As yet, the cease-fire has not been broken but the government does not seem to realise just how fragile it is. They are assuming that the ordinary people like me who want the peace to last will support them. What they do not realise is that, even though we want the peace to last, we feel that the IRA and the Loyalist paramilitaries are the ones who have given the most and not the British government. If the cease-fire fails it will not be because of the rioting which has now taken place but because of the events leading up to it. The blame will lie nowhere but at the British government's own door.

September, 1995—To celebrate one year of peace here my mother and I took my children and my nephew to Belfast for the day. It is the first time they have ever been in the city shopping because there were always the bomb scares in Belfast. It was also the first time my mother has visited Belfast since 1960 when she was there to buy her wedding clothes.

I hope my children will always feel safe to shop in Belfast whenever they want and not have to be on alert.

KIRSTY LAIRD

LONDONDERRY, COUNTY LONDONDERRY

Kirsty Laird lives with her family in the Waterside [Protestant] district of Londonderry. Now seventeen and the age when college entrance exams are the most important thing on her horizon, Kirsty still makes time to write poetry. She wrote this poem in response to an article she read about this anthology even though she and her family had just been plunged into grief by the tragic death of her brother-in-law in a traffic accident. She has had several poems published in various anthologies.

Although the Troubles have been going on for her entire life, perhaps more in Londonderry than anywhere else except Belfast, Kirsty herself has never been a victim of violence. Still, "the divide" impacts her life every day, limiting where she can go and when and causing her to worry when she mistakenly steps into the "wrong" neighborhood. She was very happy to have had the opportunity not to worry about such things for a while when she was sent to Indiana by a cross-community program and could be friends with Protestant and Catholic young people alike.

Time for Peace

(Written at age sixteen)

At sixteen years, I understand
Most goings on within this land
I grew up with the bombs and strife
Another part of daily life.
So, when a bomb came on TV
It did not shock or startle me—
I'd simply sigh and wait to hear
If it had happened somewhere near.
"A soldier killed—aged twenty-one—
Married with a baby son."
How do you tell a loving wife
Some heartless shit took the life
Of the father of her little boy—
Daddy's precious pride and joy?
And what about the three-year-old—
What the hell will he be told?
Do words exist which can explain
Why Daddy won't be home again?
The men in suits like to pretend
This bitterness has reached its end
The smiles, handshakes, papers signed
Obscure the truth which lies behind
The pictures all the world can see
But, frankly, they do not fool me.
So, people don't shoot anymore
Apart from that it's like before.
Still the fighting. Still the fear—
Am I allowed to walk down here?
I hope with time and patience too,
I'll see my prayers and dreams come true.
When people can live happily
As one. At peace. In Unity!

THOMAS GRACEY

DOWNPATRICK, COUNTY DOWN

One of nine children, Thomas Gracey was born in Downpatrick in 1975. His mother, Nancy Gracey, is well known in Northern Ireland as the founder of Families Against Intimidation and Terror in Belfast, where she still is working to end paramilitaries' punishment beatings.

While Thomas says his youth was not much affected by the Troubles, it certainly was impacted by his brother's punishment shooting in Belfast, which he writes about in his story. "I hate the Provos [IRA Provisionals]," he says. While it was true that the cease-fires held for well over a year, during which there were no sectarian shootings, Thomas says punishment beatings and murders actually increased during that time.

I asked Thomas how his brother, who lives with his wife and ten-year-old son, is doing now. "He's a nervous wreck," he said. "He doesn't really sleep. The first noise he hears then he's up. His bedroom is like an armory. He has baseball bats and all that. He's afraid of them coming back after him."

Personal Experience

(Written at age nineteen)

It was a clear crisp evening in July 1990 when a few members of my family and I were returning from a fun-filled day at Coney Island Caravan Park which is just outside Downpatrick. Some younger members of our family laughed and joked in the back of the car sharing a few jokes and gags with each other. My mother, Nancy, and I talked about numerous issues in the front of the car.

The evening was calm and the sun cast a welcoming warmth over the car. As we approached Downpatrick the five o'clock news cackled over the radio. The main story was of another kneecapping in Belfast, twenty-two miles north of Downpatrick. Belfast was notorious for kneecappings, shootings, and bombings mostly carried out by IRA terrorist squads.

We were approaching our house where two of my older sisters were waiting for us. "Ma, Paddy has been shot and we don't know whether he is dead or alive!" one of them said. For six months previous my brother Paddy had been hounded and his home wrecked for having an argument with a well-known, convicted IRA bomber.

My mother literally went berserk. Paddy had been summoned to Belfast for a meeting with the IRA to "clear the air." As instructed, my brother went to a pub on the Falls Road to have this so-called meeting with the IRA. His girlfriend, Anne Marie, and four-year-old son, Nathan, accompanied him. Instead of a meeting, Paddy was locked in by two men and then he was escorted out through the back door to a patch of waste ground. Paddy was told to lie face down on the ground. "No," he replied. "I haven't done anything wrong."

"Lie down or you're getting nutted [killed]!" one of the men exclaimed. "We're only going to kneecap you."

He had no choice but to obey their order. The first bullet ripped through his leg, destroying his knee. Then the gun was pressed against his other leg but it jammed. Then it was placed against his spine for what is known as a 50/50 (fifty percent chance of dying and fifty percent chance of being paralysed, depending on which way the bullet goes in.) Again the gun jammed.

As the IRA terrorists ran off, Paddy was faced with the option of crawling to safety or bleeding to death. At this point Anne Marie and Nathan were outside the pub and saw Paddy, covered in blood, crawling out into the street.

Eventually the ambulance arrived and Paddy was rushed to hospital to begin a long and hard battle to try to regain full use of his leg. Today he walks with a permanent limp and is a totally changed person. Instead of the caring, fun-loving brother that he was, he is now a paranoid person who trusts no one—not even his family.

God only knows if he'll ever change. Paddy feels that he is locked inside his own self. He cannot release his hatred for the IRA without resorting to violence, shouting, or arguing. I and my mother and other members of our family have tried to talk to him, to get him to talk about what he has experienced, but it just does not work. It ends in rows and fights. The IRA took a person who had everything to look forward to, tortured him, shot him, and turned him into someone that you cannot trust.

For instance, if he knew that I was writing about him right now I'm sure that he would cause trouble. I don't really know how to put this but it is getting to the point where I am growing further apart from the monster-like person that my brother is turning into.

Some things that my brother says can really hurt but at the end of the day he's still my brother.

KEVIN BYERS

PORTAFERRY, COUNTY DOWN

This autobiographical story by Kevin Byers shows how the impact of the Troubles is felt far beyond the six counties of Northern Ireland. A schoolboy on his way from England to visit his grandparents in Northern Ireland for the summer, he was detained and treated like a criminal after an IRA bomb went off in London.

Particularly since this story was written when Kevin was only eighteen, one might have expected it to include anger and a certain amount of invective against the heavy-handed British authorities. But Kevin maturely refused to see the conflict in black-and-white terms and included an event that gives the story an enigmatic, ambiguous ending.

Please see page 73 for more information about Kevin Byers.

The Leaving of Liverpool

(Written at age eighteen)

"Are you, or have you at any time been, a member of an illegal organization?" The Special Branch officer yawned as he began reading from the sheet of questions for the third time. The first time I had laughed nervously after each answer but now I cried them out.

"No, I've told you . . ."

"Where were you at two o'clock this afternoon?"

"On the train to Liverpool," I sighed.

The officer looked at me with disgust and threw his clipboard down on the desk between us. "Alright, pal, we'll leave you to the boss. It looks like the Bridewell [prison] for you to-night."

He walked out and left me alone in the office. It was the first time I'd had to think since they had taken me from the docks to the police station. I had joined the queue to board the ship for Belfast. I was looking forward to spending my summer holiday with my cousins in Ireland. I was fifteen and making the journey alone for the first time.

I noticed two men walking down the line, pointing out some of the passengers to each other. One of them stopped and pulled a man out of the line. I was watching him being taken to a white mini [small car] on the dockside when I felt a finger tapping me on the arm. Before I realized what was happening, I was in the white mini with the other passenger and the two Special Branch men who were driving us through the damp and dreary backstreets of Liverpool.

We had been taken to different rooms when we arrived. As I sat on my own staring at the walls, I wished that my unknown companion was there to tell me why we were being questioned. Perhaps he didn't know either.

The walls were covered in the shiny blue emulsion that they use in schools and hospitals and it was flaking and peeling in large patches. The desk was old and scratched and an ancient black telephone sat in the middle of an empty out-tray.

I could see the clipboard with my questionner's notes and I wondered if I had time to take a look at what he had written. No . . . what if they were watching me? Perhaps that was what they wanted me to do to prove I was guilty of whatever it was they thought I had done? I wanted a cigarette but I didn't know whether that was allowed, so I just sat waiting for the next move. I began to wonder if I really was guilty of some crime committed in a moment of mental blackout. I laughed at the thought but stopped myself. The idea that I was being watched had not left me.

I was snapped back to reality by the appearance of a tall,

bald-headed man in the doorway. "Well, son," he said softly, "you're a bit young for all of this, aren't you?"

"Yes, I . . . I suppose I am." The blood shot to my head and my cheeks coloured as the fear that I might have just incriminated myself further took hold of me. This must be the "boss" who my previous questionner had mentioned. He gave me a reassuring smile so I decided to ask the question that had been nagging me: "Am I . . . under arrest?"

"No, no lad," he said soothingly. "You're simply in for routine questioning under the Prevention of Terrorism Act." His voice had slipped abruptly into a cold, official tone with the last few words and I felt goosebumps appear on the back of my neck. He seemed to sense my fear and immediately used the opportunity.

"We want to know all about this afternoon. Now, come on, lad, it'll be better for you and all of us if you tell us the truth now."

I looked around the room in desperation, as if expecting to find someone there to help me. I was totally alone for the first time in my life. I suddenly felt guilty again. "I don't understand," I finally whimpered.

He looked at me for several minutes, staring me straight in the eyes. Eventually, he sat down. "You really don't know, do you?"

"No, honestly, I wish I did," I said, seeing a glimmer of hope and trying to sound as young and innocent as I could.

He threw down the newspaper that he had been carrying and I immediately saw the headline: "IRA Bomb in London Hotel." My eyes seemed to blur and I couldn't read anymore. "Oh, Christ, no, you can't really think that I had anything to do with this?"

He looked me in the eye again and his fatherly reassuring tone returned. He asked me my phone number and, when I told him, he moved toward the office door.

"Was there anyone . . . hurt?" I called to him, meaning to say "killed" but the word would not come out.

"No, lad," he confided. "It's just as well for you that there wasn't or you might never have got as far as me."

He walked out of the room to the next office and within seconds I could hear him talking on the phone.

"Yes, he's alright . . . nothing to worry about . . . just routine. . . . Now, you can confirm that he left London on the lunchtime train from Euston? Right, thank you very much. He'll be on his way soon."

At these last words I felt a rush of relief. I looked at my watch and realized how long I had been there. The ship would be sailing soon and the thought of being stranded in a city I had come to hate filled me with a new fear.

When the officer came back in, he picked up the receiver of the old black telephone on the desk. My mind was reeling so that I only took in the last few words. ". . . right, Jim, hold it for another ten minutes. This one's clean. Did the other one go on board yet? Good. It looks like whoever did it knew better than to come through this way. My guess is they'll lay low for a while. Right, good night, Jim."

He quickly brought me down to where the white mini was waiting to drive me back to the ship. My luggage was on the back seat where I had left it. A piece of material was just visible where one of the cases had been carelessly closed. As we drove back to the docks, I vowed to avoid Liverpool for the rest of my life.

Walking towards the gangway, I felt that everyone on the ship's decks was watching me. They knew who I was and where I had been. My ticket was hastily checked and the gangway removed as soon as I was on board the ship. I went straight to the cafeteria for a cup of coffee and the cigarette that I had been longing for all evening. I carefully avoided everyone's eyes. After a while, I became aware of someone standing beside me. I recognized him as soon as I looked up.

"Hello there, so they let you out as well then. I knew they would. The bastards were just trying to put the wind up you." He sat down and I smiled at him with the relief of having someone to talk to who had shared the same experience. We had been total strangers a few hours earlier when we were taken to the police station together but now I felt a strong affinity with him.

"I'm glad to see that you got out as well," I said, meaning every word of it.

"Who, me?" He smiled. "They let me go after five minutes . . . as soon as I showed them this." He waved a piece of paper in front of me. "It tells them that I was just let out of Long Kesh [maximum security prison outside Belfast also called The Maze] a week ago and was over in England for a job interview. I had no trouble with them . . . and I didn't get the job either!"

We both laughed and then we went up on deck and sat on a wooden bench. By one o'clock I had told him my whole story and England was just a few fading lights in the darkness.

"You can call me Gerry by the way," he said.

"And I'm Kevin . . ."

He held up his hand to stop me from saying more.

"First names are enough for us, Kevin." He spoke gently but firmly. I felt a strange fear that I could not understand. He smiled, as if he knew what I was thinking, and walked over to the railings.

"All the same, Kevin," he said after a pause, "they're terrible stupid, falling for a bit of paper like this." He tore the paper up and dropped the pieces onto the water below.

LIAM McGILL

TEMPO, COUNTY FERMANAGH

Writer Liam McGill was born in 1964 in a small village south of Derry. His father was a truck driver and his mother took care of the six children. "We had a storybook childhood," Liam recalls. "We got to work on farms . . . taking in hay . . . cutting barley . . . gathering potatoes. We had to work hard but it was a good childhood. We were a very close family."

"South Derry was a very Republican area," he told me as we sipped tea at the home he shares with his wife and children in a beautiful farming area outside the

city of Enniskillen. "I never joined the IRA and I never took a gun into my hand but there was many a time I felt like it. But my moral upbringing—'Thou shalt not kill'—that stopped me. And I was too softhearted. It takes a special kind of person to shoot somebody. But I had all this anger boiling up inside of me. I never really hated them, but everybody has a breaking point . . ."

As much as his young life was affected by the Troubles and as uncertain as he believes the chances are for peace, Liam makes a point of including humor in the stories he writes about the Troubles even when he is describing terrifying events. His story, "The Largatacky Wallop," is a tongue-in-cheek account of his serious mistreatment at the hands of the Army.

The Largatacky Wallop

A ripple of sunshine tumbled its way through the tall fir trees as I made my way down the old grassy lane and over the rugged brown gate. It is often said the weather is used much too often to fodder the mind for conversation, so I will make that subject short and describe it as what is often described in rural Ireland as a "quare day" [a fine, sunny day]. It took barely five minutes to walk to a place that as children we had christened the Plumtrees and whose name through turbulent years still plays a prominent part in the storybooks of our minds.

As I turned the key on the boot of the old Mrk 3 Ford Cortina I could not relinquish the fact that if rust was valuable this car would be priceless. It was also on my mind that above the minor things like no MOT [Ministry of Transport mechanical test], insurance, licence, road tax, and four tyres that resembled a well-scalped backside, the petrol tank was leaking and required constant attention with a jar of petrol which I placed in the boot [trunk].

I started the car within the usual clouds of black smoke and a noise came from the engine that sounded like a third world war. I proceeded to drive the six miles to some friends' house which I will name Sean, Brendan, and Jim. It was a trip I made on a regular basis and the long narrow country roads became as familiar to me as the back of my hand, unspoiled stretches of land posing to the watchful eyes.

It wasn't long until I reached the entrance to the long lane that led me to my friends' house. At the end of the lane I was greeted by three scruffy-looking characters (Beavis and Butthead types) and, after the usual insults and physical abuse, we then planned our destiny for the day and grinned inwardly at the dastardly deeds that in those teenage years we were capable of perpetrating.

The only worry I had was whether or not, when Brendan

placed the crate of empty milk bottles which was to be left at the bottom of the lane in the car boot, its decaying condition would be able to hold them. My worry was taken over by a loud explosion of Meat Loaf coming from the cassette player in which we all proceeded to make erratical movements [dancing] to the rhythm.

The few miles that we travelled we were lost in our harmonious activity when suddenly up ahead I spied an Army checkpoint set up outside the town's RUC [police] station. As would be considered rational in any normal way of thinking, especially for those who were driving on the road a year before they were legally allowed to do so and with the only licence in their possession an out-of-date dog licence, I turned up an old stone lane to escape and, after driving a hundred yards or so, I stopped.

I told my friends to sit in the car while I went to scout out the situation. As I was coming near the entrance to the lane I eased my head around the corner in the hope that the checkpoint was gone. I suddenly found myself looking into a long steel tube which resembled the barrel of a gun. And, in fact, it was a gun, at the other end of which stood a soldier with a tartan hat.

I was trying to figure out what he was saying—he sounded like a cross between an opera singer and a pair of bagpipes—when all of a sudden I thought it was night. Stars were circling round my head and I felt myself being dragged toward the car by the hair. When we reached the car I found that my friends were all lying face down on the ground. Between all the havoc I managed to understand that the soldier wanted the boot opened and that it better be quick.

As I opened the boot and stared at the sight before me I only wished that it was all a dream and that I would wake up as soon as possible, for staring at me from the boot of the car was the crate of forgotten milk bottles and the jar of petrol.

At the time, Northern Ireland was torn by rioting and petrol bombs—and the main ingredients for petrol bombs were pet-rol and milk bottles. While I tried to explain the innocense of the items in the boot, I was quickly bundled along with my friends into a Land Rover and we soon found ourselves guests of the local RUC.

A few minutes after we entered the barracks we were posi-tioned against the wall, legs spread apart and our fingertips outstretched. While I pondered on the thought that our only crime was a crate of forgotten milk bottles and a leaking petrol tank, I then became the receiver of what is known among us as a "Largatacky Wallop" [a kick between the legs], which was delivered with such force that the two scones and rhubarb jam that I had for my tea had now taken refuge on the ground be-fore me.

This form of hospitality was dished out to each of us respec-tively and, after what seemed like eternity, we were bundled into police cells and left to stew. Some time later I was taken into a room and asked to explain the items in the boot of the car. I pointed out the leak in the petrol tank and explained the forgotten milk bottles. While I waited for this to be checked out I heard the police telling my friends they could go and a dreadful pang of loneliness swept through me.

Some time later I heard the cell door open and I was told I could go. The policeman said the car was being confiscated and that the story of the milk bottles was a good one and he didn't believe it.

As I made my way down the long wide road which would lead to home, I felt empty and lost. The humiliation and abuse that I'd suffered were boiling in the very pits of my soul. A tiny drizzle was beginning to descend, slowly blackening the road before me. As I turned back I could see the barracks disappear in the thick of the rain and it was then on that rainy day in 1981 that I committed myself to the destruction of all empty milk bottles.

ALISTAIR LITTLE

LURGAN, COUNTY ARMAGH

Born in Lurgan in 1958, Alistair Little is the youngest of four children of a Scottish father who served with the Royal Auxiliary Fleet during World War II and an Irish mother from Londonderry. Alistair attended totally segregated Protestant schools until age fourteen, when he went to the "mixed" local technical college. "By this time," he says, "I already viewed Catholics as my enemy and to have nothing to do with them was the rule of the day. . . . My understanding was that we as Protestants were a better people with God on our side."

These beliefs and the experience Alistair describes in his story may go some way toward explaining how it was that he became involved with a Protestant paramilitary group and at seventeen was arrested and sent to prison for twelve years for murdering a Catholic.

Now in his thirties, Alistair is married with one child and working with the elderly in his community. Prison was a watershed experience for him, one that turned his thoughts away from bitterness and hatred.

The Death of a Soldier

In 1973 an Ulster Defense Regiment soldier was off duty and at home with his wife and daughter. His wife had just popped out to a local shop only yards from the house.

Outside, sitting in a stolen car watching the UDR man's house, was an active service unit of the Irish Republican Army. Having observed the soldier's wife leave the home and enter the local shop, two gunmen approached the front door and knocked. The soldier, who normally was very careful about opening his door, thinking that his wife had returned from the shop, sent his daughter to open the door.

When the door opened the gunmen pushed past the soldier's young daughter and entered the house as she screamed. The UDR soldier was shot dead before he was able to fire his personal weapon in defence. The IRA gunmen escaped having killed another member of the regiment, another Protestant, another Ulsterman and also having shot the soldier's young daughter in the legs.

In 1973 I was fifteen years old, I was a Protestant, I believed there was a God and that He was a Protestant also. I was in a gang called the Tartans. I hated Catholics and was proud of it. I don't recall feeling or thinking that I was any different from my peers, at least not until the death of the UDR soldier. He was the father of one of the boys who was a member of the Tartans. This made the death of the soldier more personal to me. I knew his son and witnessed the effect that his father's murder had upon him which in itself was frightening. In fact, it was all a most frightening experience. It was difficult to understand how a person could be alive one second and dead the next. At fifteen you expect to live forever.

Everyone I knew was talking about the UDR man's death and the shooting of his daughter. It seemed to me that the whole world knew about the UDR soldier having been shot in my home town and that the gunmen who had carried out the shooting would soon be caught.

A few days after the shooting I went along to the funeral. It was the first funeral I had ever attended. I think that maybe I had expected to see a dead person. As it turned out, the coffin was frightening enough. I remember finding my way to the front of the crowd outside the home. I could hear people talking about the IRA, about Taigs [Catholics] and how they needed someone to teach them a lesson for what they had done. I moved closer to the front of the home and I could see a girl, eleven or twelve years old, sitting in a wheelchair in the small garden. She was crying. I realised that it was the soldier's daughter. I felt so sorry for her as I watched friends try to comfort her.

Suddenly there was total silence as the soldier's coffin was carried out of the house and placed on two small silver stands on the pathway directly opposite the young girl in the wheelchair. A Union Jack was draped over the coffin and the soldier's beret and gloves pinned on top.

What I wasn't prepared for were the screams of the soldier's daughter when her father's coffin was lifted onto the shoulders of the coffin bearers. As they began to move away from the home she was screaming for her Daddy to come back. I began to cry. I could see other people crying, even grown men, which was something I had not expected. After all, grown men were not supposed to do that sort of thing.

I was frightened, I was angry, and I vowed that if I ever got the opportunity to take revenge on the IRA, on Catholics, and their community I would gladly take that opportunity. I came away from the funeral confused about what was going on inside of me but I knew that I hated the IRA more than I hated anything in life and I was quite sure that everyone at the funeral must be thinking the same as I was.

STEPHEN HOEY

ENNISKILLEN, COUNTY FERMANAGH

Thirty-two-year-old Stephen Hoey grew up in Enniskillen, the son of a part-time policeman. "It was a very dangerous job at the time . . . the early seventies," Stephen recalls. "The hardest time was Christmas Eve because we always wondered would he come back alive."

Stephen himself was a target of sectarian violence when he was fifteen and on his first visit to a disco. "I got severely beaten up by some guys from another school," he says, "and at the time I really did feel hatred."

As he matured, however, Stephen found himself making friends with as many Catholics as Protestants. In fact, he married a Catholic woman to whom he stayed married for ten years and with whom he parents his seven-year-old daughter, Holly.

The day that I was to interview Stephen in Enniskillen he arranged for us to meet in a pub called The Crow's Nest—a Catholic pub. Another indicator of what Stephen calls "Irish apartheid," the pubs in Enniskillen are, as he says, "all one-sided." That Stephen had chosen a Catholic pub as his local hangout spoke volumes about his political leanings. "I got a lot of trouble from other guys my age," he says, "because I was going out with a Catholic girl and that made me almost decide that I didn't want anything to do with people like that. . . . Most of my friends would be Catholic now."

Inspired by anger and disgust with the bigotry on both sides of the sectarian divide, Stephen wrote the following poem shortly after he left school in 1979.

Ireland du Nord

(Written at age seventeen)

Bombs and bullets scar this land.
People swear they'll make a stand.
They raise their voice, they raise a hand
And listen in awe to the firebrand.
They march in silence with the black armband
As they bury their dead in the borderland.
Showing their colours and following their band
They cry that the world might understand.

JOE DOHERTY

LISBURN, COUNTY ANTRIM

Forty years old now, Joe Doherty was first arrested in 1972 when he was seventeen and interned without trial in the maximum security prison called The Maze, near Belfast. He was released in 1983 but eventually was sentenced to several more prison terms, which totaled twenty years. He was one of the thirty-eight prisoners who escaped The Maze in September of 1981 in the largest prison escape in British history. He was rearrested in New York City in 1983 and nine years later was deported to Northern Ireland and sent back to The Maze, where he is today. His earliest possible date of parole is in the year 2000.

Having learned about this anthology in The Maze, Joe wrote the following account of his youth as a "second-class citizen" in Northern Ireland especially for this book. In this essay he describes the injustices he believes the Catholic community has been forced to endure and how they led him to forsake nonviolent opposition to British Unionist rule and to commit the acts that eventually landed him in a maximum security prison.

As was mentioned in the general introduction to this book, under British law there is no statute of limitations on what are considered to be terrorist acts. Perhaps for this reason and also because all of the mail going out of The Maze is reviewed by prison authorities, Joe Doherty has not described the nature of the crimes for which he was arrested.

Hopes and Dreams of Youth

Nineteen fifty-five was the year I entered the world. Unknown to me, as I let go my first screams in natural birth, I had committed an offence against the state. You see, I was born an Irish Catholic in British-controlled northeast Ireland. Naturally I was unaware of my political illegitimacy in this Anglo-created society. But being an indigenous person, a member of an underclass, one gradually develops an awareness of social inequalities, especially when one is at the receiving end of discriminatory measures, judicial imbalances, and a police baton.

My seventh year of boyhood was an introduction to racial bigotry. An Irish Catholic death in Dallas, Texas, brought much sorrow to our ghetto. "Jack Kennedy was one of our own," people whispered. Elected the first Catholic president, Kennedy's victory was a revelation as were the successive victories of Dr. King, Jr., against racial discrimination in the following years. Both were to have an effect on Irish Nationalists here in the northeast. But I was bewildered as Unionists/Protestants— those who embraced British rule in the North [of Ireland]— jeered our prayers for Kennedy. And I wondered in dismay at this blind and unwarranted hate.

As years passed, the reality of Unionist-British rule began to take shape in my young mind. I cautiously took notice of my abnormal surroundings. "A Protestant state for a Protestant people," was the Unionist government claim. Not empty rhetoric either.

I was too young to appreciate the intricate complexities of Unionist quasi-apartheid rule but I knew they permanently controlled all aspects of government (through means undemocratic) and, in turn, all other facets of society.

Partition of the country in 1922 and a gerrymandered system insured the Unionists a permanent majority as they managed and manipulated the commerce, the media, the law, the courts, and all security forces. In other words, it was their government, their law, their courts, their forces of law, and their factories. I could not help but feel alienated when I saw our differing environments. We Nationalist Catholics lived in a separate world of outcasts. Our ghetto existence consisted of the poorest housing, highest unemployment, and emigration.

Even before the present war, the police would patrol heavily armed. They seemed alien to everything around them. We did not have police stations or precincts. Instead, sandbagged barracks sprawled across the cities and countryside. No police in Europe had such weaponry or extralegal powers at their disposal.

Beneath the alienation and physical violence of our subjugation were the psychological despair and indignity of second-class citizenship. At such a young age, being despised, spat upon, and taunted because of my nationality and religion created an untrusting attitude toward the state and nurtured my will to resist systems of injustice for years to come. My compassion for other strife-torn parts of the world developed out of this formative period.

Even within the family, the Unionist environment had its effects. My father and mother sought to rid me of Belfast and their failure to provide a secure future for their children. My father insisted that I concentrate on trade class in school so as to prepare for emigration to foreign shores. "No jobs here for Nationalist Catholics," he'd say. "No chance in life with this government. Go to America, Canada, your Aunt Ann in Sydney. Work hard. Bring up a decent family with self-dignity," he'd preach. Most Nationalist youth were pained with these cultural sermons.

But in 1968, my last year of school, hope replaced despair as parents began to think that perhaps emigration was not the answer. It was then that I began to take notice of the growing movement for political change. Dr. King Jr.'s crusade in America for civil rights was everywhere and had an inspiring effect on everyone. One could not help feeling the hopes and the anxieties of that period of civil activism.

We began to gain political ground with newly founded organizations such as the People's Democracy and the Northern

Ireland Civil Rights Association. New, formidable leadership took the headlines: Bernadette Devlin, Michael Farrell, and John Hume. Their youthful, positive, and nonviolent energy gave people the inspiration to move forward. The days of the traditional, violent rebellion were closing as a new dawn of nonviolent and enlightened reformation of the state was taking hold. To a young boy this was an awakening.

But, as the world watched, basic demands for civil and political reforms were met with the full violence of the state. Police banning orders, arrests, and beatings of peaceful marchers showed the reactionary and predictable response of a regime that was undemocratic and politically bankrupt. The violent reactions of the Unionist government only reinforced the Nationalists' forward surge. The people were on the move. I remember the civil rights marchers coming back into the ghetto bleeding from baton wounds and with eyes bloodshot from something called CS gas [tear gas]. It was then that I felt a growing need to get involved; anger and frustration drove me to pick up my first stone.

Why such a lack of government response to such basic and reasonable demands for reform? Our demands were not revolutionary or impractical. There were no calls for the downfall of British sovereignty or revengeful cries about 800 years of British rule. Nationalist Catholics were submissively stating their acceptance of British rule—their head of state, flag, and other symbols. All we asked for were equal rights and justice within the system. What we received was a violent intransigence in meeting those demands.

Unlike the United States, we in northeast Ireland had no Lyndon B. Johnson to send federal troops to uphold constitutional law. We did not have any constitutional law nor a Bill of Rights, nor even a government willing to address issues of discrimination and injustice. This was the whole crux of the matter: we needed laws and protection. The government could not or would not provide that. Their refusal paved the way for a more direct form of confrontation. I began to see that throwing stones alone was not effective.

"Those who make peaceful resolutions impossible," said Kennedy, "make violent revolutions inevitable." Patience was running out and I became a part of an impatient upcoming generation. Each peaceful march was met by further state violence. Time was running short for gradual change. The state had to be overthrown. The older generation told those innocent youthful marchers that reforming the state was futile; only rebellion could secure freedom. The emergence of British troops onto the streets—although welcomed at the time by Nationalists—was a stark reminder of who was in power. The soldiers' repressive tactics hardened my attitude and marked my way to armed insurrection. The reluctance of London to take steps to alleviate the deteriorating situation paved the way to an all-out confrontation that continues to plague and threaten Ireland and Britain to this day.

Over a quarter of a century later there is little to celebrate. Yes, there may be a long-awaited welcome to the absense of (or a break from) mass violence, but the conditions that create violence still prevail. The British presense, partition, the fear of the state still persist. There is still mistrust and fear between opposing communities and a lack of direction about how to accommodate each other's aspirations. There is, however, a growing sense of cautious optimism and hope for a better future—the hope that those enlightened youth marched and sang for in the sixties. To fulfill the dreams of peace and justice for the next generation we must surely live up to the hopes and songs of that yesteryear. Then only can my children live in harmony and peace.

ALISON ÖSTNAS

BANGOR, COUNTY DOWN

One of four children, Alison Östnas was born in Belfast in 1956.
Her father was an Army officer
and her mother a college lecturer.
The family lived in an area that
was relatively undisturbed by the
Troubles, Alison says, but her ex-
tracurricular activities were curtailed and her journeys to and
from school at Victoria College in
Belfast were delayed by riots from
time to time. She especially remembers that during the Workers' Strike in 1974 young boys of
twelve and thirteen, armed with
sticks, barricaded roads and prevented people from going to work.

Asked what inspired her in 1992 to write this, the only story she
has written, Alison said, "I wanted people to know how ordinary
families were at the mercy of armed groups who always had the
advantage of surprise."

Unwelcome Callers

I was eighteen, in my first year as a student nurse. My mother
and I were relaxing after a hard day. Our dog, dozing at our
feet, suddenly pricked up his ears at the sound of crunching

gravel. The bell rang and I opened the door, to be confronted by two youths unknown to me. The smaller of the two stepped forward and thrust a revolver into my chest. "We've come for Tom's gun," he said, "and we know it is here."

My heart sank. If they knew so much, where was Tom, my policeman brother? Was he being held in some terrorist stronghold until this mission had been accomplished?

Meanwhile, I was pushed into the sitting room where our brave protective dog was cowering in the corner. The gunman ordered his mate to "go upstairs and get it." He headed straight for my brother's room and soon we could hear drawers being pulled out, contents scattered, cupboard doors wrenched open, and carpets ripped back.

Downstairs, we had time to study the other young terrorist. He was a tight little chap—tight lips, tight curls, tight jeans— but his tightly clenched hands could not control the tremor in the fingers clutching the gun. To ease the tension I had the crazy impulse to offer him a cup of tea. Instead, I asked him whether his mother knew what he was doing. He looked very uncomfortable and said that it was better to "keep the oldies in the dark." His mother was probably in her thirties.

Just then our discourse was interrupted by his mate, a big, lumbering lad with a rather vacant expression. If brawn should be required, he would supply it. He confessed, apologetically and rather desperately, that he "couldn't find it," and was dispatched upstairs again to search the other bedrooms. My mother and I exchanged a concerned glance, knowing that a hat box on top of her wardrobe contained spare ammunition. More bangings and clatterings ensued, the top was removed from the lavatory cistern [toilet tank], and the contents of the airing cupboard [for linen and clothing] came floating downstairs.

Meanwhile, my mother's car keys were demanded, the phone wires pulled out, and instructions given regarding the time lapse to be observed before reporting the incident. Once more the lumbering lad came downstairs, worry written all over his face. He had failed on his first "job." The boss was very angry but decided to settle for my brother's police uniforms which could be used in bogus road blocks.

Eventually the sidekick came down, draped in beautifully pressed trousers and tunic, a night helmet at a rakish angle on his head, and a truncheon [nightstick] under one arm. Over the other arm hung a pair of binoculars. Outraged, my mother blurted out, "You can't take those. They belong to my husband!"

Meekly and apologetically, the trainee terrorist handed them over. He had not yet learned that hard men never say sorry. Emboldened by this small triumph, my mother requested the return of her house keys, and, to her surprise, they were detached from the ring and handed over!

At last, the intruders were ready to leave and, luckily for them, their car started.

Our first act was to examine the phone. It was well and truly disconnected but would this alone constitute grounds for replacement? My mother had been agitating for months to have the old-fashioned, heavy black instrument replaced by a modern streamlined one, colour to be chosen from a limited range. Perhaps a short, sharp tap would do the trick? I fetched the hammer.

My brother arrived home later, unaware of the drama, to find the house surrounded by soldiers and police and his mother and sister poring over jigsaws of noses, foreheads, and hairlines while the features of our callers were still clear in our minds. To his great relief, his revolver was still in its ingenious hiding place.

There were several sequels to the incident. Our "semi-detached" [duplex] neighbours greeted us rather frostily next morning with mutterings about late-night parties and comings and going at all hours of the night.

My father, who had left on the morning of the "visitation"

to return to Scotland where he was working at the time, noticed two men following him onto the platform of the local railway station. They were probably ensuring that there would be no male presence in the house.

And a few months later, my brother's uniforms were discovered during a police raid on a Belfast pub. The name tapes were still sewn into each garment and the pub manager was now in trouble.

About three years later, we learned that our uptight terrorists had soon gained confidence and graduated to more serious assignments. In fact, they were currently up on a murder charge. We were lucky to have been involved in one of their first jobs.

On the plus side, our new phone, in our chosen colour, arrived next day!

JOAN FARRELL

BANGOR, COUNTY DOWN

Joan Farrell's happy childhood in a large family living on a farm that straddled the border of the two Irelands abruptly ended with the onset of the Troubles. "Our lives were blighted by the Troubles," she says. "Every time you turned on the news and you heard there'd been another bomb your heart stopped until you heard where it was."

Up until the 1970s there had been so little violent crime in Northern Ireland that people were deeply shocked by just the idea of murder. "We really didn't know that we had people in our midst in Ulster who could commit murder," Joan says.

As she describes in her story and the poem that follows it, one of the earliest murders of the Troubles devastated her and set her life on a completely different course. "There is that sorrow that I don't think ever leaves you when you've come through something like that," she says. "And there is a pain, the pain of knowing that someone you loved was treated so dreadfully and did nothing to deserve it." Joan says she became much more cynical after the murder and although knowing it sounds terrible she says, "I became much more distrustful of Roman Catholics."

In 1993, Joan found that she was finally able to write about her tragic loss. She showed me a huge notebook full of poetry, almost all of it about the murder. Her pain can at last be transmuted into writing.

Joan feels that in some ways her loss has made her a better person. "I would like to think it makes me more tolerant of other people," she says. "I would be very conscious of another person's sorrow and the problems they have to carry."

Now in her forties, Joan has two college-age children and lives in an elegant home in Bangor with her husband, Eric, manager of a local bank. Devoted to serving other people, Joan works part-time with disabled and elderly people. "My husband has been always beside me," she says, "supporting me in everything that I've done. Without the support of (a) God, (b) my family, and (c) Eric, I could never have come through what I have without tremendous bitterness."

If the Worst Should Happen

I was born near Castlederg in County Tyrone and was the youngest of nine children—eight girls and one boy. We lived on a farm which straddled the Tyrone/Donegal border so that part of the farm was in Northern Ireland and part was in the Republic of Ireland. My parents had to work very hard to get a decent living from the land.

My brother and sisters and I had a very simple but very happy upbringing, mixing with and helping all our neighbours, irrespective of religion. Never at any time did our parents instill in us any feelings of ill will towards our Roman Catholic neighbours.

It was not until the late sixties, when I was almost fifteen years old, that I had my first experience of bitterness and hostility from a Roman Catholic. It happened on my way home from school one day. The school I attended was predominantly

Protestant, although not entirely so. It was situated on the outskirts of the border town of Strabane. We were transported by bus from the centre of the town in the morning to the school—a distance of about one mile—and back again in the afternoon. The area between the school and the centre of town (locally known as "the head of the town") was almost entirely Roman Catholic and known to be an area with strong Republican sympathisers.

I had missed the last bus from the school in the afternoon and so I had to walk through this "Republican" area. I really was not worried at all because I had never experienced any difficulties with Roman Catholic people and could not imagine why anyone would want to hinder me on my way.

I was happily walking along, in full school uniform, when I was spat upon by a teenager whose mother was standing nearby talking over the fence to her neighbour. The teenager then grabbed my beret and threw it onto the road into the path of an oncoming car. She ran to the other side of the road, all the while shouting abuse and laughing. I was absolutely amazed by the whole incident which was over in a matter of minutes and was surprised that neither of the adults appeared to notice or rebuke the girl for what she had done.

I picked up my beret and walked on as quickly as possible. There were no further attacks that day but on subsequent occasions the same treatment was meted out to me and several other pupils from my school.

I realize now that we were witnessing then the start of Republicans' open hostility toward Protestants. There were also faint rumblings of "civil rights" groups and student protest marches.

Our part of the province had been so peaceful until then that we didn't take those early signs of unrest very seriously. Within three years those faint rumblings exploded into bombs and deafening gunfire. How quickly life changed for us all! The innocence and security of my childhood was torn asunder.

When I had acquired sufficiently high grades to get a creditable job in a local bank I decided not to continue with my education. I had fallen in love with the man whom I was to marry. I was still in my teens but was totally convinced that finding a job, earning money, getting married, and having children was the right thing for me to do.

I was very happy in my banking work although I had to live away from home which meant I could only see my boyfriend at weekends. Then I got a transfer to a bank in Waterside in Londonderry and we were able to see each other more often.

The situation in Londonderry at this time was very volatile and I was frequently awakened at night by bombs exploding and, from my bedroom window, I could watch exchanges of gunfire.

We were in a war-type situation but somehow we all seemed to think it would just die out and everything would return to the normal, quiet pace of life that I had grown up with. We certainly never believed that twenty-five years later we would still be feeling the effects of a massive IRA murder and bombing campaign.

Naturally, like any young couple planning to get married, Kenneth and I moved along as if in a dream world of our own. He was a contractor and was going to be able to renovate an old property we bought to live in. He was conscious of trying to earn more money for our future so he joined the newly formed Ulster Defence Regiment as a part-time member. After completing his day's work he would change into his uniform and go out on patrol along the Tyrone/Donegal border.

Many other young men like himself, from widely differing backgrounds, met up to carry out these patrols which they saw as a way of serving their country at a time when there was a very real threat to it and its people from the IRA.

In 1970 we set 14 September 1971 as our wedding date. We looked forward to this with great excitement but our excitement was soon to be overshadowed by a rumour that Kenneth's name was on a death threat list.

At first we thought someone was just trying to frighten us but Kenneth was aware of definite hostility and menacing attitudes toward him and his colleagues as they were carrying out their patrol duties in and around the Strabane/Clady area. He began to think more seriously about the threats and was careful not to take the same route to and from work each day.

Early 1971 was very restless and internment [imprisonment without trial] was finally introduced in August of that year. Within a very short time of internment being introduced, one of Kenneth's colleagues and a very good friend, Winston Donnell, was shot dead in an IRA gun attack on a UDR patrol near Clady. Kenneth should have been on that patrol but could not make it in time as he had been delayed at his construction job.

Suddenly the threats which we had tried to ignore became much more real and Kenneth realized that he was walking a tightrope between life and death.

Our wedding date was now only four weeks away and suddenly there was a great sense of urgency for us to get to the 14th of September. It seemed like being married would give us some protection, that we would have each other and that we would be safe.

Two weeks after the shooting incident Kenneth had to do some contracting work on a Sunday afternoon which meant that he took his Land Rover and left his car at home. Usually on a Sunday he and I would have been out in the car together.

That afternoon three armed men burst into Kenneth's house where he lived with his grandparents and held them at gunpoint. One man severed the telephone cable as another went to Kenneth's bedroom. Obviously the house had been watched and they had assumed that if his car was there then he must be too.

They were very agitated when they could not find him for it was their obvious intention to shoot him that day. It was a horrible and frightening experience for everyone involved and we all knew that Kenneth could not return to his home again. During the next two weeks running up to our wedding day he moved from one place to another, varying his route to work and hoping that this was all just a dreadful nightmare.

Our wedding day passed without incident. Naturally we were all nervous and worried. Kenneth carried his legally held revolver under his wedding suit. Fortunately he did not need to use it. We felt vulnerable since the date, time, and location of our wedding was well known. The church was less than half a mile from Clady.

We did not talk in any great depth about the situation in Ulster while we were on honeymoon. In fact, Kenneth seemed to block out the whole death threat issue. Perhaps that was the only way he could cope.

We returned from our honeymoon and the months of October and November passed quickly for us as we tried to settle into married life with all the new routines.

In early December another part-time member of the Ulster Defence Regiment was shot. The murder took place on a Monday and as the details became known on Tuesday we realized that he had been killed in his own house, in his bedroom, in an incident almost identical to the one which had taken place at Kenneth's house just two weeks before our wedding.

I knew then that Kenneth was very anxious and worried. That evening after we had eaten he said that we needed to talk. He spoke at length about the past year and the threats to his life. He told me of incidents which had been happening over the past few months—incidents which were geared to frighten him. He hadn't mentioned them before so that I would not be worried or afraid for him. If only he had known the fear I carried for him every day.

He said we had to acknowledge that his life was in great danger and sources had informed him that things were bleak. He said that "if the worst should happen" there were specific items belonging to him still in his grandparents' home that I was to have.

He spoke of his love for me and asked me to promise that if he was murdered that I would get married again. Many tears were shed that evening and that night we went to bed with a dreadful sense of foreboding surrounding us.

Wednesday passed without any further talk of what the days, weeks, or months might hold and on Thursday evening as I said my prayers I prayed that if Kenneth was to be killed that it would be quick and he would know nothing until it was all over.

On Friday morning, 10th December 1971, Kenneth was ambushed and shot dead going to his work. As he lay on the road, already shot several times in his right side, the gunman walked up to his body and fired three more shots into his face.

Kenneth had used the same route on two consecutive mornings and paid dearly for that mistake.

How?

They tell me now my dearest
That we all shall happy be
The killings are stopped
The bombs have ceased
We'll live in harmony. . . .
I think of you my dearest
And all the others too
Where can we lay your memories
Where can we set them by
Forgive, forget, go forward
They tell us we must try . . .
Try to forgive the murderer
Who coldly gunned you down

Who walked up to your body
And finished off his rounds
Into your face, your head, your cheek. . . .
Forgive, forget . . . but how?
Forgive, forget, go forward . . .
I do not think I can
For I know that I will never
Forgive that murdering man.

PART III

PIGS IN THE MIDDLE:
Bridges to Peace

The ball game called pig in the middle in Great Britain and Northern Ireland requires a player to stand in the middle of two other players and try to intercept a ball as they toss it back and forth over her or his head. If the ball is intercepted, the middle player wins and the player who failed to catch the ball assumes the middle position, that of the "pig."

Several writers who submitted work for this anthology used the term "pig in the middle" to describe their own position of being fully accepted by neither the Catholic nor the Protestant community in Northern Ireland. Of course, some degree of alienation from one tradition or the other is the rule in Northern Ireland: Catholics are not as likely to be accepted by Protestants as they are by Catholics and vice versa. But even more painful for these pigs in the middle is the fact that because they hold a more positive view of their neighbors across the sectarian divide than the majority of their community, they are shunned by members of their own religious tradition.

While it could be said that these people are turncoats who fail to see the oppression of their own community by the other, to the extent that these people are aware of the differences between the two traditions but are still willing to see the good in the other community, I believe they are Northern Ireland's greatest hope for peace. Such people, although paying a personal price for their convictions, are helping to bridge the sectarian divide in Northern Ireland on a grassroots level and, to my mind, their contribution to peace is as important as that of the political leaders who are conducting formal talks in an effort to construct a peace agreement. No agreement the politicians reach can bring a lasting peace to Northern Ireland unless courageous individuals from both traditions—"pigs in the middle"—are willing to risk becoming increasingly tolerant and accepting of those across the sectarian divide.

EAMON BYERS

PORTAFERRY, COUNTY DOWN

With a thick brown fringe across his forehead and a shiny round face that glows with an all-day smile, Eamon Byers looks much like any other happy eight-year-old boy. He is full of life, loves to play at the beach, and is very fond of his dog, who he told me is "a mongrel named Bruce." He is close to his two brothers, Christy and Niall, and very much the loving child of his mother, Nancy, a nurse, and his father, Kevin, a media consultant.

But far beyond what might be expected of an eight-year-old, Eamon spends hours and hours writing poetry and playing guitar and painting. He has written dozens of poems and stories, which he carefully preserves in his own special book. He reads and rereads his cherished volumes of Yeats's poetry, which he keeps in his room. Last year the family made a pilgrimage to Yeats's grave in Eamon's honor.

Eamon is so talented that he probably would be drawn to the arts no matter where he was raised or by whom. But the fact that his father, Kevin Byers (who wrote three stories in this anthology), is a writer who has encouraged Eamon every step of the way certainly can't help but add to his chances for a literary career. Eamon's poem "Hill of the Eagle" was published in a British anthology in 1994, when he was only seven. "I'd like to be a poet and an artist and a story writer when I grow up," he says.

Living in Portaferry at the southern tip of the Ards Peninsula, albeit fairly close to the major bombing two years ago in Newtown-ards, Eamon has not directly seen much violence. But it was brought home to him via television, where he says he saw the aftermath of many bombings and murders on the news. In this poem, written during the cease-fires (1994–1996), Eamon describes the changes that a temporary peace brought to Northern Ireland.

The Quiet Streets of Northern Ireland

(Written at age eight)

The terrorists who walked the streets
of Northern Ireland
have now all gone.
The screams and shouts of people
in pain
have now all gone.
The fear of being shot or bombed
at any time
is no more.
The war between good and evil
has ended
since the cease-fire.
Innocent people
have lost their lives
to the evil murderers and terrorists
in the past twenty-five years
of blood and pain in Northern Ireland.
But I am happy
and thankful that I am safe
in my warm protected house.

URSULA McSHANE

BELFAST

Now thirteen and a student at St. Louise's Comprehensive College in Belfast, Ursula McShane says that when she was younger she was afraid of Protestants. "I was afraid to go places in case I met Protestants and we got into a fight. I hated Protestants before I even knew them or even looked at them."

In this poem written when she was only eight years old, Ursula deftly puts Northern Ireland in the context of political strife around the world as she bids Catholic and Protestant religious leaders, as well as Saddam Hussein and George Bush, to take a more playful and cooperative approach to life.

Ursula's poem won second prize for her age group (eight to eleven) in the poetry competition of Women Together for Peace and was first published in their collection, *Poems for Peace,* in 1993.

Bouncing on the Bed

(Written at age eight)

Bouncing on the bed tumbling over
and over and falling off the edge,
Come on Nichola bounce with me.
Bouncing on the bed tumbling over
and over and falling off the edge,
Come on Mum and Dad bounce with me.
Bouncing on the bed tumbling over
and over and falling off the edge,
Come on priest bounce with me.
Bouncing on the bed tumbling over
and over and falling off the edge,
Come on minister bounce with me.
Bouncing on the bed tumbling over
and over and falling off the edge,
Come on Bush bounce with me.
Bouncing on the bed tumbling over
and over and falling off the edge,
Come on Saddam bounce with me.
Bouncing on the bed tumbling over
and over and falling off the edge.

RICHARD FALLIS

GLENGORMLEY, NEWTOWNABBEY, COUNTY ANTRIM

"**B**eing in the middle and having a feeling of alienation" is really what his autobiographical story is about, says sixteen-year-old Richard Fallis, a student at St. Malachy's College, a Catholic school in Belfast.

In his story, written especially for this anthology, Richard depicts the derision he has endured for not being anti-Protestant. Using a variety of techniques most often seen in fiction, he powerfully conveys the painful reality of being a pig in the middle.

Bussing It

(Written at age sixteen)

Pete and I saw the bus moving along the road before the others did, but as usual we were the last to go and get on. Had we moved, we would have been knocked down by the vast body of juniors which swamped the road within an instant of one of its parts spying the approaching vehicle. The youngsters dragged their overpacked bags along the asphalt after them as they ran to attack the bus before it had even begun to decelerate. They waved their passes and tickets wildly and cried out in a piercingly high pitch. They pushed and shoved each other against the doors, those at the front being squashed against the chipped Perspex [acrylic plastic] sheets by those behind who were screaming for the driver to hurry up and let them on.

I sighed from behind the sheltered bus stop, trying hard not to cough, while Pete stubbed out his fag on the back of the drunk who was standing to his left emptying his bladder over the wall behind the crowded bus stop, the same wall against which Pete and I were leaning, our right legs tucked in tight under our backsides, one or both of our hands plunged deep into our trouser pockets, our blazered backs pressed hard against the graffitied stone wall. The drunk was too caught up in the pleasure arising from his act of micturition to notice the stubbing of the fag, and Pete frowned.

"He's got the back of a Terminator," he remarked.

I smiled, not because I found the remark particularly funny, but because I was watching the antics of the squeaky-voiced juniors. There were no seniors here, apart from Pete and me. To my left, out of the corner of my eye, I saw Pete shoving the drunk away. "Aw, for God's sake go pee over someone else!" he screamed at the old guy. And then to me he said, "It's only Monday and that knob's [slang for penis] gone and sprayed me with—"

"Let's go," I said, cutting Pete short. I lifted my blue rag-bag [knapsack] and hooked the worn strap over my shoulder as Pete stopped drying his trousers with a bloodied tissue and made a brief examination of the patch of empty space which had formed around the bus door. Amazingly, the juniors were already on board and were busy fighting over those few seats which remained unoccupied, while the bus driver, glaring into his rear-view mirror, was bellowing the command which is as synonymous with Belfast's bus drivers as the phrase " 'Allo 'allo 'allo" is with English bobbies. "Move up the bus!" the driver was yelling to a shrill, profane chorus from the junior mob he was addressing. Meanwhile, back outside the bus, the platoon of "bloody-young-people"-muttering old people made their way towards the ascension ramp, having been pushed back by the black-uniformed multitude. I reckoned that when they all got on and had made some gullible wee girl and lad get up from their seats with the excuse that it was the duty of the youthful to give up their seats to their elders, there would be enough room for just two more people—i.e., Pete and I—to squeeze on, provided the driver was still in a good enough mood.

Unfortunately for us, he wasn't. In fact it turned out not to be a "he" at all. It was a "she," and a very large "she" at that. "Sorry, lads," she said in an accent which was a cross between that of your average West Belfast dweller and the raucous Swedish tone of Greta Garbo. "No more room."

"No more room my hole," Pete said, trying desperately to push his near-done concession ticket into the driver's hand.

"Just get off the bus, lad," the driver said, her voice quiet but malevolent, her hand refusing to close around Pete's ticket.

"Aw for fu—"

"Let's just get off, Pete," I said quickly, and off I got, pulling Pete along behind me, trying to shut my ears to the verbal abuse Pete was hurling at the driver, who simply gave Pete the finger, shut the doors, and slammed her foot down upon the accelerator to the joy of those drivers stuck on the road behind her.

"That bus was never full," Pete said.

"Och, sure another one'll be along shortly and I bet you we'll end up overtaking that one anyway," I said. "Now come on. There's room for us under the shelter now."

"Aye. So there is."

The two of us moved away from the curb and went under the empty shelter, which was marked "Bus Stop: Citybus and Ulsterbus." We put down our bags and fell back hard against the sheet of reinforced glass which formed one of the shelter's two walls. We adopted our habitual slouching stance, bending our right legs double, bringing our right feet up tight under our backsides once again. Pete pulled his lighter and a fag from his inside blazer pocket and I screwed up my face in disgust.

"How many of those things can you smoke in five minutes?" I asked.

"Look, stop your whinging," Pete said, lighting the appropriate end of the fag and placing the unlit end to his lips. His chest swelled as he inhaled the smoke. "If you don't like it," Pete went on, "why don't you just go off round the back—" from behind the shelter came a sound which could best be described as "bloik"—"and swim in that wino's puke?"

"Just don't breathe it over me," I said. The warm wind swirled round my face and so did the gaseous muck Pete had breathed out. I gave up and tried to breathe normally as best I could.

Then, after a while, another bus came along the road. Purring along in front of it, like a Special Weapon Dalek [an alien machine/organism seen in a BBC science fiction television series], was a grey, armour-plated police van. As I lifted my bag and searched for my pass, which I'd forgotten I'd slipped into one of my blazer pockets, I tried to shut my ears to what I knew would soon be coming from Pete's blackened larynx.

"HUNS GO HOME!" Pete bellowed as the police van rolled past. His words were partially drowned out by the sound of the bus screeching to a halt. There was a flatulent hiss as the doors opened to let me and an unrepentant Pete on board.

"I wish to God you wouldn't do that," I said after we had both dumped our bags in the buggy pen [luggage rack] and headed to the back of the bus, the two of us falling down into the only empty double seat, all the others being occupied by the usual, discreetly rowdy assortment of out-of-school teenagers and plain-clothed young people.

"You wish I wouldn't do what?" Pete said, looking genuinely

puzzled as he shifted from left to right in the seat, trying to make himself comfortable.

"I wish you wouldn't shout stuff like that," I said, watching the scenery start to change as the bus moved off.

"Like *what?*"

"God, it's like it's a reflex action with you! You see a Peeler [police] van and you automatically scream at it. You don't think about what you're doing at all!"

"It's not my fault I can't warm up to Prod [Protestant] Huns!"

"Oh stop being so sad!" I snapped.

"No, you stop being so sad!" Pete snapped back, glaring intensely at me. "The way you get on it's like you're a Hun-lover or something. My mates would go *through* me if they knew I let you hang around with me. You're a Taig [slang for Catholic], for God's sake. Taigs hate Huns. Taigs hate the Brits. That's the way it's always been. So why don't *you* do the wising up and leave me be, okay?"

I paid no heed to this. I sat in silence for about a minute, staring out the window, first at the sky, then at the passing buildings, people, and vehicles, ignoring the quizzical looks the two of us were getting from our fellow passengers thanks to Pete's rather sonorous outburst. The sky was altogether unobscured. There were only two substantial clouds. One of them was large and grey and heavy with rain. The other was just as large but altogether whiter and less baleful looking. The two clouds were coming together to form one restless expanse of grey, the separate components of the two of them not seeming to mix very well. If anything it seemed like the two of them wanted to get away from each other as quickly as possible.

I imagined I had eyes in the back of my head and that I could see St. Jude's Grammar [Catholic high school] disappearing from view as the bus put more and more tarmac between itself and the bus stop beside the school gates. I saw a pigeon being squashed by a car going the other way. The driver only had to swerve slightly to avoid it but instead he had willingly transformed the bird from a daft-looking, mobile lump of grey and white fluff into a daft-looking, squat glob of red gloop and white tufty bits. I laughed. I thought I saw flecks of the pigeon's blood shoot into the car cabin through the open windows, the blood landing on the driver's beard and splattering all over his glasses.

"And anyway," I said, watching an Irish Waste lorry [garbage truck] trundle over the goo which had been the pigeon, "the Peelers are home. You only shout 'Go home' at the Brits. That is, if you're going to shout anything at them at all."

"Aw, Brits, Peelers—they're all the same. Scum the lot of them. They should all be sent back to Britain and the whole of Britain should be blown up, Peelers and all."

I smiled. "Oh? Would that be with or without Oasis [British band]? Don't you like Oasis?"

"Aw, shut up," Pete said, after a moment's hesitation.

"And what about Eternal [British band]? Well, maybe you don't like their music, but you do fancy *them*, don't you?"

"Sure, okay."

The bus came to a halt at another bus stop. After a pair of girls from our school had got on and flashed their bus passes at the driver, the bus started moving again, and it was soon trundling along the road in its usual way.

I sighed. Pete watched the girls select a double seat about halfway up the bus. He was trying to give the nicest of the two of them "the eye," whatever that was, but she didn't look up the bus at all. Then he tried his luck with the other one but he had no success there either.

"Bugger that one," he said.

"Do you know them?" I asked.

"No. They look like third-year students and I don't know any third-years. I'd *like* to know them, though. Hey, we could have one each."

"I thought you and Paula were still together," I said.

"Sure you know we aren't. I told . . . Oh, maybe I didn't tell you. You must be the only one I haven't said anything to." Pete leaned a bit closer to me and I tried not to choke on the smell of tobacco smoke. "You see I found out the other night she's a flipping *Hun!*" Pete said, his voice becoming slightly more hushed than before.

"She is?" In spite of myself, I was a bit surprised by this. "I thought she went to East Tower."

"She *does,* but they've made the place multidenominational or something."

"I didn't know that. Since when?"

"Dee says it's been like that since September."

"Seriously?"

"Yeah," Pete said. "Well, anyway, like I said it was Dee who told me. He says to me, he says, 'She's a ride [good time] and all that but do you know what school she goes to?' and I say sure I do, she goes to East Tower and Dee says, 'Yeah she does but that place is integrated,' and I says sure it is, they take in both blokes and wee girls and he says, 'Not like *that*—it's integrated the *other* way,' and I tell him to catch himself on that, Paula can't be a Hun because she doesn't mind when I slag off [insult] Paisley [Ian Paisley, ultraconservative Protestant politician] and all them ones but Dee says that she's a neutralist or something, I don't know, and he says he seen her going into that dump of a Hun church down on Stockman Road with her ma and da last Sunday and I says I don't believe you so I go and ask Paula and she says, yeah, she's a Prod and she says she thought I knew! I mean, can you believe it? For a month I was out drinking and snogging [kissing and cuddling] with a Hun! Not that she did any drinking, mind you, which was a bit of a pain. Well I told her to shag off there and then, and then I went home to wash my mouth out because just before Dee had come on the scene I'd had my tongue halfway down her throat!"

"This must only be her first year at East Tower."

"Yeah. I mean I knew she'd only just moved here, but I

didn't know she was a Hun. Right enough I never seen her going to Mass but I just thought she was an atheist or something. Now that I wouldn't have minded at all. But God, it was awful. I felt sick for ages."

"I'm sure you did," I said. "I did read somewhere that Hun gob [spit] is particularly toxic if Taigs drink it in huge amounts."

"You wouldn't be taking the mickey out of me [teasing me], would you?"

" 'Course not," I said.

"Just as well. I've had enough stick [criticism] from you today."

"Sure you have. I'll leave you be," I said and I went back to looking out the window.

So Paula O'Brien was a Protestant. I knew her pretty well, and I did stop and chat with her if we met in the street, but I hadn't known she was a Protestant. This didn't particularly bother me, however, since she was, it seemed, a neutralist, and I liked neutralists, be they Catholic or non-Catholic, unlike Pete, who liked only Catholics and who was perhaps *the* teenaged human embodiment of the word "sectarian."

I sighed. I'd been sighing a lot lately. My Mum had been complaining about it. She said it gave the impression to those around me that they were boring me and that I should stop it as a matter of courtesy. I was a bit sick of courtesy. I sighed again, just to convince myself that this was the case.

The bus was drawing near Pete's stop. Soon I'd be alone. I was glad of that. Pete expressed his own gladness that he was departing. "I sort of hope I don't see you tomorrow," he said, getting up. "You've been a bit of a pain today."

I shrugged.

"And anyway," Pete said, "I only fancy the white one, but then not in the same way that I do, say, Pamela Anderson [Canadian/American actress who sometimes appears in television shows like *Baywatch* and *Home Improvement*].

"Hmmm?"

"You know, Louise [Louise Nordling] from Eternal?"

"Oh, right. I see."

"Right. Well, see you." And off Pete stalked up the length of the bus, dinging one of the bells as he went, almost forgetting to lift his tatty bag from the buggy pen. The bus came to a halt after the driver had pinpointed the bus stop. The doors swung open and Pete hopped off. As the bus moved off again and trundled past Pete, out of the corner of my eye I saw Pete turn and try to make eye contact with one or both of the girls he liked the look of. He did not succeed, however, and he said the F-word very loudly, so loud, in fact, that I and everyone else on the bus heard him over the sickly rumbling of the bus engine.

I rolled my eyes and looked briefly up at the sky as some of the older passengers *tut-tutted* to themselves or to their partners. The two clouds had separated and were each going their own way, the grey one tagging along with the bus, it seemed, which was probably a trick of parallax. The textbook definition of parallax briefly came to the front of my mind, but I pushed it forcefully to the back of my head. I was too tired for a technical dissection of the passing world. I just wanted to sit and observe until it was time for me to get off, which would be soon enough.

Since I was on my own now, I instinctively felt very exposed and weak. I knew it was silly, but I felt I had to get a good look at the people around me, just to make sure no one particularly sinister or sectarian-looking was sitting near me. Pretending to be watching something on the pavement outside the bus, I turned my head through as close to a straight angle as I could manage. Then I twisted my neck and brought my head back to its original position as quickly as possible. I was safe enough. Almost everyone around me was wearing the uniform of a Catholic school, and you seldom got serious stick from someone of your own religion. There were two people, a boy and a girl, wearing the uniform of some Protestant grammar school [high school], the name of which I knew but couldn't remember. But they looked too sophisticated and, indeed, too absorbed in the contours of one another's faces to bother with me. Yes, I was safe enough here, where I was sitting.

But what about when I got off the bus? I was at risk of being attacked then. There was a particularly rough non-Catholic school close to where I lived and some of the lads from it sometimes gathered at the bus-stop and hassled just about anyone who walked past. But they were especially keen on making life difficult for passing Catholics. I had been abused verbally once or twice before, which I could tolerate, but some people didn't get off so lightly. Beatings did occur from time to time, though usually only in winter when daytime was short and the mob could seek refuge from the Law in the early darkness. And then sometimes a rival Catholic gang would assemble on the other side of the road and you occasionally got caught in the crossfire between the two masses, though only verbal missiles were thrown most of the time, neither side having the guts to get involved in a serious conflict.

I always checked before I got off to see what the bus-stop I wanted to alight at was like. If it was populated by a particularly rough-looking crowd I sometimes waited and got off at the next stop, which was rarely the scene of mob battles but which was a good deal further away from my house. But more often than not the handier of the two bus-stops was free of trouble and I could get off without having to worry about the slaggings [insults] or the kickings or whatever.

The bus drove past St. Columba's Church, the church where my family and I attended Mass most Sunday mornings or Saturday evenings. A few of the old women at the head of the bus blessed themselves without actually looking at the Church, but I did look and I saw that the words "Irish Out Now!" had been sprayed in black paint over the church door, which had only recently been painted pillar-box [public mailbox] red. I surveyed the church's elaborate stained-glass windows. Usually, such graffiti attacks were accompanied by the casual flinging of a brick through one or all of the windows, but this time that had not happened. The windows were all still intact. Instead the vandals had climbed up onto the church's flat roof and kicked over the ringed cross which rose up from the tiled surface. I couldn't help but smile, even though I didn't find any of what I saw particularly funny. Perhaps it was the small-minded stupidity of it all which amused me. I didn't know for certain. But certainly many of my fellow passengers would have been deeply offended had they seen me smirking so openly.

St. Columba's was soon left behind and the bus started to make its way through the mixed suburbs. In five minutes I would be getting off. Time had flown. I felt as if I had only just settled down in my seat. I wasn't ready for getting off. I just wanted to sit here, in this blissful state of solitude and oblivion. All I could look forward to if I got off was, perhaps, a fist or two in the face and, most definitely, a huge number of RE [religious education] scripture questions to do for the next day's class. Yes, to go home and do *that* homework was really worth risking getting my head kicked in over.

I sighed and rummaged about in my inside blazer pocket, looking to see if I could find something interesting to fiddle with for the next few minutes. There was nothing there with a high fiddleability rating, so I pulled out my homework diary and gazed intently at the satellite photograph of planet Earth I had stuck there with cellotape and which I had ripped out of a geography textbook the other day when the teacher had been sitting sleeping at his desk. It was a beautiful photograph. Since the textbook was a British one, the British Isles were at the centre of the photograph, and the more I looked at the photograph, the more I became aware of Ireland's tininess. And that only emphasised my own lack of substantiality in comparison to the whole planet and, indeed, the whole Universe. I raised my eyes and looked at the people who sat around me. Forty-odd people—all walking insubstantialities—some in all likelihood thinking they were better than those around them, blind to the fact that they didn't matter, that they were really all the same. I looked back at the photograph and at the tiny blotch of green which was Northern Ireland and I thought, *it just doesn't matter, does it?*

The entrance of the local park caught my eye and I pocketed my homework diary. I was almost home.

There was a particularly awkward crossroads ahead. I looked out the window and saw that two drivers were locked in combat. They were in opposing lanes. The driver of a blue Cavalier on the same side of the road as our bus was wanting to turn off the main road onto the road running away from the main road on the same side as the bus, while the driver of a red Cavalier on the other side of the road was wanting to turn off the main road onto the road running away from the main road on the same side as the bus. Both cars were blocking each other and neither driver could go where he wanted and this seemed to annoy the two of them immensely. The obvious solution to the problem was for one of them to reverse and let the other one pass but the two of them were too determined to go exactly where they wanted to think of doing that.

And as the two drivers quarrelled in the middle of the road, the rest of the traffic, with horns tooting and engines revving, tried to squeeze past the two Cavaliers and be on their way. The bus found this a little more difficult than its fellow vehicles but get past the obstruction it did and soon it was back to trundling along the road, drawing steadily nearer to my stop.

Two minutes after passing the slight jam at the crossroads, I moved over in my seat to look up the aisle and out the front window in order to check what state the bus-stop was in. I was relieved to see it was devoid of human life. *I had made it.* I went to lift my bag from the buggy pen.

"Next stop please," I said when I came to stand beside the

driver who was sitting in his protective plastic bubble. He stopped where I wanted and the doors opened.

"Thanks," I said and I hopped off.

"Right, son," the driver mumbled, watching to see that my feet were clear of the doors before he closed them.

I came down too hard on my right foot and I felt a sharp pain shoot up my leg. I had to stop for a moment until the pain passed and, as I stood rubbing my leg, I watched the bus go past me along the road. Involuntarily my eyes were drawn to the part of the bus where the third-year girls were sitting and to my surprise I saw that the nicest looking of the pair had turned in her seat and was staring straight at me. I quickly forgot about the pain in my leg and concentrated on the girl.

Her eyes were big and wide and blue and they were looking fixedly into mine. I was aware only of her eyes and a certain glint in them told me she wasn't looking at me because she was in any way freakish—that her attention was not directed towards a horrible, huge, pus-packed spot which had suddenly developed somewhere on my face. She was looking at me for another reason. That was clear. And that reason was . . .

My line of vision was broken by the movement of the accelerating bus and, before I could lock onto the girl's eyes again, my own eyes had drifted and settled on the girl's hands which she had clutched clenched against her chest. I saw her bring one of her hands up to her face. I saw her extend the hand's index and middle fingers, each finger blocking from view a luscious eye. I felt the blood rushing into my ears and cheeks and I felt my forehead furrow into a frown. The girl's V-sign [an obscene gesture] stayed constant and I now saw a malicious grin forming on the girl's face. And now her friend was turned round, laughing at me. Everyone on the bus was laughing at me. Even the bus itself was chortling away; the roar of its engine now seemed to resemble a rubble of rowdy, drunken laughter. And I felt my hand going to my inside blazer pocket and from the pocket I pulled a gun. And from the gun I shot a bullet. The bullet exploded through the window behind which the girl was sitting. It slammed bloodily into the girl's forehead. It burst out of the back of the girl's head. It raced through the air between the girl and the driver. It hit the driver's body, and the corpse which resulted slumped over the vast steering wheel, causing the wheel to turn to the left. The bus careened out of control, going up onto the footpath. The passengers screamed pathetically as it smashed into a wall which ran parallel to the road. The bus continued to roll along, scraping its left side against the wall. It eventually came to rest and, when it did, it exploded. I saw the dying passengers writhing and groaning in the heat and I saw the flames which consumed them shooting upwards to lick the sky. Each flame rose like a finger of the Red Hand of Ulster [Protestant symbol] and as I watched I saw the crimson digits arrange themselves into V's to fly away like a gaggle of geese.

And then I came back to reality. I became painfully aware that I was standing in isolation on the pavement. I saw the bus, now in the distance, and through the glass in its side I thought I saw the third-year girls, alive and well and hugging each other as they laughed hysterically. And I noticed a pain was still lingering within me, though not specifically in my leg and certainly not an irksome physical pain. It ran much deeper than that. It filled my limbs, my head, and my torso, plaguing each and every organ in my body, but in particular my heart. I felt my eyes becoming bloodshot and I felt my fists clench and my toes curl in the confined space of my shoes. I was halfway to screaming a primordial cry of intense, burning, indescribable anguish and frustration when someone came up softly behind me, touched me gently on the shoulder and asked, "Are you all right?"

It took me a while to actually realise someone was speaking to me.

"Are you all right?"

I turned slowly and found myself staring into another pair of big, wide, blue eyes. I was initially repulsed but when I really looked I saw that the blue of the eyes was tinged with a hint of genuine concern. Then I moved my eyes to take in the whole of the person's face and I was comforted when it turned out to be a familiar enough sight to me.

"Oh, I'm—I'm fine," I said eventually. "I was just a bit—a bit . . ."

Paula cocked both her eyebrows, as if to say, "A bit what?"

"Yes, well," I said, lifting my bag which had slipped off my shoulder without my noticing. "I, eh, haven't seen you about for a bit."

"No, I haven't been out all that much," Paula said. "Peter dumped me, you see. I really thought we had something going. Anyway, I haven't really felt in the mood for socialising since. I go to school, come home and stay in. I'm on my way home now."

"So am I. I heard about you and Pete. He only told me today."

"Oh. You and him are pretty good mates, aren't you?"

I hesitated. "Ye-es," I said. But then, "We-ell . . ." Again I sidled awkwardly into silence.

"You really don't look or sound a hundred percent. Are you sure you're okay?"

The lovely, warm look of concern was back.

"Yes, I'm sure. It's just been a bugger of a day at school, that's all. You know, between teachers' nagging and homework and all. The usual. I just want to go home and relax a bit before I get started on the homework."

"Oh, I see. Well, I can, eh, walk with you if you want. I'm going that way anyway."

I smiled. "Sure," I said. "Okay."

And off we walked, chatting away, with me feeling totally at ease since I knew that whatever I said, my words would be heard and analysed and respected. I no longer felt it necessary to escape by looking up at the sky and watching the clouds, so I did not notice when the cloud which had followed the path of the bus came together with another, identical, ominous-looking rain cloud, forming one turbulent, billowing mass which presently began to water the Earth.

FIVE STUDENTS FROM ST. BRIDGETT'S PRIMARY SCHOOL

CROSSMAGLEN, COUNTY ARMAGH

Front row (left to right): Edel McArdle, Carol Rowland
Back row (left to right): Paul Murphy, Michelle MaGuire, Rosemarie Daly

For its size, Crossmaglen has known more violence than any other town in Northern Ireland. Situated very close to the border with the

Republic of Ireland, it has served as a hideout and ammunition depot for the Irish Republican Army. In fact, the Republican cause is so highly regarded in Crossmaglen that there is a monument to the IRA in the town square.

Sitting high above the town on a winding country road is St. Bridgett's, a modern brick primary school for the town's Catholic children. As was not the case in many of the schools that I visited, the Troubles are openly discussed at St. Bridgett's and the children are invited to write about what they've experienced.

The following five letters to Prime Minister John Major were written as a class assignment. The poem by two of the letter writers, Carol Rowland and Michelle MaGuire, was written especially for this book and handed to me personally by the girls when I visited the school in September 1995.

Letters to the Prime Minister

(Written at age ten)

Dear Sir,

I live around the Crossmaglen area and I am ten years old. I remember a Saturday night when I was at Crossmaglen mass. It was half past eight and I said to Mammy, "Is it nearly? . . ." As soon as she said "no" a bomb went off. The lights went out.

All the girls in the gallery started to cry. When I came out of mass I saw fire brigades and ambulances everywhere. I will never forget that incident.

I want to thank everybody that has made peace in Northern Ireland.

Paul Murphy

(Written at age eleven)

Dear Sir:

I am eleven years old and I live in South Armagh. I remember one night when I was at mass in Crossmaglen and a bomb went off. It was in the middle of mass when suddenly the lights went out. They were out for a couple of seconds when there was a loud bang. Children started crying and people started crying as well. We found out on the news that night that it was a bomb.

I was very scared that night and I will never forget it.

Yours sincerely,
Rosemarie Daly

(Written at age ten)

Dear Sir,

When the Troubles were on here in Ireland you would never see any police or soldiers walking around the streets without guns in their hands. But now that there is peace, police and soldiers can go about their business without being worried about being shot. I hope the cease-fire holds out as it is great to be able to go and get on with our lives.

Yours sincerely,
Carol Rowland

(Written at age eleven)

Dear Sir,

I have lived in the Bronx in New York City for the past nine years. I am now living in Crossmaglen. My name is Michelle

MaGuire. I am living in South Armagh nine months now. The change is unbelievable.

In New York it was a very busy place. Here in Ireland it's peaceful and safer on the roads than New York City. I have heard about the Troubles of the Irish Army and the British Army but now thankfully the Troubles have ended for a while.

Yours Sincerely,
Michelle MaGuire

(Written at age eleven)

Dear Prime Minister:

My name is Edel McArdle. I am writing to you on behalf of the people of Northern Ireland, the Republic, and the people of England who want peace in our time. Peace to love, peace to grow . . .

Peace to love my family and neighbours and hopefully grow up to make new friends. Peace to grow up with a new generation of young people who don't hate their neighbours but love and respect them. Peace in my country without being afraid that I have stepped over a border line I don't know. Finally peace to know my neighbours and people of different faiths and religions without fear.

Please, Mr. Major, give peace a chance.

Yours hopefully,
Edel McArdle

Troubles

(Written by Michelle MaGuire, age eleven, and Carol Rowland, age ten)

Over the years since the troubles began
Bombs and explosives scared every woman, child, and man
Parents afraid to let children roam
In case the children didn't return home.

People were so scared in the past
But now there is a cease-fire we hope will last.
A lot of people have suffered such pain
But now we can start all over again.

CATHERINE O'NEILL

BELFAST

I visited with thirteen-year-old Catherine O'Neill in the library of Rathmore Grammar School in Belfast, where she is a student. As Miss O'Reilly, Catherine's teacher who had told her about this anthology, made tea for us and a photographer snapped our pictures for the school newsletter, Catherine and I talked about the impact of the Troubles.

"The Troubles were always part of your life," Catherine said. "Although you may not have known someone directly who was killed or injured, it was always in the background." The thing that has struck her most about the Troubles is the "waste of all the lives . . . especially all the young children who happened just to be in the wrong place at the wrong time."

The cease-fires (1994 to 1996) made a definite difference in Catherine's young life. For the first time, she was allowed to go to the cinema or shopping in downtown Belfast unsupervised. "It's just brilliant!" she said. And, she told me, one of her aunts who lives in Dublin and who would never risk coming to Northern Ireland finally visited Catherine's family in Belfast during the cease-fires.

If You Didn't Laugh You'd Cry

(Written at age thirteen)

"There's a bomb in the cabbages!"
  is the cry
Startling people
  walking by.

Everyone panics.
  Police arrive.
They say, "Don't worry
  we're all still alive."

However, the search
  reveals nothing at all.
It's back to normal
  but soon comes the call,
"There's a bomb in the cabbages!
  That chap was right.
What a thing to happen.
  And in broad daylight!"
Pandemonium reigns,
  the police come again
and seal off the area.
  It's all quiet when . . .

. . . the bomb goes off
  gives everyone a fright
and soon shreds of cabbage
  are all that's in sight.

This story I heard
   from an aunt who was there
on the infamous day
   of the "cabbage bomb" scare.

Now, twenty years later
   after years of such fear
true, lasting peace
   is finally here.

                              We hope.

SHARON INGRAM

GOTHENBURG, SWEDEN

Sharon Ingram, the second of four children, grew up in the town of Ballygawley, County Tyrone, where her father was a Church of Ireland minister and her mother was a justice of the peace. She was ten years old when the Troubles began in 1968, and from then on, she says, "there was always the worry about what might happen."

Sharon and her classmates at Dungannon High School for Girls avoided certain streets for fear of bombs and walked well away from parked cars for the same reason. When areas were cordoned off she remembers lying on the ground and covering her head. "The worst was feeling that sickly suspense before the bomb exploded," she says, "the unspeakable thud . . . and the worry about who might have been hurt or killed."

Although the Ballygawley area was certainly no stranger to the Troubles, Sharon says that Catholics and Protestants got on better together there perhaps than in some other areas: "It was not the sectarian divide which disrupted *our* area—people were too kind for that—it was the IRA," she says.

"For me by far the worst event of all the Troubles," Sharon says, "was a certain news report on TV showing the aftermath of an IRA bomb . . . Belfast people having to put bits of loved ones' bodies into plastic bags. To this day I am haunted by it. . . ."

While certainly the Troubles impacted Sharon's growing up, as she shows in her story, she thinks it very important not to convey the idea that the Troubles were all that was happening in Northern Ireland after 1968. "It was not just blood and tragedy," as some of the writers of the time would seem to be indicating. "I was particularly upset," she says, "that the greatest landscape poet of them all—Seamus Heaney—turned his back on the depiction of purely rural scenes in favour of more obviously political poetry."

Although events in the following story occurred as Sharon describes them, she has chosen not to use the real name of the poet who visited her school and around whom the story centers in order to make it clear that she had a problem with all the poets in Northern Ireland who turned from pastoral to political writing, not just one in particular. "McSweeney," therefore, is a fictional, generic name for a number of such poets and Sharon, herself, has written "his" poetry.

Sharon has been writing since she was seven years old. As she grew older, she focused on playwriting and short story writing. "My one small ambition," she says, "is to be able to produce at least ten good short stories. Maybe it's my own private attempt to offer an alternative to the 'blood' poetry that was so prevalent in Ulster throughout the seventies and eighties."

Sharon says she also writes to stay in touch with Ulster and her mother tongue. She has lived in Gothenburg, Sweden, since she married a Swede, her pen pal of five years, in 1986.

McSweeney Astray?

There is an alarming tendency among some of my friends to look on happiness as the ultimate goal in life and yet to ridicule those who have actually reached that goal. It is as though, by definition, it must forever remain beyond one's grasp. "How dare they be happy," mutter my friends. "No one has any right to be happy at the present time."

I have noticed this particularly in the domain of school where intellectual or artistic brilliance (surely an expression of happiness?) is more often than not condemned. The strength of such a mentality and how it can influence even the most steadfast admirers of our island life was brought home to me recently in a school seminar on Ulster poetry. My English teacher, Mr. Craig, had invited Shay McSweeney to come and give a reading of his latest creations. Oh, how I looked forward to meeting him, hearing him read, absorbing those cameos of Ulster life which are so dear to me—the sound of blackbirds after April rain, visions of primroses on mossy banks in Tyrone, and the pungency of turf [peat] fires all along the Findrum Valley. McSweeney's poetry had always delighted me. Remarkably, he had even managed to make a name for himself on the international market, sold twenty thousand copies of his first collection in six months, and been short-listed for the Nobel Prize.

Shay McSweeney was a feast to be relished by all so, for weeks before his arrival at our school, I would take pages of his poetry out to the field above our house and listen as they became one with my immediate surroundings. Granted, he said very little about city life, about conflicts, or squalour, or bomb throwing. But did this matter when he still managed to capture so much of what to me was reality? He might have disappointed the media but he was constantly touching the depths of my soul. He portrayed not the terrorist or bloodshed but the local man, the countryman, the farmer, the fisherman, the turf-cutter. He was *mine*.

> "When I awake
> it is dawn in the Findrum Valley and
> twilight in the Sperrins . . .
> And the long lazy sunshafts give to
> lines of wandering cattle
> that exhilarating sense of being

three-dimensional
which rarely exists elsewhere,
be it on the Plains of Picardy or in the
forests of Denmark
where terrain and illumination combine to contrive
flatness,
flatness of vision, flatness of mind and
flatness of aspiration.
Dwelling here in this country is like being
part of a pop-up storybook.
Hardship gnaws the soul
but we are eternally the landscape.
Here are our shades of green."
            —"Entre'acte Verte," by Shay McSweeney

My teacher decided that, although Shay McSweeney was
very famous, we would meet him in as comfortable surroundings as possible. Consequently, he arranged easy chairs for
himself and McSweeney not in the big assembly hall but in one
of our sunny classrooms.

I arrived about half an hour early. Some of my classmates
thought that I was obsessed. "Really!" they said. "There's no
need to be so obvious about your infatuation. We all know he's
a great poet but there's no need to keep on proclaiming it from
the rooftops. It's enough that he gets his perpetual interviews
on television."

But I did not care. For me, this was a once-in-a-lifetime
event. I was not only going to meet one of Ulster's most famous
poets but at a time when I needed him most. My classmates
had been jeering at me a great deal lately. The town girls, especially, had found my own attempts at poetry naive, and even
my comments on the political situation were considered short-
sighted, idealistic, out of touch. "Nonsense!" they said. "It's not
that great to live here—a hellhole if you ask us. No opportuni-

ties for teenagers and, with parents on the booze, it's getting
worse."

So, for me, meeting Shay McSweeney was to be like a public pat on the back for my attachment to the more positive aspects of life in Ulster. I waited patiently in the classroom whilst
Mr. Craig arranged the chairs. He had left some of the windows open so now and again spring air shunted into the room
and I could hear the subdued *biff baff* of a tennis match under-
way on the courts below.

As I waited, I mulled over a myriad of lines which I looked
forward to hearing the great man recite in front of everybody
. . . and for my sake.

Gradually the room filled up. All forty sixth-formers had
been invited plus a couple of enthusiastic "O" levelers, and
Mrs. Jackson, the art teacher, who had a particular partiality
for the visual aspects of Shay McSweeney's poetry and was
even writing a paper on the subject.

At precisely ten to three Shay McSweeney arrived in the
school courtyard in a bright and glossy new BMW, probably
earned from his recent successful stay at Yale. The car was sophisticated but he himself looked less refined—the same old
tweed jacket we had grown to associate with him, the tousled
white hair and gently hooded eyes.

Within minutes he was in our room being introduced by
Mr. Craig and the seminar began.

"I realise," he said, "some of you may have come here today
hoping to hear me recite some of my earlier poetry. It is poetry
which depicts our traditional way of life in the Ulster countryside—farming, turf-cutting, the warm handshake, the intimate
landscape—a life which I value very much and which, thankfully, still goes on. Sadly, however, I don't think I can afford to
confine myself to these rural scenes any longer.

"My recent sabbatical in North America has at long last
convinced me that the present strife is really much more important as subject matter. As an artist, I feel a tremendous obli-

gation to try and make sense of what has been happening to us. If I ignore it I think ultimately I do us all an injustice. After all, we have now lived with the agony for nearly ten years and there is no sign of it finishing for maybe even another ten years. I turn to it with great reluctance because it makes such horrendous material. But it is unavoidable. There is no point in going around with our heads in the clouds. So bear with me. Listen to some of my new poems. They are full of regret but, I hope, as true for you as they are to me."

The town girls drew their breath. I was shell-shocked. Were all my hopes to be confounded in one short speech? How could I continue to sit here in front of everybody even another minute? I felt sick and my ear lobes were suddenly very hot. I ought to have guessed that something was brewing when, to my surprise, Mr. Craig had not asked us to read Shay McSweeney in the weeks leading up to this meeting.

What followed was the outpouring of a woeful tale. If I heard it at all (for I could hardly bear to listen) it was about horror, blood, terror, the bomb, the lethal road, the darkening cloud, and, as far as I was concerned, the rejection of anything called hope.

Gone were my visions of springtime, clear weather, and the enjoyment of our rural communities. Gone was that miraculous perspective he had once given me. Gone was the one man who might have been able to verbalise my sensations of delight in autumn on Knockmanny Hill where the roe deer leapt and the gold and orange seemed to last longer than it did anywhere else. And gone was my exhilaration in the (oh so genuine) greenness and dampness of moss and dripping ferns on the floor of Altadavin. Above all, gone was the one true link with myself and my past—Ulster *before* 1968, 1921, 1916, *before* the Famine, *before* the Gaelic Celts and the Brittonic Celts. Ulster as the land, the soil, the scattered shower, the sunny spell, without any nuclear waste, without pollution; untouched, verdant, primeval. It was as though he had suddenly joined the other poets. Was it a case of not wanting to feel left out?

In the late afternoon sunshine I could hear tennis balls *biff baffing* back and forth as if the players down on the court had started an argument. "McSweeney astray?" I wondered. "Do you really find innocence and hope naive? Do you really prefer shades of red to shades of green?"

Meanwhile, the wide-eyed, identical town girls sat in their corners and smirked.

KIMLOUISE McCLEAN

BELFAST

Kimlouise McClean's Scottish father was serving with the Army in
Northern Ireland when he met her
mother. They married in 1977 and
Kimlouise was born in 1980, the
eldest of four children. She began
her schooling in Scotland but the
family later returned to Northern
Ireland.

Kimlouise says that her childhood was not much affected by
the Troubles except that "it was
difficult to understand why there
were certain areas we couldn't go
into or even pass by." As is true
for many children in Northern Ire-
land, some of the worst of what she has experienced of the Troubles
has been via television. "The most horrific event was sitting watching TV and seeing news footage of two soldiers being surrounded
by a huge mob and pulled out of their car and beaten and killed."
Several other writers for this anthology witnessed this live coverage
of two brutal murders and, like Kimlouise, they say they will never
forget it.

Kimlouise started writing poems when she was six, a response to
her father's reading poems to her instead of bedtime stories. This
poem was written in 1990 and was subsequently printed in *Poems
for Peace,* a Belfast anthology published by Women Together for
Peace.

Birds Flying Gracefully Through the Air

(Written at age ten)

Birds flying gracefully through the air,
Snow falling softly into my hair,
Children laughing having fun,
At the beach feeling the heat of the sun.
The dog with no tail chasing the cat,
The old ladies at the corner having a chat,
Girls getting dressed up, boyfriends to meet,
Flowers in the garden smelling so sweet.
Clouds in the sky so silvery white,
Stars in the night shining so bright,
Corn in the meadow swaying to and fro,
In the middle stands Mr. Scarecrow.
So far remembered are my thoughts this day,
To what's happening at home and so far away.
I hope it will end soon, for I feel so sad,
For all of the children who are missing their dads.

JOHN McDOWELL

Recently ordained a deacon in the Church of Ireland [a Protestant denomination], forty-one-year-old Belfast-born John Mc-Dowell sees cooperation across the sectarian divide as a very important goal for the churches of Northern Ireland. As he dramatically depicts in his story, even in his teens John had the utmost respect and admiration for the Catholic people of his country. "I was very taken by the fact that the Catholic community is an extremely coherent community," he says. "Protestantism by and large tends to divide . . . to separate sheep from goats."

I met John McDowell for the first time in the cafe of Belfast's Europa Hotel. As we sipped our drinks and tried to talk over the loud music, I thought that he might seem an unlikely candidate for the priesthood. He graduated from Queen's University in Belfast (the major state-supported university, which now has a majority Catholic student body) with a degree in history in 1978, did postgraduate work at the London School of Economics, and then went on to a career in international business, which included consulting for Short Brothers Aerospace Company, well known in the airplane and missile business. He is married to a professional actress.

"Being a priest is something I've always wanted to do," John said. "It was like a very mild toothache for twenty years and I chose to ignore it, but the time came when I was thirty-six or thirty-seven when I started thinking I really should have a go at this vocation if I'm going to." Not long after, he enrolled in the theology program at Trinity College. He was ordained a deacon in June 1996.

John says he hopes that he can "open up some new vistas" for people who are still stuck in ancient animosities. "I may take some flak for it," he said, "but so what?"

In this story, which he wrote over a period of years and revised for this book, John McDowell reveals how his adolescent admiration for the Catholic people led to his collecting Roman Catholic tracts and artifacts. It was an unusual "hobby" for a young boy; one that would be seen by some Protestants in Northern Ireland as bordering on traitorous.

The Mission

It was 1973. Belfast was a very different city then. It didn't appear so to many of its inhabitants but it was at the nadir of its fortunes. "Polarisation," as the politicians had begun to call it, was at its most arctic extreme. The consequences of the protagonists' gambits—Bloody Sunday, the Abercorn, Oxford Street—were fresh in the air. "The nearer the source, the clearer the stream," and religious hatred had never been more crystal clear. As I sat on the No. 33 bus I too was unaware of the horrifying depths to which the morals and morale of my countrymen had sunk. I was feeling most content.

I amused myself by thinking what my fellow travellers would feel had they been aware of the purpose of my mission. I knew the answer. Each would have been utterly sickened. But I knew my own mind. I was seventeen and intelligent; very intelligent indeed some of my teachers had said at the grammar [academic high] school. This thought was constantly in

my mind and as though to corroborate it I recited to myself
some lines from Pope:

> So clocks to lead their nimble motions owe,
> The Springs above urged by the weight below;
> The ponderous Ballance keeps its poise the same,
> Actuates, Maintains, and rules the moving frame.

Today I felt purposeful and adult. I felt self-sufficient in a
way I had never felt before and, although I did not know it, I
would never feel again. Today was the culmination of eighteen
months of thought and preparation.

I had begun by writing to England. Month by month the
plain buff envelopes had arrived and I had built up a sound
knowledge of the principles involved and felt able to defend
them in argument. I had practised at home with my mother
and father but they had been reduced to incoherent rage after
the opening sallies. Nevertheless, I thought I would make a
good apologist in any company. I was much less sure of the
practical issues, but I knew that better men than I had lived by
them, and today's mission was the first step towards putting
the theory into practise.

I alighted from the bus at Wellington Place, taking care not
to bang the plastic bag which had been resting at my feet. The
first thing I noticed was the burnt-out shell of a lately bombed
restaurant. I walked over to the building to take a closer look.
An older man was standing in what, until the previous night,
had been the entranceway to the building. "Probably a policeman," I thought.

"Any casualties?"

"No—Thanks be to God."

Good, I thought. I lit a cigarette.

I walked down to Donegall Place and stood for a minute
looking across at the City Hall, a mock Palladian building con-
siderably out of proportion with the rest of the buildings in

the Square. I thought of the councillors and local government officials within. I remembered a story told to me by the politics teacher at school about Belfast Corporation in the 1930s. A Unionist [Protestant] Alderman had been inveighing against the high rate of inflation and describing how it would reduce the council's ability to build new houses and repair old ones, particularly in the west of the city. At the end of the speech one of his colleagues had stood up to support the mayor's prudence. His words were to the effect that all reasonable men were aware of the difficulties which the Corporation faced in administering its processes, especially at this time when inflation, like a giant octopus, was spreading its tentacles over Northern Ireland. For me the story summed up the crassness and boorishness of Unionism . . . a creed which was supposed to be my heritage.

As I turned sharply to go, I collided with two nuns who had been queuing behind me to cross the road. The bag I was carrying dropped from my hand and fell to the ground. Unknown to me, the minute hand of the clock inside broke off. (I got into trouble for that I can tell you.)

"Shit!—Sorry, sister."

I picked the bag up and walked on. I glanced at my watch—11:50 A.M.—time for a pint.

I already knew many of the bars in town and liked most of them. There was nothing quite like the atmosphere in a Belfast pub, and nothing in Belfast pubs was quite like the atmosphere in McGlade's. I headed off towards the far end of Royal Avenue and within ten minutes was sitting on a high stool in the upstairs lounge contemplating a pint of Harp. I had first drunk in town when I was just sixteen, when the fashion for long hair and heavy sideboards had made the discernment of age almost impossible for publicans.

I had come to know Siobhan, the barmaid at McGlade's, quite well. She came from Divis Street in the lower Falls and I was fairly certain that she knew me to be under age but ignored it. I knew that she liked me. One day when I was sitting alone reading a book on Irish history she had come over and sat beside me during her lunch hour. Seeing the book, she assumed I was a Catholic and had told me stories about her brother's ordeal in Long Kesh, the prison outside Belfast. That's what I liked about Irish Catholics. They were a community; one faith, one nation—a freemasonry of sanctified adversity.

Unfortunately Siobhan wasn't on today and the barman, the proprietor's son, was chatting to some journalists at the far end of the bar. I reached down into the bag and, groping carefully among the contents, took out a book and began to read. It was *The Great Hunger*, Cecil Woodham-Smith's account of the condition of Ireland during the years of the Famine. I read intently, occasionally marking important passages. More often than not they were quotations from the letters of Charles Edward Trevelyan, Assistant Secretary to the Treasury, Clapham Seat philanthropist and incorruptible zealot for the improvement of public administration.

In October 1846, during the second year of the Famine when the potato crop had failed completely, he had written, "all we can safely aim at is to accomplish such a just distribution and equalisation of the existing stock of food that the people in every part of Ireland may have the opportunity of purchasing food at current prices, if they have the means to do so."

Those who had not the means to buy "must be placed on a charitable footing." I thought that this statement would look ordinary, even benign, out of its historical context. However, on the following page I read the report of a postmortem on a man engaged in a poor relief scheme [make-work public assistance program] of road building. "There was no food whatever in Dennis Kennedy's small intestine, but in the large intestine was a portion of undigested raw cabbage, mixed with excrement."

When I left the bar at about one-thirty my mind was suffused with the vicarious indignation which is the prerogative of the remotest onlooker to a distant tragedy. I walked down Donegall Street and on to High Street, turned right into Church Lane. I pushed open a glass door and walked up to the counter.

"I've an appointment for one-thirty."

"Okay. You're a bit late. You can go over to the basin now. Shelley, your one-thirty's here now. Can I take your coat and bag?"

I took my coat off. "I'll just hold on to the bag if you don't mind."

I sat down in the chair and placed my neck in the cleft made by the V-shaped protrusion of the hairdresser's wash-basin and focused on a large damp spot on the ceiling. Twenty seconds later I was peering at the face of the assistant.

"Water all right for you?"

"Yes, fine, thanks."

I enjoyed having my hair washed, and involuntarily closed my eyes to savour the experience. As the girl was working in the second shampoo I thought I could hear her whispering about me to her colleague and imagined her glancing at my relaxed face, fancying me.

When she had finished I got up to take my seat in front of a mirror. As I was passing out of earshot the assistant said to her friend, "I hate it when they come in stinking of drink."

"Silly tart," I thought, "no judgement, no looks, no future."

As usual the haircut was not what I had hoped it would be. I had a double crown and my hair sat up like a semi-beehive on the side opposite the parting. I thought that it destroyed the symmetry of my face and looked a little effeminate.

"How's that, will that do?"

"Yes, fine." I tipped the receptionist on the way out.

I had one more call to make before I could set about the proper purpose of my journey. On my way back through town

I stopped to look in the window of Burton's. "The fifty-shilling tailor," my father called it.

At that time it was still a brightly lit sanctuary where the surplus of working-class thrift could be converted into the benison [blessing] of a bespoke [custom-made] suit of sombre Presbyterian cut and colour. These people (just like my father and uncles) were ministered to by antique tailors vested in fustian, with tape measure stoles, confidently elevating their chalk to take the measure of respectability's inside leg. Here poverty of thought and aspiration were coutoured to cut a figure at church or meeting-house or demonstration.

I thought of a joke I had heard recently.

"What do you call a Catholic in a three-piece suit?"

"I don't know."

"The accused."

The spirit of three-piece-suit respectability drove me back to the wilderness of my thoughts and confirmed me in my mission.

I walked back into Donegall Place. The city was not as busy as it had been. People were afraid to come out at night because of the bombs but the shops and bars were doing good trade that Saturday afternoon. It always amazed me how much people smiled as they walked and chatted through town. I was used to coming in alone, drinking and reading. I was not resentful of them but my earlier contentment had faded and I was feeling irritable. Perhaps it was the hair cuttings lodged in my shirt.

I walked towards Castle Junction and cut into a narrow street, almost an alleyway. I approached a building which looked derelict, pushed open the heavy metal door, and began to climb the five flights of stairs which led me to the workshop at the top. I tried the handle but the door was locked as I had known it would be. First removing my book, I set the bag down carefully beside the doorway, turned and descended the stairs.

It was raining now and I walked swiftly towards St. Mary's

Church, blessing myself as I passed by. I opened the door of the little Repository opposite and stepped inside. I walked up to the counter and, pointing high to the right-hand side of the display window, said: "I would like that crucifix, please—the large dark brown one for seven pound ninety-nine."

The shop assistant, an elderly shabbily dressed man, picked up a bamboo cane, took aim, flicked the bottom of the crucifix with the cane, and caught it just before it hit a little delft Madonna and Child. He wrapped it in brown paper and gave it to me.

The anxieties which had begun to afflict me became worse as I got on the bus to go home. I felt sure that people were staring at the oddly shaped parcel which was swinging casually in my right hand. My anxiety worsened as I thought about what my father would say when I got home. Anxiety became panic when a man I knew sat down beside me for several stops.

"What's in the parcel?"

"An aeroplane."

"Are you not a bit old for that?"

"No, it's one of those remote control ones. I'm in the club at school."

The man looked pityingly at me for a moment.

"What's that then?"

The head of Christ with an unusually sharp crown of thorns had torn through the brown paper package.

"I don't know, I haven't looked at it properly yet. My stop—excuse me."

I walked slowly home. I opened the door and shouted. There was nobody there. I unwrapped the Crucifix and tried it in various positions on my bedroom wall. It looked best in the place where Picasso's "Blue Nude" usually hung. I was fed up with that anyway. I opened my wardrobe and put the offending masterpiece behind a pile of shoe boxes. I had closed the wardrobe door but opened it again, kneeling down to pull out the bottommost box.

I opened it and removed twelve buff-coloured envelopes. I took out the contents of the first envelope. It was a letter marked "Catholic Enquiry Centre, 120 Westheath Road, London, WNW3 7TY." Attached to it was a small pamphlet—No. 44—"The Catholic Church." I glanced at the contents, put it back in the envelope, and replaced the shoebox. I returned to the Crucifix. I had just hammered in a nail when I heard the front door open and my mother and father come in.

"Hello, hello, are you home, son?"

I heard my father's steps begin to climb the stairs.

"Did you leave your granny's clock into your Uncle Albert's to get fixed?"

"Yes; he wasn't in so I left it at the workshop door like you told me."

"Good lad."

I could just see my father's hand as it rested on the top of the bannister.

"Hey, Dad," I said, "you'll never guess what I've bought."

JENNIFER STEAD

LISBURN, COUNTY ANTRIM

Now eleven years old, Jennifer Stead is a student at Harmony Hill Primary School in Lambeg, as is her seven-year-old brother. Her mother works as a "home help" looking after the elderly and her father works at Short Brothers Aerospace Company in Belfast.

When we met at her school in October 1995, I asked Jennifer how her life had been affected by the Troubles. "I didn't like the news very much," she said. "It was just really sad to hear that these people were dying because stupid people were killing them."

Angry with the killers, Jennifer said she hopes that her anger comes across in her poem. "I wanted to tell them, 'Why don't you go and kill yourself if you want to kill . . . instead of killing other people. If you were sent out to kill then God would have made you with guns and knives in your hands.' "

"It's nice that the killing is over now," Jennifer said, referring to the cease-fires. Referring to the so-called "punishment beatings," she said, "If the beatings would stop it would really be over but they seem to keep happening."

I asked her why she thinks this is. "Their bosses say it's over but they're still angry and they're taking it out on other people. They take iron poles and baseball bats and such and clobber people."

"In this case, their own people," I said.

"Yes," Jennifer sadly agreed, all too aware of the reality of continuing violence in Northern Ireland.

Change

(Written at age ten)

Bombs, bullets, murders and strife
This is all I have known
For the ten years of my life.
I don't understand how it all started
But hundreds of families have been left broken-hearted.

A cease-fire came in August 1994
More tourists and shoppers than ever before.
People are smiling now, living without fears.
We've been trapped in this nightmare for twenty-five years.

So let us all look ahead now
Forget the pain of the past
We can all live together
There is peace at last.

ZELDA CONN

ENNISKILLEN, COUNTY FERMANAGH

Eighteen-year-old Zelda Conn, the youngest of four children, has grown up in Enniskillen, where, in 1987, thirteen people were killed and many wounded when a bomb exploded during a war memorial observance in the town center.

As a child Zelda says she "couldn't bear to watch the news as there was always another person announced dead." In her poem, written at age twelve and first published in 1993 by Women Together for Peace *Poems for Peace,* she directs her readers to find peace within if they would hope for an end to the bloodshed in Northern Ireland.

Looking for Peace

(Written at age twelve)

We look for peace
And search around;
Inside or out
Where is it found?

Life on earth
Gets so involved,
Endless problems
That can't be solved.

Close your eyes
Open your heart,
Feel your worries
And cares depart.

The answer's easy
For all to see,
It's in your heart
So let it be.

LISA BURROWS

MOY, COUNTY TYRONE

Seventeen-year-old Lisa Burrows says her childhood wasn't much affected by the Troubles, but she does remember having to be especially wary of bombs at Christmas time. "I remember the hotel near our house was bombed—devastated and in ruins," she says, "but it was accepted as normal, a day-to-day happening . . . the shootings and bombings were so frequent that it was just accepted."

In the following account of her coming of age, Lisa shows how she gradually came to be more and more accepting of Catholics as she grew older and how, even though a romantic relationship was forbidden her, she was able to build a close friendship with a Catholic boy.

Neil

(Written at age seventeen)

You know how it is. When you're eleven or twelve, impressionable and a Protestant, the Catholics are always the bad guys. Then you move on—thirteen, fourteen—you don't have much contact with them. They're still bad, but more of a curiosity.

293

Fifteen—your best friend goes out with one, loses her virginity to him, and you begin to accept them more. Then she falls out with him and you're back to the eleven- or twelve-year-old stage. Once you're in college you're basically outnumbered and all the old prejudices have to be left at home with your teddy bear. You enter into a friendly world with Catholics, ignoring what it says on television about the latest bombing or shooting, forgetting the things your parents told you about "them ould Micks."

Sixteen. Sweet sixteen, the magical age. What is it about the teenager that makes the older generation cry, "Oh, no, not the teenager—it's a curse!" Being a teenager is tough. There's the "Does he or does he not like me?" stage, the "I'm not a baby, let me curse, smoke, drink, go out with my friends stage," the "Let me dress how I want and express myself" stage. But try including any of these stages with something major like . . . moving house for instance. Not a good idea.

I was sixteen when I left my old school and all my old friends behind to go to Downpatrick College of Further Education. My first day was disastrous. I knew nobody, had to take a strange bus to a strange place whose doors I'd darkened only once in August. Worst of all, I had to hang about with myself. I'm normally a gregarious person and horribly conservative; so, as normally I loathe changes, you can imagine what my first day was like. Come Monday, I began to fit in more, find my niche, and stay in it. Tuesday, I'd gone to dinner with two girls. They were Catholics. Wednesday, I pleased my mother and fell in with some Protestants whom I stuck tightly to and whom I am still with. College gradually improved and now, eight months after I first got here, lonely and frightened, I feel I fit in.

After two months we had to move house. We had sold our house on the day my GCSE [college exams] results came out.

We were moving to Ardglass, to a brand new house which was supposed to be built and finished for June 1994, September 1994, November 1994, December 1994, January 1995 . . . It was eventually finished in March 1995—nine months late. We had to be out of our old house in the second week of September. Since rented houses were too expensive—and it was only to be for a month, two at most—we moved in with my Granny at her house in Killyleagh. We were to live there six months, during which I discovered that Catholics could be friendly and that I as a Protestant could be accepted by them for who I was, not what I was. It was especially surprising when one took me under his wing, so to speak, and went out of his way to make me welcome.

There were no Protestants in Killyleagh for me to hang about with. In fact, the girl I did hang about with was and is going steady with a Catholic. This left me on my own pretty much as she was always with him and I had no wish to play gooseberry [chaperone, or an unwanted party to a couple]. So what did I do when I was bored in the evenings? I certainly didn't sit in the house! I called for Neil. Neil was the only guy in Killyleagh whom I could confide in. Sure, everyone was friendly enough, but Neil had that something which prompted me to see more and more of him. It got to the stage where everyone thought we were, to use an old-fashioned phrase, walking out together. It was actually rather funny because some of the girls thought we were an item and were jealous. This led them to ignore me. It's not even as though Neil's the best-looking fellow among the guys—because he's not—but he's definitely the easiest to talk to and the friendliest. Everyone knows Neil. So there I was, a newcomer and I had snitched the nicest guy from right under the residents' noses—no wonder they all whispered about me. But they'd all got the wrong idea! After my initial shyness, which I soon got over, I was always with "the guys," as they were known. I ran with the pack nearly every night, except the nights I was working. There were many times when I guess I could have been raped. I mean frequently there was just me and around six to ten boys. That makes me sound like a slut and I'm not, but that's just the way it was. The guys respected me and I was an unknown quantity too, I guess, so no one ever tried anything. I was also under Neil's protection and his word seemed to matter a great deal within the group.

I was still hanging around with Neil and company. My parents made it clear that they didn't approve and Granny nearly had a canary the night that Peter and Neil called at the door for me. Mum and Dad definitely didn't encourage this but they didn't forbid me from seeing them. As Daddy said, "If I say that you aren't allowed to see them then you'll just be all the more determined to do it. So you can continue your relationships provided that you don't go out with one of them. I don't want to see you hurt."

I was always slipping down the road to see them. As Mum said later, I didn't think about anything else, didn't have time for anything else. The crunch came when by accident Mum read part of an old jotter I keep my diary in. It told her that I was "cracked" on Neil. . . .

"So what?" I hear you say. But for me this was an invasion of my privacy and it had a profound effect on me. After my six-month sojourn in Killyleagh, moving house again was a big wrench. I must have been weepy for about a week after it. Mum thought that when we had moved I would forget about "McArdle." Not so. I was still infatuated of course. Every Thursday I went "home" on the Killyleagh bus to Granny's house just to see him. Every Sunday I was making excuses to go down to the Priory to him.

It would have made my life so much easier if we had been of the same religion. The peace process had begun at the same time as I had moved to Killyleagh, but it had no effect on attitudes. Why do Catholics and Protestants hate each other? Is it the inbred fear that comes with hatred? Always there's the "them" and "us" factor. Why should religion have to matter? The whole world seems split by religion: Bosnia, Iran/Iraq, Ireland. . . . Why do we as a people always see our opinions to be correct? From an early age we are told that it is not what is outside a person but what is inside that counts. Why does this not seem to matter where religion is concerned?

I seem to have portrayed my family in an awful light. My parents tolerate the relationships and Granny helps me escape down the street sometimes. But what of the rest of my family? What do they think? Do I want to know?

I still continue my relationships in Killyleagh. Sure I get strange looks and all sorts of comments, but I don't really mind anymore. You could say that I'm conditioned to it now. My aunt is forever putting in barbed comments about my friends and because her daughter is going with a staunch Protestant she thinks that she is in the right. There's no problem with her daughter going into town to meet him and no problem with her going off with him for the whole evening, yet I have to beg, plead and cajole to stand fifteen minutes on the street corner with Neil.

There are times when I think that Neil isn't worth the hassle, but other times I get determined and ask myself why should religion have to matter. Surely it's the person's psyche that matters. For example, I called down for Neil on Sunday, after obtaining permission from Mum to go down the street for fifteen minutes. Neil was on his way out so he answered the door coat-in-hand. We went down to the hut and I was greeted vociferously by everyone. When my allotted time was up I had some time alone with Neil when he walked me home. Now that was the Neil I know—friendly, funny but intimate. On Tuesday I met everyone again at the bus stop. I met a different Neil then—even the rest of the guys were different. Indifferent, trying to act the smart ass. . . . Only Neil was quiet and begged me with his eyes to put up with the teasing. On days like Sunday when we're down at the hut or on our own, I know that the hassle I sometimes go through is worth it. On days like Tuesday I begin to wonder.

I'm not allowed to go out with Neil. I respect my Dad's opinion on that score, but the attraction is there between us. I realise that here in Northern Ireland relationships between Catholics and Protestants are strained. But should religion affect how you view a person? Surely not. However, old prejudices run deep.

Religion? Two differing ways of worshipping God. Does He really mind how we worship him? The most important thing is that we do it.

DONAL P. SAYERS

COLERAINE, COUNTY (LONDON)DERRY

A resident of Coleraine but currently studying for a masters degree in law at Queen's University in Belfast, twenty-one-year-old Donal Sayers has been writing for as long as he remembers.

In this personal essay, which Donal wrote just in time to be included in this book, he graphically displays how a person can, by hearing from different parts of the self, feel a bit like a pig in the middle in a game for one. He says his intention in this writing was "to redress an imbalance in the perceptions of people outside the situation looking in through the lens of a TV camera."

In his essay Donal points out that despite the bombs and bullets, many people like himself aren't all that directly affected by the Troubles and are glad to have grown up in Northern Ireland.

Teenage Kicks

(Written at age twenty-one)

F*riday afternoon and, as always, I'm downtown with Emmett and Barry. We're all about fifteen years old. We're in a tiny, dark, faintly grubby amusement arcade near the cinema. And we're* *crowded round either Dynamite Dux, 1942, or the racing one I was never any good at . . . laughing, shouting, battering buttons dementedly. I'm wearing a heavy green duffle coat my father wore in the sixties. I know that in an hour or two I will eat fish with my family and afterwards everyone but me will drink tea and I will laugh a lot. I know that* Whose Line Is It Anyway? *is on television tonight and I can't wait, knowing that on Monday we will yell the funniest lines at each other throughout the school day and laugh a lot again. I know that I really like these dry-roasted peanuts and the radiator I'm leaning against. I'm not sure but I think I'm aware that this may be as close to happiness as it is possible to be.*

Having been born in 1974, I can't deny my status as an authentic, never-known-it-no-different Child Of The Troubles, TM [literally, trademark, suggesting that the narrator regards this as an overused term.] Yet what I want to explain is that during the Troubles the Northern Ireland now being sold so fervently by the Tourist Board never actually went away; it just didn't make very good television. Others can explain the devastation done to their lives by the Troubles. I don't presume to understand. I simply want to make sure that the record is not left completely without balance for there is plenty about Northern Ireland and its people of which I am very proud. And I want it known that growing up in Northern Ireland during the Troubles was not an unbroken cloud over the lives of all those under the age of twenty-seven. There has always been a Northern Ireland where it is possible to lead a happy, secure, and *almost* normal childhood and I was fortunate enough to live in it. So it happened like this, too, and it should never be forgotten.

My last day of school at Loreto College Coleraine involves Clare and I, as Head Girl and Boy, making speeches to the assembled pupils, staff, and guests at Prizegiving. Spirits are high. Sister Philomena, the headmistress, thanks Clare and I in the course of her speech and, as the school claps and cheers, I am close to bursting with joy. I speak first and the upper-sixths, my class, get to their feet at the end of my speech as they will for Clare's too. My grin is so wide by now it's beginning to hurt.

And then again how like a Child Of The Troubles TM it makes me sound to claim that my upbringing could ever be thought of as normal. How distorted my perception is. Even living in a comfortable middle-class home near the north coast, I did not live through the violence of the last decades oblivious. My closest experience of terrorism came when my mother was in the orthopaedic ward of Musgrave Park Hospital and the military wing across the lawn was decimated by a bomb. My father and I were visiting and the three of us were watching a televised rugby international with varying levels of interest. When the explosion came, the noise was obviously enormous but, even more, I remember what it *looked* like—as though I was watching the world on a TV screen and the cameraman had shaken the camera with a violent, wrenching motion. The dust began to fall from the ceiling tiles and smoke filtered in in clouds. Then I saw the hospital staff begin the evacuation of a ward full of people who weren't fit to walk.

The school operated a "guardian angel" scheme that year, assigning each final-year student at least one first-year to look out for, in the hope that a friendly older face might help ease the transition between primary and secondary schools. Outside, after Prizegiving, Niall attempts to take a photograph of me with Catherine, for whom I was guardian angel, and two of her friends. As we get into place another of the first-years, not wishing to be left out, comes down the hill behind us at speed and takes a flying leap onto my back a second before the camera clicks. It's my favourite photograph ever.

I can remember seeing the wreckage of the military wing from across the grass and realising how much of the horror of such an event is filtered when viewed from the cosiness of an armchair. Much of the outrage following the Musgrave Park Hospital bomb focused on the new low to which terrorists had stooped in attacking a hospital. A code, apparently, had been broken. I never quite understood this. Bombs are indiscriminate by their very nature. The ability to plant a bomb indicates a potential in the bomber to pick off little blind girls in wheelchairs with a sniper's rifle. This wasn't a new low—simply the continuation of the same old low we'd been witnessing for over twenty years.

Age thirteen again—the monthly parcel from London's Forbidden Planet comic shop arrives on Friday morning. I choose, with staggering willpower, to leave it unopened until I return from school and can lie on the floor of the living room with my shoes off and my feet up against the radiator poring over the superhero adventures that mean so much to me as the smell of toasting pancakes floats in from the kitchen where my mother is busy with lemon juice and sugar.

Two or three soldiers died that day. Three, I think, but I honestly can't remember and that alone is *absolutely terrible*. Such desensitisation, ugly but inevitable, is no doubt visible in a great number of my generation—along with a taste for black humour which may or may not be a subconscious coping mechanism. Local poet Damien Gorman believes that the very name we have given to the violence of the last quarter-century is an attempt to reduce and make manageable something beyond comprehension. A phrase like "the Troubles," pitched somewhere between "a wee bit of bother" and "civil war," makes this violence our own, nearly homely—as distinctively *Norn Iron* as calling armpits "oxters" or serving up potato bread. That's not the way it should be. The numbness to horrific violence is hopefully fading now but, no matter what, there was never any romance to any of this, no terrible beauty here. The belief that there was remains, perhaps, the single biggest barrier to permanent peace in Northern Ireland, a place which should be known instead for *Astral Weeks* [an album by Van Morrison] and "Teenage Kicks" [a 1979 pop song classic by the Undertones], for breathtaking natural beauty and the humour of its people.

Late-night shopping with Emmett and Barry on the Tuesday evening just before Christmas 1989. We walk into Bradley's, news agents [news stand] at the top of Railway Road, and I turn a corner on my life. On the front cover of the New Musical Express, *the four members of The Stone Roses are pictured, arms aloft and hands linked, atop a snow-covered mountain. The legend reads* TOP OF THE WORLD, *above a line in smaller type announcing "The Stone Roses: Band of the Year." Since Emmett (who was always into cool bands long before everyone else) had tracked down the album in September, The Stone Roses had become everything—simply the most important band ever. It was a realisation we somehow imagined had been arrived at by only a privileged few. We were wrong, of course—by this stage the Roses were a full-fledged phenomenon whose place in British pop history was assured—but to find out like this was the most exciting thing in the world. Words fail utterly to capture the heart-stopping glory of seeing my band pictured like this—world-mighty, the authors of three out of the* New Musical Express's *top four singles of the year and an album the* NME *would later declare the best of the eighties. Copies duly purchased, and sprawled later on the floor of Emmett's room, I see for the first time what the Pixies actually look like and realise I know less than I had thought about The Stone Roses. We fail to win an original John Squire painting called "Don't Stop" because we cannot name the Roses song which refers to a Jackson Pollock painting and our hearts break briefly. For the rest of that evening, mine is full.*

Have I made any sense? My childhood was nearly normal, I seem to be saying, because I only heard a *few* bombs and they didn't really intrude on my everyday life. There's probably no way such a statement can be understood from outside the situation itself. All I know is that, as a teenager, the Troubles were mostly just a backdrop to the things that really mattered to me—how to get past the wall of death in *Double Dragon, X-men* comics, my tragically unrequited passion for Deirdre McA. It seems somehow important that people know that this is how life was for many, many people. Maybe growing up in Northern Ireland during the Troubles wasn't normal. But that's not to say it wasn't special.

STEPHEN HOEY

ENNISKILLEN, COUNTY FERMANAGH

Sometimes the gap between Protestants and Catholics can be bridged in simple and unexpected ways, as Stephen Hoey indicates in this autobiographical story that he wrote especially for this book. When he almost accidentally learned that he had much in common with Catholic boys and enjoyed their company, he took a radical turn away from the sentiments of many if not most in the Protestant community. Today Stephen says that most of his friends are Catholics and that, in fact, his best friend is from a Catholic family.

Please see page 219 for more information about Stephen Hoey.

The Road Rats Cometh

"There's fourteen Fenians [slang for Nationalist Catholics] in the morgue."

So said D with an air of subdued delight in his voice as he ran up to me that Saturday morning in June.

D was one of the younger boys on my estate [housing project] and prone to exaggerate but even by Northern Ireland standards this was big news. "What happened?" I asked. "What's going on?"

"Last night," he went on enthusiastically, "at the dance in the marquee [entertainment tent] there was a riot, I tell you, and there's fourteen Catholics dead and fifty of them in the Erne Hospital."

Fourteen of my archenemies dead? Loads more hurt? Sounds okay to me, I thought. I hope the one who beat me up last Christmas is among the fatalities. I must watch out for his name on the casualty list in next week's paper.

I kicked my motorcycle into stuttering, two-stroke life. I'll go for a spin downtown and try to find out more about last night's trouble. It must have something to do with that bike gang who rode into town last night. Who were they? Where did they come from? And how come they killed so many Catholics?

I rode around town which, even on a busy Saturday morning, doesn't take very long in Enniskillen. My eyes were peeled for the high security presence which follows incidents like this. But there was nothing. I rode on to the scene of the alleged massacre but there was nothing much there either—just some broken fencing, one or two sightseers, and an empty marquee. So what did happen?

Over the next few days the true story came out. The biker gang was from Lurgan, a town fifty miles away. They had come to the dance at the marquee, by now an annual event, to hear a rock band and have a bit of a wild time. Owing to some high spirits on their part, some non-biking locals had taken offence and a major brawl had broken out. Nobody had died—no Catholics, no Protestants. There were some injuries including, unfortunately, the loss of one biker's eye but certainly no death toll of fourteen. Exaggerations abound in the teenage mind.

Deaths or not, this was a major event to a seventeen-year-old aspiring Hell's Angel and to confine its contemplation to the boys from my estate seemed to be a bit of a waste. But who else could I discuss it with from a biker's point of view?

The answer was to come the following Thursday afternoon. I was sitting on my bike outside the local bike shop which was, and still is, the meeting place for anyone on two wheels. A purple Yamaha pulled up alongside me. But this was no ordinary Yamaha because when its rider removed his helmet I saw he was a Catholic!

I tried to casually finish my cigarette without appearing to rush things, put on my helmet, and prepared to go.

"What about Friday night?" he asked, straight at me. "Heavy scene or what?"

I switched off my ignition partly through shock, partly through having flooded the engine in my eagerness to be gone. "Aye, it was some night!" I answered. "Were you there?"

"No," he went on, "I just went down on Saturday morning after I'd heard about it. I heard there were loads of people killed and injured but the whole thing was blown out of all proportion."

We discussed the night's events at length and, when I finally did ride away, my head was spinning faster than my motor. Here was I, some Protestant biker rebel without a clue having just shared a conversation and a cigarette with a Catholic who was quite possibly a real rebel with a clue.

Well, things changed dramatically after that first encounter. The next time I met Michael at the bike shop he was with some of his friends and we talked some more about that Friday night. Then a few of my friends joined in and before too long we all began calling at each other's houses in different parts of town—parts where, prior to that, we wouldn't have dared venture.

Shortly afterwards we even formed our own bike club. "Road Rats" it said on the colours that we proudly wore. We were, perhaps, the first cross-community organisation by the youth, for the youth, in Enniskillen. We, of course, didn't see it that way. We just wanted to be outlaws, man!

Over the next few years many lifelong friendships were formed—not only between us riders but with each other's families, friends, and neighbours—and we all agreed that we should have gotten together much sooner.

Looking back now, we were just boys trying to become men and, thankfully, we did it well enough, I think, because, even though most of us have sold our motorcycles years ago, we can still drink a beer together whenever the opportunity arises and we can talk about those biking years. And in the same breath we can discuss the politics and problems that still exist in this country that we share. We can do it in a way that does not offend each other nor, hopefully, anyone else.

Sometimes I like to think that it was just our passion for motorcycles that brought us together then—that we were some special breed, that we had our own colours to nail to the mast so we didn't need anyone else's. Sometimes I like to think that, for me at least, it was the example set by my parents. After all, it was they who had encouraged me to buy a bike in the first place and to always respect the views of others.

But deep down I hope that it was something more. I hope that all boys to men can do what we did, that they can all find something—anything—that can break the ties that bind and make them start talking.

SHARON INGRAM

GOTHENBURG, SWEDEN

In these excerpts from the diary she kept between the ages of eight and twenty, Sharon Ingram first expresses her regrets over how sectarian violence limits her freedom and then resolves that her romantic choices will not be limited by sectarianism.

Please see page 271 for more on Sharon Ingram.

Diary

(Written from age twelve to twenty)

AUGUST 26, 1971

INTERNMENT [imprisonment without formal charges or the presentation of evidence]—Dad suddenly announced at 8 P.M. that we would have to cut short our holiday in Sligo. He had been listening to the radio and heard that serious trouble as a result of internment was expected the following day. Started packing at 8:10. Took two hours to pack. Had a gorgeous midnight feast at Lower Lough Macnean. Arrived home at 1:45 A.M. Went to bed at 2:45. Woken about 5:00 by a terrible bang. The Ballygawley electricity transformer was up in flames. I fumbled my way along the landing to my parents' bedroom, keeping as close to the floor as possible. I think I was shaking.

OCTOBER 20, 1973

Gladys [her sister] was wearing blue mascara and pink eyelid stuff when she sat on my bed. She chattered on about Wellworth's. It's such a beautiful shop. You can stroll in there anytime but, if you carry baggage, a man at the door has to search you. Wellworth's has been blown up about twice and it opened again just a fortnight ago.

OCTOBER 23, 1973

Ugh! I'm sickened. The IRA won't shut up their stupid bombs.

DECEMBER 1, 1973

The IRA have been blocking roads but I'm sick of their killings, so I won't mention them any further.

DECEMBER 2, 1973

My coat has never been out of Ulster. It trudges along to church on Sunday mornings when the weather's cold. If the IRA would shut up it would probably go to theatres in Belfast and concerts all over the country.

MARCH 15, 1974

I was really disappointed that my Catholic friend Jane did not turn up at orchestra practice tonight.

APRIL 22, 1974

I wasn't allowed to go to Enniskillen tonight with Mummy to choral practice because Mummy was afraid for my safety. The IRA are getting more bloodthirsty than ever.

DECEMBER 20, 1976

I would love to risk sleeping some Christmas night with curtains flung back from the windows, nothing but shiny black glass between me and the stars and sky, the drizzle and the horses, but bombs ruthlessly silence my wishes, for a while at least.

JANUARY 29, 1977

Oh to lie thinking in bed without having to have the curtains drawn which the blasted terrorists have taught us to do.

AUGUST 30, 1978

CORRYMEELA—CENTRE FOR RECONCILIATION, BALLYCASTLE

I'm concerned about Corrymeela for I love it. It has great potential for helping us but I just hope and pray it's not on the wrong track. It needs something more than what it has at the minute. It shows itself outwardly in a very moving way: hugs, smiles, laughter. There is a great sense of caring about the place and that I'm thankful for.

Alf McCreary talks of a certain "tension" about the place. From my own experience there was, indeed, tension . . . it seemed to involve wondering how much one could talk and what one could talk about. Okay, so there was freedom—great freedom—to do what one liked. But I felt that the line was drawn at the expression of political and religious views.

We need to put across more strongly the message of freedom—if that is what Corrymeela is all about—so that thoughts on these subjects won't be suppressed. My own experience of suppression: Mike saying "Good!" with a vengeance when he heard that the Pope had died. And then being shooshed up. Jeffrey playing the first few bars of "The Sash" [Protestant anthem] on the mouth organ, much to the chagrin of some people. And then being shooshed. Jeffrey repeating them two more times for the pleasure of hearing even more moans and shooshing. I thought Corrymeela was "the place where you don't have to whisper."

JULY 25, 1979

DEAR GLADYS,

I had a fantastic time in Corrymeela. I prefer to remember the first week for reasons which will soon become evident to you—if they haven't done already—because, by golly, you discerning old beetle, you know right well when some man or other has caught my eye. And he *has* this time. . . .

I met him a year ago. His name begins with L—but I won't tell you it yet because that'll let out some of the irony of the situation. I only knew him for a couple of hours last year. I'd forgotten what he was like but when I met him again this year it all flooded back quite vividly . . .

One afternoon I asked him to look at my camera. It was faulty: the film wouldn't wind on. So he had a go. Soon I realised he was shaking as much as I was, though he probably didn't know I was nervous and overjoyed at being with him because I'm too used to covering up nerves. (I think singing at the Dungannon Festival got me well into practice). When I saw his hands I just wanted him to stop. So I said it was okay, I'd take the camera to a shop.

We were sitting in my chalet. He looked at the camera again and said suddenly that he'd been talking with my father on the phone and had asked him for my college address but Daddy had said I'd be home at Easter and that he could write to me at home. L. was upset about this. So was I. I said to him: "Daddy didn't know who he was speaking to." *Why* Daddy wouldn't give him my address baffles me . . . unless it was that Daddy asked him for his name and he gave it—Liam O'Farran. That says a lot, doesn't it? Especially at the present time. Of course religion matters, but is religion an excuse for trying to keep a person away? It'll be interesting to hear what Daddy says. When he comes home I'll ask him if he remembers someone ringing up and asking for my address. What good it'll do I don't know but I'd be interested to hear Daddy's reaction.

If Daddy is surprised at my infatuation with a Catholic he's not the only one. I am myself. After spending the past year convinced that I don't want to marry an Ulsterman, I spend the last fortnight knowing that many of my ideas, values, ambitions have been called into question. Go to Corrymeela, I grow a little, learn a lot, meet more and more wonderful people than I ever thought possible . . . and then I have to go and love *him*. After this I'll never be able to talk about love in the same cynical way again. It really is indescribable. I'm *astounded* . . .

Will I ever marry? It's like asking if the sun will be shining this day twelve years. Furthermore, I know now how little control one has over feelings of love. They just happen and that's that. I won't get very far if I restrict my vision to nice clean British Protestants with third-level education. As far as I'm concerned, that is like asking me to fall in love only with men who are five feet four inches tall and have grey eyes.

NIALL McGRATH

BALLYCLARE, COUNTY ANTRIM

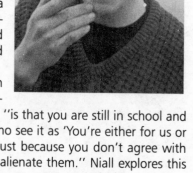

As we talked in the parlor of the bed and breakfast I was staying at in Belfast, thirty-year-old Niall Mc-Grath told me how he came to be a "pig in the middle." Because his mother spent a lot of time visiting various countries and his father had a strong interest in history, archaeology, and pre-Christian times, Niall believes they had a wider perspective than many parents in Northern Ireland and raised him to try to understand and respect all points of view.

"But one of the problems with growing up in a more open-minded environment," Niall says, "is that you are still in school and growing up with some people who see it as 'You're either for us or against us,' who don't see that just because you don't agree with people you don't have to totally alienate them." Niall explores this awkward position in the story he wrote over a period of several years and then revised especially for this book.

Niall thinks that, increasingly, young people in Northern Ireland really don't want to be identified with the "limiting and insular" political squabbles of the country. "You've got TV—satellite TV—and you can appreciate all kinds of cultures," he says. "And you go abroad." He thinks it is particularly important for writers to get beyond the particular beliefs of their culture. "A writer should be focused on how the human individual feels about things," he says.

Writing is very important to Niall, who works by day in the National Income Tax Office in Belfast. He has had short stories and poems published in Northern Ireland and England, and his novel, *Heart of a Heartless World*, was published by Minerva Press in 1995.

Pig in the Middle

Harry, Gervase and I were in the dim, dusty farrowing unit. The long, low wooden-walled building was sultry with the body heat of sows, glares from infrared lamps warming piglets, and heavy aroma of dung.

I was tearing my way through a meal-dust-festooned cobweb when I heard Harry's grunts. He had got besieged in the corner of a boar pen. The agricultural college's prize breeding Duroc's pig's name was stencilled on the high steel door. Harry darted out from the pen with his empty bucket, almost colliding with me in the passageway.

"Big Red's in a frisky mood. Near got me. Where's Gervase?"

"Scraping the slatted pens beyond the farrowing crates."

"Gervase! Gervase!"

Harry called our mate over. I had begun to realise, now that we'd all been at the college for three weeks, that I wasn't keen on Harry. Harry Campbell was one of the hardnuts of our 1985 intake of students. He was a chubby, true-blue Loyalist [pro-British Protestant] from a village twenty miles the other side of Belfast, about as far into County Down as this college was the Antrim side of the capital city. Gervase O'Brien came strolling up the aisle. He was, in contrast to Harry, a tall, skinny fellow. He was from a border area, the so-called "bandit country" of south Armagh. Gervase was a mild-mannered lad, yet I found it as difficult to talk to him as I did to Harry.

Gervase gangled towards us, dragging a hand scraper behind him. His hands were, like the implement's shaft, spotted with muck. Sweat was soaked around the armpits of his blue overalls and was glistening on his brow. His Wellington boots flapped against his shins as he stepped along.

"Yeah, what's up?"

"Are you finished down there? You're lucky this morning. Big Red's is the only boar pen that needs a clean-out."

Gervase grunted and went into the high-walled pen. Harry put his hand over his mouth to stifle his laughter as he bolted the pen door. His eyes bulged, signalling to me that he expected his humour to be appreciated. I faked a grin. I heard Gervase grunting more loudly, then shouting at the boar. The boar was squealing, high-pitched and incessantly. Hands appeared at the top of the two-metres-high wall. Gervase's red face appeared; he leaned forward and rapidly heaved himself over the top. Harry was in hysterics as Gervase flopped down into the slippery passageway. I couldn't help sniggering myself.

"The brute nearly chewed the calves off me!" Gervase fumed. "You did that on purpose!"

"Can't you take a gag?" Harry gasped.

"I've had enough!" Gervase said, making to leave.

"You can't leave your scraper in there," Harry told him.

"Bloody can!"

Gervase stormed out of the farrowing unit. Harry and I finished our pig unit morning duty chores without him. As we were washing down the passageway Harry began whistling.

"Maybe I'm annoying you?" Harry asked, looking up warily from his stooped posture where he was brushing the concrete.

"Why should I be annoyed?"

" 'os me tune's 'The Sash' [Protestant anthem]." Pregnant silence. "Right enough, Billy Quinn was tellin' us you're supposed to be one of us."

"There's never been any Orangemen [members of a Protestant organization with anti-Catholic sentiments] in our family. Though I have been reared Protestant, if you must know."

"But isn't O'Neill a funny name for a Prod? Are you a half-caste, like yon wee Debbie Muldoon, or something?"

I sighed deeply, exasperated. "No, I'm one hundred percent Presbyterian. Wasn't one of Northern Ireland's oul' prime ministers called O'Neill? And he was a Protestant—he was Church of Ireland."

"Aye. Traitor he was, invitin' thon [that] Fenian [slang for Catholic] Prime Minister Lemass up from Dublin! It was his wishy-washy sort that let the Taigs [slang for Catholics] start the trouble in the first place. He should've kept them in their place. After all, Ulster is British; what's it got to do with them down there?"

"Oh, I'm not interested in politics, really. All I know is plenty of people up here would like more to do with them 'uns."

"And us the majority don't!" Harry eyed me suspiciously. "An' them rebels needn't think, neither, that if they get a few percent of a majority by outbreedin' us, that we'll just lay down an' take it. This is *our* country. If you're a Prod, how come you're called 'Sean'? Damn funny name for a Prod."

"It was the sixties, before the Troubles began. My Mum liked Sean Connery in those James Bond movies. Besides, I've been told there was a fad in those days for Prods to give their kids Irish names, especially among the middle classes. I can't help being what I am—I had no say in the way I was born or brought up, did I? Anyway, sure, we're all Celts, aren't we?"

"Us Campbells are Scotch! We're British!"

"The Scots were originally Irish. They were a Celtic tribe, same as the Picts they invaded and took some of Caledonia from. And the ancient British were the Celts who invaded England and Wales from Brittany. Besides, we're all human beings. Does it matter what race or tribe we might be?"

Harry's lower jaw jutted pugnaciously. "It matters that we're free as Prods. We shouldn't want to kowtow to the superstitions and tyranny of Papishness [Pope worship, slang for Catholicism]. Are you some kind of Fenian [Catholic] lover or summat [something]? Hardly surprisin', with a name like yours!"

I barked back, "I don't like Irish Catholicism either. I think it's a dreary old ideology. But I'm not particularly religious so I've no time for Protestant preachers and stuff either. All I'm saying is things aren't black and white. Ian Paisley's [ultraconservative Protestant politician] as much anathema to me as Cardinal O'Fiaich [outspoken Nationalist]. Aye, it was bad enough being brought up Protestant. I'd loathe to have been reared Catholic!" I tried to joke with him about it to lighten the atmosphere.

Shaking his head, Harry muttered some curses under his breath as we finished our work. But we put the discussion behind us, changing the subject to soccer as we dandered down the lane, back to the dormitory block to get washed up for breakfast.

After an Ulster fry [big breakfast] in the college canteen, I went back to my single room in the accommodation block. I sorted out my folders for the morning's dairy hygiene lecture. There was over half an hour before classes began. I unpadlocked my top locker and got down the spirits bottle. Cracking open a can of Coca-Cola, I drained a few swigs from it and added a small measure of Cossack [brand of vodka] into the can. I slouched in the chair by my desk and looked out over the college's fields where the dairy herd of Friesian cows were grazing, swinging their tails as if they were being blown by the breeze.

I felt disappointed with myself. I'd made a bit of a scene this morning, spouting off like that to Harry. I knew I shouldn't have voiced my controversial opinions like that. Like my Mum said, "Whatever you say, say nothing" was best in Northern Ireland. Speaking out, calling a spade a spade, only got you in trouble. My parents' generation were always saying it's best not to be too outspoken, it only gets people's backs up. Living in

Northern Irish society often felt like one long McCarthy witch-hunt: so many folks were on the lookout for a real or imagined offence against the sacred tenets of their particular tradition. If you didn't show clearly that you were for them, they made sure you were treated as if you were against them.

No doubt Harry and his true-blue mates would give me a hard time. But they were doing that anyway, for the Hell of it. Those hardnuts were only here for the nights out and the raking about [self-indulgent and/or promiscuous pleasure seeking]. I could have told Harry that I'd a second cousin who was a UDR [Ulster Defense Regiment, a government militia] part-timer. That might make me sound a more kosher Protestant. But I knew even that was a complicated matter. That relative, Dave, had joined to do his bit to help keep the peace after the Troubles began but had left after a few years because he was frustrated by the few of the lads in his regiment who threw their weight around, who were tactless and too heavy-handed, too bitter towards their Catholic neighbours.

As I sipped my drink I wallowed in self-pity. I felt isolated, ill at ease among these new people. Over the past few weeks I had begun to rely on these tipples to get me through the day.

I mulled over my predicament. Out the window, clouds were drifting over the ploughed hill field behind the college buildings. I thought about how life was so similar for these lads, growing up on farms, helping their fathers to look after cattle, sheep and pigs, to plough and drive tractors. The differences between their lives weren't all that great, really. They all watched the same TV programmes; liked the same brands of beer; enthused about Eastwood, Stallone, and Schwarzenegger videos; took an interest in the motorbike or Formula One races; and they all had the hots for Debbie Muldoon, the only girl doing our course. She was, rumour had it, a half-caste from Enniskillen—the offspring of a mixed Protestant-Catholic marriage. I reckoned guys like Harry or Gervase would never think of getting serious about Debbie since she wasn't "purebred," but that didn't stop them lusting after her.

I had done well in my "A" levels [college entrance exams] and had come to do this one-year agriculture certificate because I wanted to learn more about farming so that I could follow in my Dad's footsteps. I had preferred history at school to the physics and chemistry I'd done in order to get a place here. I was denying to myself any regrets about not going on to university, but deep down I knew now that really I had wanted to go. I was beginning to realise my sense of loyalty to family tradition might have been misplaced: I was living a lie, trying to make myself into something I didn't really want to be, a farmer. My own sense of duty towards carrying on the family farm (I had no brothers) made me aware of how people like Harry could need to cling to the beliefs they had been brought up with. Beliefs that I, with my more liberal upbringing, thanks to my broad-minded parents, did not share. Yet Irish history and British history had turned me off studying. I could only see in it a catalogue of inglorious skirmishes.

As the alcohol bit into my brain I smirked at the Coke can in my hands. I knew I was staring out at the countryside numbly now. And I was remembering last night—how I had stood in the off license [liquor store usually attached to a pub] in town, perplexed by the shelves of booze. I'd already had a few pints in the pub by then. What type should I buy? As the staff became impatient, I had perused the bottles of spirits intensely. Whiskey? But if I offered some of it one evening to some of the other lads Scotch might offend the Catholics, Irish the Prods. I liked Southern Comfort but the likes of Harry might take exception to *Southern*, equating it with the South of Ireland rather than the U.S.A. Gin, then? But the only gin on the shelf was Beefeater—too English a connotation to safely assume Catholics could stomach it. I knew I was only being paranoid—things weren't that zany, really, were they? In the end I chose vodka because Commie red wasn't a contentious colour in Northern Ireland. At least not in comparison to orange [signifying Protestant] and green [signifying Catholic].

I could hear faint music coming through the wall. Finishing my drink, I went round to the next room, leaving my key in the door as was the lads' habit at the college. The door was ajar and I nipped into Damian's room. Gervase was there and the other Armagh [county on the border with the Republic of Ireland] lads—Phelim, Seamus and Niall. They were chatting and listening to a Clannad tape. They ignored me as I loitered near the door beside Gervase. They were talking about their trip to the cinema the previous evening. Suddenly they shifted their chatting into Gaelic. Their faces all inspected my reaction. I realised they were waiting for answers to some questions. Having been to a Protestant, state school and not having had the opportunity to learn the Irish language, as I sometimes half-heartedly wished I could, I simply asked Gervase, wasn't it time for our class.

He followed me out. As I was pushing my door to go in and collect my notes folder, Gervase grabbed my Red Hand of Ulster [Protestant symbol] key-fob. I thought it was a joke, stealing my key-ring to tease me. I'd seen similar things done to others with scarves and so on during the past fortnight. So I played along and tried to wrestle it back from Gervase. But he tossed it to Seamus who tightened his fists around it and tugged the chain from the plastic decoration. Phelim got the ring and key which he let Sean retrieve without too much of a struggle. Niall lit up his cigarette lighter and melted the plastic fob in the flame as Seamus held me back.

Niall whispered, "When our day comes the Prods'll suffer for fifty years like we did under Unionist [pro-British Protestant] Stormont fascism."

He dumped the shrivelled lump of plastic on the corridor tiles. The Catholic boys went charging down the passageway to the stairs as the bell sounded for classes. Alone, I tried to pick up the vandalised fob but it burnt my fingers. Kicking it, I realised that it was now stuck to the floor. I got my folder and went down to our class.

At lunchtime I headed to the TV room to catch the news. I wasn't hungry. On the way I paused by the notice board to see the results of our "Crops" class test. I'd gotten a "Pass." There was one "Distinction"—Charlie Murphy. His middle name was on the list—Ignatius. I laughed out loud and said to big Hugh Moore, a Prod, that it was a daft name. Just then, Charlie was coming up behind us. He was a decent spud [slang for a short, stocky person] and ignored my inanity. Hugh Moore gave me a withering stare which clearly said, "You asshole!" My heart dropped into my boots. Okay, so I knew it was Charlie's confirmation name and a lot of Catholics took their religion seriously. But that didn't mean I had to. It sounded like a silly, old-fashioned name to me, full stop [period]. I wasn't being sectarian, even though both Charlie and Hugh were thinking I was. Sometimes in Ulster you just couldn't do or say hardly anything without it being taken up the wrong way by one side or the other.

Glumly I slumped down in an armchair in the TV room. There was a report on the news about an incident in the capital city. Billy Quinn came in. Billy and I were from the same area and belonged to the same church congregation (although I didn't attend anymore) but we had gone to different schools.

"There's been a shooting in a shop in Belfast," I told him.

"Whereabouts? Was it another tit-for-tat?"

"Ssh, till we hear."

We listened to the report. A man was behind the counter in his grocer's corner shop when two gunmen had walked in and gunned him down in front of his fourteen-year-old son.

"A Protestant area. There you go, it was the Republicans that did it. Say, I hear you're in Gervase's bad books today!"

"Me? Why for? Sure didn't I stick up for him when Harry mocked him in the pig unit this morning!"

"I heard him saying you laughed at him."

"Couldn't help laughin'. It was a gag no matter who it was."

"Alasdair Henry says he saw your cawfuffle [raucous disagreement] in the corridor. That was a bit silly, taunting them Catholics with a Red Hand of Ulster key-ring! Like a red rag to a bull that! I thought you had more sense."

"Yeah . . ." I sighed. "I guess it was silly to have it. I didn't think. To them it's a straightforward Loyalist badge, their 'enemy's' propaganda. But to me it's not a Unionist symbol. That's not really my culture. To me, as an O'Neill, it's special because of the myth of the Red Hand of Ulster. You know it?

"The legend is that some early O'Neill and a rival were competing for the ancient kingdom of Ulster [the northern nine counties of Ireland, six of which comprise Northern Ireland today] after the reigning chieftan died. The first to get his fighting hand on Ulster won the territory. They both sailed from Scotland or somewhere to stake their claim. Their ships were neck and neck as they approached the northern coast. The O'Neill was so eager to win that as his ship neared the shore he chopped off his free hand with his sword and threw it onto the land. It was, of course, covered in blood—hence the Red Hand motif. He was worried ever after about how he'd keep the peace without a good hand to fight with. To me, as an O'Neill, it's a reminder about the senselessness of bloodletting."

Billy Quinn shook his head. I knew instantly that he was incredulous at my naivety. I knew he was thinking I wasn't living in the real Northern Ireland at all. And I knew that, for most people, I wasn't. But I was living in *my* Northern Ireland and wasn't it as valid as anyone else's?

Lunch was soon over and so the TV room began to fill up with students. Debbie Muldoon came in for a few minutes but the lads' jokes and comments, now aimed in her direction, soon became crude and she went out in a huff. Gervase and Seamus came in and sat to my left, eyeing me cagily. Harry, Alasdair, and a few other Protestant lads entered. They sat to my right-hand side.

Alasdair called, "Hey, Billy, come over here and sit beside me a minute . . ."

A chorus of whoos and whistles erupted.

"Naw, nothin' dirty, you guys! Billy, you're a whizz-kid at this dairy hygiene stuff. I want to ask you about what we were doing this morning. I'm not sure about it yet."

Billy deserted me. I felt a flush of embarrassment rise from my collar as the lads chatted in their two cliques to either side of me. I sensed that I was being shunned. But I sat on, regardless, not buckling under the pressure of their silence towards me and scuttling off to my room.

That afternoon our class was taken in a minibus on a field trip to a farm some thirty or so miles away. Billy Quinn sat beside me but I found myself surrounded by a subtle barrier of indifference. I was being excluded, ostracised. As we were inspecting the drainage system we were there to learn about, the other lads chatted among themselves. But I was left standing on my own a few metres from the others.

It was Harry Campbell who started the mud pie fight when we were returning to the minibus. He scooped up a handful of fresh cow dung and hurled it at my back. I felt obliged to stand up for myself so I retaliated. But I missed Harry and, ironically, splattered Gervase instead. Chaos ensued. Shit flew in all directions. The farmer and our teacher stood their distance and chortled at the young lads' messing. Before long most of the dirt was flying in my direction. A makeshift circle formed around me and the others were soon pelting me viciously, whooping as they did so. I put my arms over my head as clod after clod of muck thumped into my limbs, hair, and body. I thought of Montgomery Clift in that movie *Red River* where he stands up to John Wayne and asserts his spiritual strength even if he isn't physically able to stand up to the macho violence of the Wild West around him. Was it the same film or some other one in which Clift came out with that line, "A man who doesn't go his own way, he ain't nothin' "?

"That's enough!" our teacher yelled.

But the lads didn't stop until they'd run out of ammo. By the time we got back to the college I was as relieved as the rest of them to be escaping the minibus.

Billy Quinn gave me a shove from behind and said, "Get outta here, ya smelly pig!"

I stripped off in my room and showered quickly so as to be able to make it to dinner before going to my pig unit duty chores that evening. As I was on my way to the canteen I was pulled up by the accommodation block warden.

"There's someone waiting here for you, O'Neill. I've been trying to get hold of you for half an hour."

Puzzled, I looked into the warden's office. It was my girlfriend Deirdre.

As she approached me I noticed that her face was quite pale. She pursed her lips in that distinctive way that always turned me on. But this time behind the thick lenses of her spectacles her eyes were glazed by tears. She hugged me tightly. I sensed that something was badly wrong.

"Your mother asked me to collect you. The man who was shot today—he's her cousin Dave . . ."

". . . My God! We were playing tennis with him only last weekend."

"Can you come home with me?"

I glanced at the warden who looked away. "I'm on pig unit duties this week . . ."

"It's okay, lad, in the circumstances. Go."

I followed Deirdre out. As she drove up the college lane I asked her if Dave was really dead.

She nodded. "Your mum asked, could we meet her at Tim's house. Uncle George let me skip work at The China Garden tonight. The worst thing is not knowing what's going on. There are supposed to be riots in the city. Are you alright, Sean?"

"Yes. It just hasn't sunk in yet. Are *you* alright?"

Deirdre nodded solemnly. As she drove eastwards I switched on the car radio.

The news report was depressing. ". . . Today's shooting is believed by security sources to have been in retaliation for the Loyalist paramilitary murder of a young Catholic shop assistant last night. That attack in turn is believed to have been in retaliation for the IRA blowing up a middle-aged woman in her car in the driveway of her home last week. The retired school teacher is still recovering in hospital following the amputation of both legs. She was injured by mistake since it is believed that a neighbouring policeman was the real target of the car bombing rather than her husband who is a college lecturer . . ."

"Christ!" I said. "It's not that any of those paramilitary bastards give a damn who they kill. It's all publicity for them and their causes. And no offence to a recently dead man but things were simple for Dave. He was a Prod, he was British, this is part of the UK and he liked it that way. But Christ, when Tim's Catholic mate Marty had relatives up from Tipperary a few years ago and they'd no spare bed, Dave gave him a room at their place. He just wanted to help keep the peace here. I guess at times he could be uncompromising too. But he loathed thugs on either side. He was a Unionist alright and he was in the UDR to help keep law and order. But he didn't like the thuggery some Prods show towards Catholics."

I sat bemused as we travelled towards Belfast. The pop music was annoying so I switched the radio off. "It's been one of those days." I sighed. I told Deirdre about how I'd probably upset Charlie Murphy.

"You shouldn't be treating him like that!" she scolded.

"Oh, I don't mind other people being Catholic and I'd defend their right to be if they want to. But how can any of us be interested in a united Ireland when the Catholic Church influences the South's society so much? I don't want to be told by priests how I should think and behave. I wouldn't want my kids—if I had some—to be brainwashed into believing in what I consider to be superstitious nonsense. Fiddling with rosary beads, chanting like primitives, worshipping statues of virgins who've had babies, believing in life after death and ghosts and supreme beings like eejits [idiots]. If I had kids I'd accept them converting to any religion when they grow up, apart from some of these cranky ones like the Moonies."

"You might be wrong . . ."

"About God's existence? Yeah, I might be. I've just got to *have faith* that there's no supernatural plane," I joked. "If there's a God there's a God. If there ain't there ain't. What's the big deal? But if he exists, is he Catholic or Protestant? Christian or Confucian—or what?"

"Now you're being silly. And boring. Maybe this . . . incident's getting on top of you?"

"Don't worry," I whispered, teasing her. "I'm coping. Though how I don't know. How have any of us coped with this carry-on for all these years? All either side cares about is winner take all. There's no time here for live and let live. We don't have to forgive, but can't we all just *forget* about the past?"

I switched on the radio again and changed stations. There was a chat show on. The presenter was chairing a discussion about discrimination. Someone telephoned in to complain that their local Gaelic language centre wasn't given any government funding, yet it was part of their tradition.

"Tradition!" Deirdre scoffed. "They want street name plates in Gaelic put up as well as ones in English because of *tradition*. Yet the second language in Ireland is Cantonese, not Gaelic. I don't hear anyone crying 'discrimination' when there's no Chinese street name plates erected!"

"Oh, who's getting ratty now, eh?" I teased her.

The laugh we shared helped to ease the tension.

"You can erect Chinese street name plates if you want. I'm

not prejudiced against that! Unfortunately too many would be. So many people here don't want to see each other as they really are but as they want to think the other person is. *Other*. And what future do our wise political representatives propose for us? The utopian Irish 'Soviet' that Sinn Fein [Catholic Nationalist organization wanting a united Ireland] has in store for this island or the ethnically cleansed Protestant northern enclave that the Loyalist high command appears to aspire to?"

"You're being flippant again," Deirdre commented.

"I hope so," I replied grimly.

We had reached Belfast. It was nearly dark as Deirdre drove towards Dave's home. There were youths screaming in the streets, jogging along, their faces contorted with energy. Of course, I realised the spoilers-for-a-brawl were out for the evening. Butterflies began to swarm in my gut.

The red, orange, and blue lights of emergency services vehicles were dancing in the gloaming as Deirdre slowed the car in the street. Grey police and khaki Army Land Rovers were speeding around us, heading both to and away from the area we were about to pass through. Yellow, luminous-strip-marked jackets were glowing beneath the neon streetlights as ambulancemen tried to ferry away both rioters and policemen with bleeding heads or wounded limbs.

"We'll have to turn," Deirdre said. "The road's blocked."

Sure enough, there in the middle of the road squatted a heavy, resolute, Army saracen [tank], known locally as a "pig." A wee boy, maybe ten years old, slung a milk bottle at the soldier who was perched in the top hatch, cradling his rifle in his arms. The rag of the petrol bomb trailed after the Molotov cocktail like a comet's tail in the darkness. The homemade weapon landed on the front of the vehicle. The squaddie leaned way out of his hatch to try and swipe it off but in the split-second he made this wrong move he slithered out of the vehicle completely. The saracen was trundling away from the stone- and petrol-throwing youngsters, moving in an arc in front of Deirdre's car. The soldier bounced out in front of the saracen.

Deirdre braked. We sat dumbfounded for a few moments, mesmerised by the mayhem about us. The young Brit had been run over by his own vehicle. From somewhere other soldiers appeared and guarded their mate with their rifles as another gave him First Aid. As the kids skipped away chortling, one soldier fired furiously at them. His bullets caused little clouds of dust to erupt from the walls where they contacted. If he was aiming in his rage to hit one of the messers [muddlers, bun- glers] they were lucky this time. Another soldier was giving the injured man mouth-to-mouth resuscitation. But the unfortu- nate lad merely coughed, spitting out blood and gunge [sticky, viscous substance] as he did so. He'd been crushed across his belly and was vomiting up his intestines.

Deirdre reversed quickly and we sped away from the trou- ble spot, taking a different route toward Dave's family's house. Staring through the windscreen at the armour-plated monster in front of me at first I thought it had begun to rain. But then I discovered to my surprise that I was weeping.

"Don't worry. Let it out," Deirdre consoled me. "As long as some of us are still able to cry, maybe there's hope for us all."

"I've just realised," I said to Deirdre, wiping my eyes and feeling foolish, "this is just the kind of position I'm in. The Brits like to think of themselves as holding the ring here, while the Republicans [Catholics] and Loyalists [Protestants] slug it out. Well, maybe in my own way I'm a 'pig in the middle' too," I said. "I'm very much caught up in it all . . . a reluctant partici- pant. Maybe I'm Irish, maybe I'm British—I dunno. I dunno about anything anymore. It's all so confusing. And confused! It's not even just the violence that galls me. I'm sickened by the fierce hatred and small-mindedness all around me. And maybe it's in me, too, to an extent. It's hard for any of us not to allow ourselves to be corrupted, isn't it? Maybe it's in us all, like a virus infecting a whole herd, driving us crazy until we fling ourselves over the edge, into the abyss of our uncertain future, foaming at the mouth like the Bible's Gadarene (possessed) swine. For how much longer will we have to put up with this madness?"

KEVIN BYERS

PORTAFERRY, COUNTY DOWN

This, one of three stories by Kevin Byers in this book, very powerfully conveys how confused and trapped children of Irish immigrants to England can feel when they are forced to choose between their Irishness and their Englishness. Finding himself in this pig-in-the-middle position from his early school days on, Kevin calls himself a "mongrel" and in this melancholy reverie depicts the tragic displacement and alienation caused by the Troubles.

For more about Kevin Byers, see page 73.

Second Generation

(Written at age twenty-one)

I walked quickly into the cold, unwelcoming bedsit [studio apartment] and went straight to the record player in the corner. By the time I reached the small gas cooker the record I had just placed on the stereo began to play and, as I made a much-needed cup of coffee, I began to sing along. I noted with some amusement that whenever I sang I slipped almost unconsciously into the same Irish accent as the singer on the record. My speaking voice was that of a South Londoner but sometimes, especially during an argument, it would become a strange mixture of inflections. It was something which I had noticed in many of my friends whose parents also came from Ireland.

Still singing, I carried the steaming mug of coffee over to the bed and sat cross-legged on the purple quilt, the one touch of home which I had brought to the new room. It had been nearly five months since my parents had sold the house in which I had been born and moved back to Ireland. They had gone home, after more than twenty-five years in England, and the only thing they had left behind them to show that they had been there was me. I perfectly understood their need to go. They had never accepted England as a permanent home, just as England had never really accepted them, although the pretense had been kept up for a quarter of a century. They had worked for all that time to pay off the mortgage, to feed, clothe and educate my sister and myself, but with only one goal in mind—to go home to Ireland. Now they had achieved it. With the money from the sale of the house, they had bought and rebuilt an old cottage in their home village. And now they could begin to live the dream which had sustained them during their long years of exile. I was truly happy for them. But sometimes it was hard.

I sipped the coffee and lit a cigarette. The voice of the singer was replaced by the sound of a lament played on the Uillean pipes [Irish bagpipes]. The solitary, haunting sound quickly filled the room and the drones seemed to vibrate through my body. Suddenly a tear began to form in my eye and the cigarette smoke seemed to harden in my throat. It was a strange feeling. I was totally aware of my actions as I put the cup down on the bedside cabinet and carefully placed the cigarette in the ashtray. It was like watching someone else cry . . . and being unable to do anything to help.

Later, as I resumed drinking my now lukewarm coffee, I began to try to put my thoughts in order, to try to stop the stream of conflicting emotions which raced through my body. I felt so totally alone—like a stranger in the land in which I had been born and raised. For as long as I could remember I had considered Ireland to be home. Every summer the whole family would set off for the small village in County Down and, whenever anyone asked us where we were going for the holidays, the answer was simple—we were "going home." To me,

Ireland meant summer, sunshine, and freedom. England was winter, school, and loneliness.

At school I was known as "Paddy," in deference to my often-defended claim to be Irish. "Of course you're not bleeding Irish, Pad," would come the retort which everyone knew would send me into a rage. "You was born in England like the rest of us. You're as English as we are whether you like it or not!"

"Christ was born in a stable but he wasn't a fucking horse, was he?" That was my favorite reply and it never failed to silence my tormentors, at least until the next time.

But it was much the same when I'd gone to Ireland when I was younger. I so much wanted to be accepted by my cousins and their friends. It took many years before I gained that acceptance. There was one day in the summer of my eleventh year which I will never forget. I was walking along the main street of the village when I saw a small group of older boys smoking on the street corner. Suddenly I felt a stone hit me on the side of the face and then came a shout of "English bastard!" The boy stood face to face with me, proud and defiant, relishing the laughter of his friends. One by one, they all started picking up small stones and hurling them in my direction. Few of them hit me, and those that did couldn't have hurt me, but I turned and ran to my grandmother's house as the tears started to fall, the boys' shouts growing fainter in the distance.

The stones hadn't hurt me, they probably were not intended to, but their words had cut me to the bone. Even now, all these years later, the memory stands out in my mind. Later I came to know the ringleader of the group. Although I forgave him a long time ago, I have never forgotten and I doubt if I ever will.

Who was right? Was I English, as everyone seemed determined to tell me, or Irish as I told myself? I sometimes thought that I and others like me should be made to live on the Isle of Man, halfway between England and Ireland, as a compromise, a new master race of mongrels. But there comes a time in the life of all children of immigrant families in England when they must make a conscious or unconscious decision about their identity. For me it was a mixture of both. Later I realized that the seed of the idea had always been there, carefully planted in my childhood and nurtured by my parents, although they were hardly aware that they were doing it. The final conscious decision had come at school, just after the Birmingham bombs, when the Fleet Street anti-Irish campaign was at its height.

Waiting at the bus-stop, I felt a hand grasp my shoulder. I turned to acknowledge the friend I expected to see and was met instead by a fist to the jaw. I did not fight back—I was too shocked as the blows of several fists and feet thudded into my body. I had seen the boys at school. Although I didn't know them I will remember their words forever. "Irish bastard, tell your fucking IRA pals they'll get the same!" I never told anyone about that day. In a way I understand why they did it. The politics of Ireland was no longer something distant from me, I was very much a part of it—even on the streets of London. Ireland was no longer merely the bright summerland of my childhood. It had become far more important. Ireland was now part of me and I was part of it.

Now, as I lay on my bed going over these familiar memories, I realized that I was entering a new stage of my life. With the sale of my parents' house had gone the last real ties which bound me to England. I had not moved over with my parents for a simple reason—the same reason which had brought them and thousands of other Irish men and women over to England for hundreds of years—and that reason was work. It is ironic that now that I had finally been accepted over there, and Ireland was "home" in every sense of the word, I could not go there to live. I had watched my friends in Ireland as they walked each Monday to "sign on" the dole and I saw their acceptance that this was the way it had always been and always would be. And I had watched them in the pubs as they drank themselves into nightly oblivion.

My life in England had taught me to expect more. So I remained in England, in the lonely, unfriendly bedsit room, listening to the Irish songs of oppression and exile, and continued the dream of my parents. One day I would go home.

BRENDAN HAMILL

BELFAST

Having just turned fifty, Belfast poet Brendan Hamill did not grow up during the Troubles but, living and teaching most of his life on the Falls Road, he certainly knows what it is like for young people to grow up in a war zone.

This poem, written at age eighteen and the first of Brendan's poems to be published, commemorates the loss of his brother David who, in 1958, was forced to leave the family and emigrate to London in order to find work. "David went when he was twenty-one," Brendan says, "because he was a Catholic and couldn't get work here in Belfast. Most every Catholic family would have had family members who had to emigrate because of the employment discrimination . . . because they couldn't get jobs here. To this day," Brendan says, "a Catholic is two and a half times more likely to be unemployed in Northern Ireland than a Protestant, according to statistics from the Northern Ireland Office."

Brendan felt his brother's loss very deeply. Their family of three girls and three boys had been very loving and supportive and this, it seemed to him, signaled the end of the closeness of the family. He was sad but he was also very angry and indignant that, because of his religion, a young person would have to leave the country of his birth in order to survive.

A writer and a teacher of English literature for most of his adult life, Brendan is very excited that this book will showcase the work of young people from Northern Ireland and allow them full expression of their feelings about the Troubles.

Emigrant Brother

(Written at age eighteen)

They said you would be back soon
But it is seven years now
Since I stood childishly choked
At the Heysham boat
Spilling through my eyes goodbye.
Remember Saturday morning pillow-fights
And headstones in the sun
Seen through dimpled glass
Of our small box room window.

London drank you in like new beer
To tube trains towing fog in winter
And kites, like pet hawks riding high
Over Hampstead Heath in summer.
This summer, strangers for a year
We'll drink in Highgate Village.
They said you would be back soon
But you asked "What for?"

MARK RUSSELL

RICHHILL, COUNTY ARMAGH

A recent graduate of the law program at Queen's University in Belfast, twenty-one-year-old Mark Russell lives with his parents and younger brother in a spacious, modern home to which I was invited for a family dinner.

Personable and intelligent, Mark is extraordinarily articulate about the political situation in Northern Ireland. And, unlike some people who have a lot to say about politics, it seems that Mark has given a great deal of thought to understanding the views of all sides: "My parents tried to make me grow up in a way that I wouldn't harbor ideas of the differences [between Catholics and Protestants] the way some people do," he said. "This is a Christian, very strong churchgoing family. My parents believe in 'love thy neighbour.' You would not show animosity or hatred toward other people even if you disagreed with their political viewpoint. And they bred that into me."

The Legacy of the Past and Hope for the Future: Reflections on Growing Up in Northern Ireland

(Written at age twenty-one)

It was a Saturday morning in May 1993. Our family was preparing to make our weekly shopping trip into Portadown. As we sat in our lounge [living room], the ground shook. There was a roar and a thudding sound as an IRA bomb exploded.

Such sounds were common in Northern Ireland until very recently. Each signalled the destruction of another town or city and lives lost.

As we sat in our lounge we hoped and prayed that no people had died. I switched on my radio to hear the news:

> BBC Radio Ulster News: "The IRA has admitted planting the 2,000-pound bomb that ripped the heart out of Portadown this morning. There was a fifteen-minute warning to clear the busy town centre. It was a miracle that no one was killed."

Another town destroyed and more jobs lost. The telephone rang—a friend who worked in a department store in the town telling his harrowing tale of cheating death. As he stood on the River Bann Bridge where the evacuated masses were directed, the bomb exploded and a large strip of metal from the van that held the bomb flew past him just missing him by inches. It hit an eighty-year-old lady in the leg.

I was born into a Protestant family during the first few years of what has become known as the "Troubles" in Northern Ireland. I grew up in a province where murder and outrage came on a daily basis, each terrorist group keen to outdo the heinous and barbaric acts of the others. I was fortunate to live outside the really violent and ghettoised parts of the province but the vicious circle of violence had a profound effect upon my childhood. There were places I never visited, people I never saw, and things I could not do because it would involve crossing the invisible line into what was Catholic territory.

As I grew older I began to realise that Northern Ireland is an insular and polarised community. Catholic and Protestant children grow up in separate areas, go to separate schools, and live separate social lives. Religious division even permeates the world of sport. I discovered that to wear the wrong coloured football scarf in the wrong place was a dangerous mistake to make.

In this segregated environment, lies told by one community about the other grow into the truth. Children are bred to mistrust the other community. Children are indoctrinated with hatred and attitudes that lead to murder and bloodshed. The net result is that wives lose their husbands and children lose their parents.

I left school in 1992 and was awarded a place at the Queen's University of Belfast to read law. For the first time in my life I began to interact with Catholics in classes, in the library, in our residences, and at social activities. The barriers began to come down, a trust developed, and now I have some good Catholic friends. Once the ice was broken the friendships grew but not without a slip of the tongue or two!

I soon realised that Catholics suffered the same problems as Protestants. We had so much in common—if only we would talk.

Growing up in Northern Ireland can lead to a hard heart and mine was no exception. As murder and mayhem came on a daily basis I became hardened to violence and suffering.

In 1993 the violence began to spiral out of control. In October it reached its peak. The IRA murdered nine innocent people in a fish shop on the Shankill Road in Belfast. The bomber was killed by his bomb. Days later, Gerry Adams [head of Sinn Fein, the political arm of the Irish Republican Army], "the man of peace," carried his coffin, causing stomachs to churn throughout the province.

Then the Loyalist [Protestant] paramilitaries responded a week later in Greysteel near Derry. Eight died as they sat around laughing in a pub. The gunman shouted "trick or treat" before spraying the pub with bullets.

These two events shocked a province used to horror. Protestants and Catholics alike reeled in the shock. The streets became quiet as people were afraid to go out. At University the bars went quiet, the cinemas were deserted, and people were even too afraid to study in the library.

Fear stalked the streets. . . . I can remember lying in my bed in Belfast, too terrified to sleep. I shook whenever there was a knock on the door. I thought that our house must have been the "Heads" on a gunman's coin. And then it would turn out to be only a neighbour.

In Number Ten Downing Street [residence of the Prime Minister], the Greysteel and Shankill murders burdened the mind of John Major, the British Prime Minister. He was determined to try to broker a peace in Northern Ireland, something every other prime minister had failed to do. He devoted great amounts of time and energy to this and in December 1993 Mr. Major and the Taoiseach Albert Reynolds [head of the Republic of Ireland] published the Joint Downing Street Declaration. This paved the way for the August and October 1994 cease-fires by the IRA and UDA/UVF [Protestant paramilitary groups] respectively. Mr. Major had achieved what all his predecessors had failed to achieve and the guns went quiet in Northern Ireland.

Northern Ireland has had peace for nearly a year. We have come a long way in that year. There have been many physical changes: the security walls have come down, the checkpoints have gone, roads opened, and investment conferences in Belfast and Washington, D.C., herald new industrial development. Even the President of the United States is taking an intimate interest in Northern Ireland and proposing an official visit. Tourist books are up by 70 percent. Certainly in economic terms the province is basking in a revival. The government hopes this economic growth will cement the peace process.

This is all very welcome. Certainly living in a postviolence Ulster is very different. I no longer have to carry photo identification everywhere. I am no longer stopped whilst driving and my car is no longer searched. Now a trip to the seaside takes twenty minutes instead of over an hour as it did whenever the Army sealed the border.

In the first seven months of 1994, sixty-seven people were murdered. From August 1994 to August 1995 no one has been murdered as a result of terrorism. Our local news programmes have difficulty now in filling their time slot!

A way must be found to ensure that the peace process carries all people with it. History teaches us that solutions that do not answer the fears of both traditions will founder. A sustainable settlement will require compromise. I am prepared to concede some of my demands to aid a peaceful future—are others?

I believe that the young people of Northern Ireland will have to lead the way in the slaying of some sacred cows and the losing of some historical baggage. "Blood and thunder" politics must be consigned to the past as must the soul-stirring rhetoric of "sell-out and surrender." It is a time for calm and cool heads . . . not short fuses.

The peace process depends not upon a cessation of violence but upon an acceptance by all of the citizens of Northern Ireland of the responsibilities of a mature democracy and a conviction that the goal of peace and change is worth persuing.

With each person playing his or her part we can build a real peace. I want my children and grandchildren to grow up in a Northern Ireland free from hatred, murder, and bloodshed. That hope *is* attainable.

In the words of the Old Testament, there is "a time of war, and a time of peace" [Ecclesiastes 3:8]. Northern Ireland has had its time of war and it is now time for peace. The challenge facing all of our people is to look to the future with confidence and to grasp this historic opportunity to turn our hopes into reality.

CLEAVER PATTERSON

LONDON, ENGLAND

Twenty-seven-year-old Cleaver Patterson is the middle of three children in what he describes as "a close-knit, Protestant family." His father is a civil engineer with his own steel fabrication business and his mother is a mathematics teacher. It was his mother who saw my request for writing in the *Antrim Guardian* and sent a clipping to Cleaver, who is now living in London, to see if he would be interested in submitting some writing.

Cleaver's essay makes the important point that people who have grown up in the Troubles have had a wide variety of experiences, the less sensational of which are rarely portrayed in the media. Cleaver reminds us that even though Northern Ireland has been beset by violence for nearly three decades, it was still a beautiful place to grow up and, in certain areas, a peaceful one as well.

Outside Looking In

There is a long-standing joke in my family that 1968 saw two significant happenings take place in Northern Ireland: I was born, and the recent, and thankfully abated, spate of violence

344

started. I hasten to add at this point that the only thing these two incidents share is a common date!

Although I was born and spent my early years in Belfast, the majority of my life has taken place amongst the green fields and quiet lanes of County Antrim. What, I hear you say, peaceful countryside does actually exist—and not just in the brochures produced by the Northern Ireland Tourist Board? Yes! And no more so than in the village of Ballinderry.

It was here that my parents discovered the ruin of a watermill and decided, much to the amusement of many of their friends, that it would provide the ideal environment to bring up their young family. Looking back—now that we have all grown up, left the mill behind, and moved on—it is my parents who have had the last laugh. It's hard to believe that the sweeping lawns with the waterfall and river running through them, the tall trees which overlooked the winding driveway and housed the bats which flew at dusk, and the twisting road which ran past our house and lost itself amongst endless green fields, all lay less than twenty miles from the back streets of the Shankill and the Falls [Protestant and Catholic districts of Belfast].

This was a Northern Ireland where it was safe to go on holiday for a week and leave a window lying open without fear of being burgled. A Northern Ireland where Protestant and Catholic children got the same school bus home and the only fight that broke out was if someone broke your prize conker [a horse chestnut used in a game]!

I must admit that we were conscious, when visiting any of the larger towns or cities, of a level of security and policing that was peculiar within Britain to the streets of Ulster. Visitors have often asked me how I could cope with the countless road checks or bag searches but when you have known nothing else you get used to it. And, unless you had something to hide, why should you have to worry anyway?

Having said all this, I did come close to the reality of the

Troubles as well. Towards the end of the 1980s a large bomb devastated the centre of the market town of Lisburn where I was attending the local technical college. My mother and I were less than a quarter of a mile from the explosion and, although we weren't hurt, knowing that we were so close and seeing firsthand the aftermath of the bomb brought home the real horror of the situation in which we were living. Northern Ireland might have been a happy, peaceful place to me but I could see how it might appear frightening and oppressive to those looking in from the outside.

September 1994 saw me move to London in order, so I hope, to further a career in writing. The week that I left home saw the current cease-fire take place. I again hasten to point out that there is no significance between these incidents!

Now I was on the outside looking in. The only time I heard about Northern Ireland was if some trouble or the latest protest made the national news headlines. It is easy to see how, if television is your only contact with the province, you might think of it as a dangerous, lawless country.

When I returned home for Christmas I felt an air of relaxation even after only four short months. No more road checks or bag searches. No bomb scares at Christmas—a popular time of the year in the past for the terrorists of both communities to intensify their campaigns.

So, yes, things seemed to indeed be changing for the better. Yet some things were still the same. Ballinderry was still peaceful, the mill was still there, and the road still followed its twisting path to nowhere.

Someday I hope to return to live in Northern Ireland—and surely that says it all.

SARAH HILL

BANGOR, COUNTY DOWN

Twenty-three-year-old Sarah Hill was born in Ballymena, County Antrim. Because her father was a rector in the Church of Ireland, the family moved about from one parish to another until his retirement. Sarah grew up in three counties in Northern Ireland plus one in the Republic of Ireland.

Not only did her young life straddle the two Irelands, her education straddled the religious divide as well. She went to Protestant primary schools and then to a Catholic secondary school for two years in Donegal. "It was every bit as bad on both sides," she says of the "ignorance and bigotry of fellow school children."

When she and her brother moved back to Northern Ireland, "we were both referred to as 'Fenians' [slang for Nationalist Catholics] at school," Sarah says. "Some of my schoolmates still think I am Roman Catholic when in actual fact I was confirmed into the Church of Ireland; as I do not worship in a church I do not count myself as one or the other."

Having graduated with a BA in English and scholastic philosophy in 1995, Sarah is now about to take a job as a promotions agent. But her real love, it seems, is writing. She has written a fiction trilogy as well as a screenplay.

This poem of Sarah's, written in 1992, won first prize for her age group (fifteen to eighteen) in the Women Together for Peace competition and was published in their anthology, *Poems for Peace*, in 1993. Seamus Heaney, who attended the book launch, read it out loud and said it was one of his two favorites; hence, Sarah says, "It was featured on the teatime news that day."

River of Peace

(Written at age eighteen)

Slowly it starts,
Barely recognizable glimmer
In a raucous menagerie of darkness.
Slowly, it starts.

Slowly it grows,
A noise, something stirs,
Like a finger's touch to an open palm.
Slowly, it grows.
Slowly, it shows,
A source rediscovered,
A handshake across a borderline.
Slowly, it shows.
Slowly, it flows,
A river unbroken,
Swelling and gurgling to a tranquil sea.
Slowly, it flows.
Gathering momentum as it goes.

MYRA VENNARD

BANGOR, COUNTY DOWN

In this essay, Myra Vennard forgoes examining the circumstances of her own individual life in order to focus on the life of her country. Written at the time of the cease-fires (1994 to 1996), this essay and the poem that accompanies it suggest that the return of people who have emigrated because of the Troubles could bring new hopes for peace to Northern Ireland.

For more about Myra Vennard, please see page 142.

The Long Shadow

> . . . the worlds we sought were never those we saw, the worlds we bargained for were never the worlds we got.
>
> —Saul Bellow

Joseph, in Saul Bellow's novel *Dangling Man*, asks himself if the urban ugliness he sees from his window equates with the interior life of the people who live there. He comes to the conclusion that there has to be a doubt that "what men created they also were." There is at least a possibility that, underneath the chaos, there is a common humanity; an elusive quality; "a difference between things and persons and even between acts and persons."

In Northern Ireland we live with labels. Whether we like it or not we are either/or—either Catholic or Protestant; either Nationalist or Unionist. For some, these labels only tend to exacerbate the innate sense of alienation that lies in the psyche of every living person. For some, these labels impede creativity. For some, these labels spell disintegration.

Born as we are in Ireland, we have inherited as our birthright a land of awesome beauty and, as Irish people, we are part and parcel of a rich heritage of saints and scholars. Unfortunately, part of our inheritance is also a cyclical violence—perhaps the voice of the unheard. Through centuries of exploitation, deprivation, and famine, fires of resentment have blazed. In the flames have danced the spirits of Nationalist [Irish home rule] idealism and Unionist [pro-British, Protestant] ambition.

Many disillusioned young people have left Ireland over the last twenty-five years and now, in a tentative period of peace, they are drawn back in hope. Will they be returning with the old labels around their necks or will they bring with them world identity cards? Will this quarter-century's revolution in Ireland's wheel of violence be a positive turn in a search for a common humanity?

From the window of the world will Ireland be seen as a people who, out of suffering, have been brought to a new awareness of our common birthright of beauty and imagination? Will we harness the energy of that birthright to universal evolution?

> After storm
> There is a cleanness
> Of sky and sea
>
> Standing here
> On the unwalked shore
> In winter's red sunglow
> I am alone on purged sand
> —Beside a long shadow.

BIBLIOGRAPHY

Adams, Gerry. *Falls Memories.* Dingle, Ireland: Brandon, 1982. Niwot, Colorado: Roberts Rinehart Publishers, 1994.

Bell, D. *Acts of Union: Youth Culture and Sectarianism in Northern Ireland.* London: Macmillan, 1990.

Bell, J. Bowyer. *The Irish Troubles: A Generation of Violence 1967–1992.* New York: St. Martin's Press, 1993.

Cairns, Ed. *Caught in Crossfire: Children and Young People in Northern Ireland.* Syracuse, N.Y.: Syracuse University Press, 1987. Belfast: Appletree Press, 1987.

Coles, Robert. *The Political Life of Children.* Boston: Atlantic Monthly Press, 1986.

Devlin, Bernadette. *Price of My Soul.* New York: Alfred A. Knopf, 1969.

Fraser, Morris. *Children in Conflict: Growing Up in Northern Ireland.* New York: Basic Books, 1973.

Harbison, Joan, ed. *Growing Up in Northern Ireland.* Belfast: Stranmillis College, 1989.

Jenkins, Richard. *Hightown Rules: Growing Up in a Belfast Estate.* Leicester, England: National Youth Bureau, 1982.

Jenkins, Richard. *Lads, Citizens & Ordinary Kids: Working-Class Youth Life-Styles in Belfast.* London: Routledge & Kegan Paul, 1983.

Jennings, Peter, and Maggie Duran. *Children of the Troubles: Growing Up in Northern Ireland.* Basingstoke, England: Marshall Pickering, 1986.

Muldoon, Paul, ed. *The Scrake of Dawn: Poems by Young People from Northern Ireland.* Belfast: Blackstaff Press, 1979. Toronto: McCelland and Stewart, 1983.

Murray, Dominic. *Worlds Apart: Segregated Schools in Northern Ireland*. Belfast: Appletree Press, 1985.

Parker, Tony. *May the Lord in His Mercy Be Kind to Belfast*. New York: Henry Holt, 1993.

Rosenblatt, Roger. *Children of War*. New York: Doubleday, 1983.

Whitman, Lois, for Helsinki Watch, a Division of Human Rights Watch. *Children in Northern Ireland: Abused by Security Forces and Paramilitaries*. New York: Human Rights Watch, 1992.

Women Together for Peace. *Poems for Peace: An Anthology of Children's Poetry from Northern Ireland*. Belfast: Women Together for Peace, 1993.

CREDITS

PHOTO CREDITS

Photo of James Bailie, © John Bailie, Belfast, Northern Ireland, 1995.

Photo of Lisa Burrows, © Derek Burrows, Moy, County Tyrone, Northern Ireland, 1995.

Photo of Eamon Byers, © Laurel Holliday, Seattle, Washington, U.S.A., 1996.

Photo of Joyce Cathcart, © Betty Campbell, Templepatrick, County Antrim, Northern Ireland, 1995.

Photo of Zelda Conn, © Twyla Conn, Enniskillen, County Fermanagh, Northern Ireland, 1995.

Photo of Laragh Cullen, © Greba Cullen, Dungannon, County Tyrone, Northern Ireland, 1995.

Photo of Pearse Elliott, © Sarah Elliott, Belfast, Northern Ireland, 1995.

Photo of Jeffrey Glenn, © Norman Glenn, Holywood, Northern Ireland, 1995.

Photo of Frank Higgins, © George Potts, Belfast, Northern Ireland, 1996.

Photo of Sharon Ingram, © Richard Montgomery of *The Tyrone Courier*, Dungannon, Northern Ireland, 1995.

Photo of Kirsty Laird, © Laurel Holliday, Seattle, Washington, U.S.A., 1996.

Photo of Alistair Little, © Alexander Little, Lurgan, Northern Ireland, 1996.

Photo of Martin McClurg, © L. McClurg, Greenisland, County Antrim, Northern Ireland, 1995.

Photo of Margaret McCrory, © Bridgett Timony, Boston, Massachusetts, U.S.A., 1995.

Photo of Liam McGill, © Kathleen Moore, Maghera, County Derry, Northern Ireland, 1995.

Photo of Niall McGrath, © Christopher Blair, Belfast, Northern Ireland, 1995.

Photo of Gemma McHenry, © Peter Brady, Ballycastle, County Antrim, Northern Ireland, 1995.

Photo of Kimlouise McLean, © Trevor James McLean, Holywood, County Down, Northern Ireland, 1995.

Photo of Ursula McShane, © Carrie McShane, Belfast, Northern Ireland, 1995.

Photo of Peter SJ Merrigan, © Myra Merrigan, Derry, Northern Ireland, 1996.

Photo of Brenda Murphy, © Bridget Murphy, Belfast, Northern Ireland, 1996.

Photo of Bridie Murphy, © Brenda Murphy, Belfast, Northern Ireland, 1996.

Photo of Catherine O'Neill, © Stephen O'Neill, Belfast, Northern Ireland, 1995.

Photo of Alison Östnas, © Teresa Hughes, Bangor, County Down, Northern Ireland, 1996.

Photo of Cleaver Patterson, © Patricia Patterson, Lisburn, Northern Ireland, 1995.

Photo of Mark Russell, © Laurel Holliday, Seattle, Washington, U.S.A., 1996.

Photo of Donal P. Sayers, © Niall Tierney, Limavady, Northern Ireland, 1996.

Photo of St. Bridgett's Primary School students, © Laurel Holliday, Seattle, Washington, U.S.A., 1996.

Photo of Aine da Silva, © Laurel Holliday, Seattle, Washington, U.S.A., 1996.

Photo of Neil Southern, © J. Southern, Bangor, County Down, Northern Ireland, 1995.

Photo of Jennifer Stead, © Laurel Holliday, Seattle, Washington, U.S.A., 1996.

Uncredited photographs were either taken by machine or the photographers' identities and whereabouts are unknown. If you took a photograph in this book and your work was not credited, please contact the publisher so that credit can be arranged for future editions.

CHRONOLOGY

1000–500 B.C.: Coming mainly from France and Spain, the Celts roust the native Firbolgs, or "Big Men."

5th century A.D.: (St.) Patrick converts the Celts in Ireland to Christianity.

1171: King Henry II begins what will become eight centuries of English attempts to conquer/colonize Ireland.

1609: The beginning of Great Britain's "plantation" of Scottish Presbyterians in Ireland.

1641: Catholic uprising in which as many as 12,000 Protestants were said to be killed.

1652: The English Protector Oliver Cromwell and his 20,000 Ironside troops murder about a third of the Catholics in Ireland and turn most of their land over to Protestants.

1690: Catholic King James II of England defeated at the Battle of the Boyne on July 12 in Dublin. The anniversary of this Catholic defeat is celebrated every year on July 12 by members of the Protestant community in Northern Ireland.

1845–1848: The Great (Potato) Famine, in which over a million people die as a result of greedy landlords' use of oppressive eviction laws and England's refusal to provide relief for the starving Irish.

1872: Sectarian riots in Belfast. Four thousand soldiers and police called to duty.

1905: Ulster Unionist Council (Protestant organization) formed.

1900: Sinn Fein ("We Ourselves"—Catholic Nationalist organization) founded by Arthur Griffith.

1916: April 24—Easter Rising of Irish Republicans in Dublin. After a week of fighting, British troops quash the rebellion and execute fifteen of its leaders.

1920: War between the Irish Republican Army and British forces.

1921: December 5—A partition document is signed but the boundaries are in dispute.

1922: Civil war in Northern Ireland. One thousand wounded and 264 dead. Treaty between the British and Sinn Fein creates a twenty-six-county free state and a six-county "Northern Ireland" that is still a part of the United Kingdom. Irish Free State Act receives Royal agreement.

1966: Formation of Ulster Volunteer Force (Protestant paramilitary organization). They kill two people before the organization is legally banned.

1968: October and November—Civil rights marchers are attacked by Protestants and the police as the world watches on television. Riots throughout the country. Violence escalates and by the end of the year thirteen people are dead.

1969: January—Students' civil rights march from Belfast to Derry is attacked by Loyalists, including the Reverend Ian Paisley.

March–April—Bombings damage public utilities throughout Northern Ireland.—Bernadette Devlin (twenty-one-year-old, outspoken Catholic Nationalist) wins a seat in Parliament.

August 15—British Army troops brought in to put down serious rioting in Belfast and (London)Derry. Many people regard this as the official beginning of the Troubles.

1970: The Reverend Ian Paisley is elected to Parliament as a Protestant Unionist.

1971: The first British soldier is killed in Northern Ireland.

August—Internment is introduced and over three hundred people are imprisoned without trial. This leads to major rioting, arson, and the deaths of no fewer than twenty-six people. By the end of the year 1,576 people have been imprisoned without trial.

1972: January 30—"Bloody Sunday." After a civil rights march in Derry, British paratroopers shoot thirteen civilians dead, seven of them under age nineteen.

July 21—"Bloody Friday." As many as thirteen people die as a result of twenty-two IRA bombs in Belfast.

The worst year of the Troubles. Four hundred sixty-eight people die of bombings, shootings, and arson.

1975: December—The end of internment is announced. Since its inception in 1971, 1,981 people were interned, 1,774 of them Republicans.

1980: The hunger strike is begun by seven Republican prisoners in The Maze (Long Kesh) prison.

1981: May—Bobby Sands's death, after sixty-six days of a hunger strike in the Maze, leads to rioting throughout Northern Ireland.

1983: June—Sinn Fein's Gerry Adams is elected Member of Parliament for West Belfast.

November—Gerry Adams is elected president of Sinn Fein.

1984: Gerry Adams is wounded by gunshot.

1987: November 8—Huge bomb explodes at a Remembrance Day ceremony in Enniskillen injuring over sixty people and killing eleven.

1992: The three thousandth victim of the Troubles dies.

1994: August—Irish Republican Army institutes a unilateral cease-fire.

October 13—Protestant paramilitary groups call a cease-fire.

1995: January 12—British Army troops withdraw from the streets of Belfast during daytime hours.

1996: February 9—Irish Republican Army cease-fire ends with a bombing in London in which two people are killed. Several other bombings in London and one in Manchester soon follow causing massive structural damage and high economic losses.

June 10—Peace talks begin in Belfast but elected Sinn Fein representatives are excluded, bringing any conclusive results of the talks into serious question.

July 8–15—Some of the most widespread violence of the Troubles occurs during the annual Protestant commemoration of the defeat of Catholic King James II by William of Orange in 1690.

There are massive economic losses throughout the country and two Catholic men lose their lives. During this week of violence many Unionist representatives walk out of the peace talks to protest police limitations on annual Protestant marches through Catholic neighborhoods. When the police back down and allow the marchers to follow their traditional parade routes, the moderate Catholic S.D.L.P. representatives walk out to protest what they see as the betrayal of the Catholic people by the government and, in particular, by the 90 percent Protestant police force. The talks are suspended until early September.

(This chronology is based on chronologies published in *The Belfast Telegraph* and *Fortnight,* as well as those appearing in several history texts. Some dates and figures are approximate as there is often disagreement between sources.)

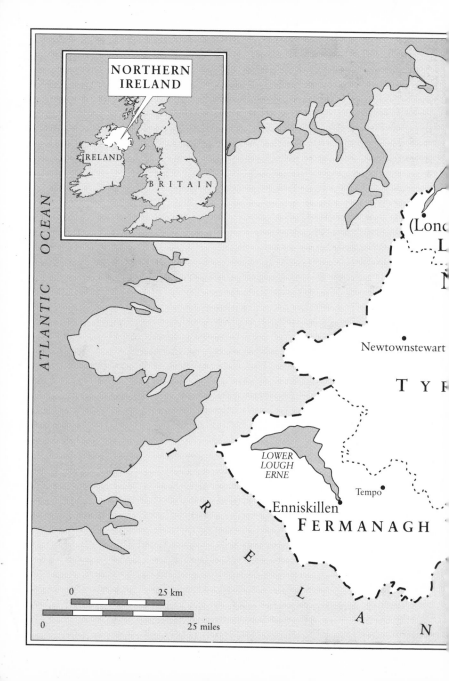